THE CREDIBILITY CHALLENGE

THE CREDIBILITY CHALLENGE

How Democracy Aid Influences
Election Violence

Inken von Borzyskowski

CORNELL UNIVERSITY PRESS   ITHACA AND LONDON

Cornell University Press gratefully acknowledges receipt of a grant from Florida State University, which aided in the publication of this book.

First published 2019 by Cornell University Press

Library of Congress Cataloging-in-Publication Data

Names: Borzyskowski, Inken von, author.
Title: The credibility challenge : how democracy aid influences
    election violence / Inken von Borzyskowski.
Description: Ithaca [New York] : Cornell University Press, 2019. |
    Includes bibliographical references and index.
Identifiers: LCCN 2018047445 (print) | LCCN 2018048574 (ebook) |
    ISBN 9781501736551 (pdf) | ISBN 9781501736568 (epub/mobi) |
ISBN 9781501736544 | ISBN 9781501736544 (cloth)
Subjects: LCSH: Elections—Developing countries. | Political
    violence—Developing countries. | Election monitoring—Developing
    countries. | Democratization—Developing countries. | Developing
    countries—Politics and government.
Classification: LCC JF1001 (ebook) | LCC JF1001 .B675 2019 (print) |
    DDC 303.6—dc23
LC record available at https://lccn.loc.gov/2018047445

For Hanna

Contents

Figures

Tables

Acknowledgments

Election quality has fascinated me for a long time. Elections in the former East Germany, where I was born, were not credible: the electoral field was tilted heavily toward the Socialist Unity Party (SED) and the "candidates" of the National Front, and voting was not secret, free, or truly voluntary. People were "encouraged" to turn out by getting time off from work and walking as a group to the polling station in "celebration." Once there, the motto was "folding, not voting" (*falten statt wählen*). The expected procedure was to get a ballot, fold it, and drop it in the ballot box (unmarked ballots were a vote for the SED/National Front). Voting booths—if available—were rarely used, as that would signal potential opposition to the one-party regime, which could result in political and economic consequences for nonconformist voters and their families.

My interest in credible elections, violence, and democracy promotion was rekindled at the University of Wisconsin-Madison. For reviving these interests, teaching me how to study them, and offering generous support, I am grateful to Lisa Martin, Andy Kydd, Jon Pevehouse, Scott Straus and to Susan Hyde at Berkeley. Each has helped me improve the project and imparted a drive for research. Other faculty have provided feedback and supported my work in graduate school and beyond, including Ed Friedman, Dave Weimer, Melanie Manion, Jonathan Renshon, Mark Copelovitch, and Nils Ringe. Friends and peers have also contributed to parts—and frequently revised parts—of the project, most of all Sanja Badanjak, Jess Clayton, and Mert Kartal, although many others weighed in as well. On the home front, I thank my father and grandparents for their encouragement since the early days of my studies. I thank my husband, Carlton Henson, for his unwavering support during the last thirteen years.

The book has greatly benefited from a manuscript workshop during my postdoc year. For traveling to Berlin just for the workshop, I thank Irfan Nooruddin, Nikolay Marinov, Sarah Birch, Andrea Ruggeri, and Tess McEnery, who all provided tough questions and great suggestions to further shape the work. I thank Tanja Börzel and Thomas Risse for sponsoring the postdoc year and workshop through the German National Science Foundation (DFG) as well as Emanuel Adler, Ed Stoddard, Elin Hellquist, and Mathis Lohaus for making that year productive and enjoyable.

Colleagues at Florida State University have supported my research since my arrival. I am particularly grateful to Charles Barrilleaux, Sean Ehrlich, Mark Souva, Will Moore, Amanda Driscoll, Matt Pietryka, Quintin Beazer, and Holger Kern as well as my research assistants Rebecca Saylor, Zach Houser, and Richard Saunders. I owe thanks to my collaborators on other research projects—Felicity Vabulas, Patrick Kuhn, Michael Wahman, and Clara Portela—who provided insights and were patient on more than one occasion. For their support and comments on my work, I also thank Emily Beaulieu, Sarah Bush, Allison Carnegie, Jeff Colgan, David Cunningham, Hanne Fjelde, Tom Flores, Kristine Höglund, Anna Lührmann, Paulina Pospieszna, Meg Shannon, and Jaroslav Tir. The book benefited from the advice and suggestions from faculty and graduate students at a number of conferences, seminars, and workshops.

I thank my editor at Cornell University Press, Roger Haydon, for his enthusiastic support, excellent suggestions, and guidance. The book was published with assistance from FSU's Office of Research. In earlier stages, I was fortunate to receive support for this research through grants, fellowships, and prizes from several institutions, including from the Electoral Integrity Project at Harvard/ Sydney, University of Wisconsin-Madison; Florida State University; European University Institute; the International Studies Association; the U.S. Institute of Peace (USIP); and the International Foundation for Electoral Systems (IFES).

Many practitioners in the election observation and election assistance community have greatly improved this book. Gabrielle Bardall, Eric Bjornlund, Oscar Bloh, Tom Carothers, David Carroll, Joshua Changwong, Jonas Claes, Glenn Cowan, Almami Cyllah, Staffan Darnolf, Aleida Ferreya, Jeff Fischer, Maarten Halff, David Jandura, Lisa Kammerud, Robin Ludwig, Manar Hassan, Hiroko Miyamura, Vasu Mohan, David Pottie, Bhojraj Pokharel, and Barry Weinberg have all been generous with their time and influenced my thinking on policy interventions and election violence. All remaining errors are my own.

Last but not least, special "thanks" go to the Kenya National Police for allowing me to experience election violence firsthand. After Kenya's 2017 repeat election, I was on Nairobi's Moi Avenue near a group of loudly celebrating young citizens when they were confronted by the police. The police used physical measures and tear gas to disperse the crowd, and the tear gas quickly affected civilians around the scene. This event has further strengthened my motivation to understand what drives election violence and how it can be mitigated.

Abbreviations

AU	African Union
CC	Carter Center
CIS	Commonwealth of Independent States
CW	Commonwealth of Nations
EC	European Commission
ECOWAS	Economic Community of West African States
EU	European Union
IFES	International Foundation for Electoral Systems
IGO	Intergovernmental Organization
IO	International Organization
IRI	International Republican Institute
NDI	National Democratic Institute
NEC	National Election Commission
NGO	Non-governmental Organization
OAS	Organization of American States
OSCE	Organization for Security and Cooperation in Europe
SADC	Southern African Development Community
UN	United Nations
UNDP	United Nations Development Programme
UNDPA	United Nations Department of Political Affairs
UNEAD	United Nations Electoral Assistance Division
USAID	United States Agency for International Development
USIP	United States Institute of Peace

THE CREDIBILITY CHALLENGE

THE QUESTION OF DEMOCRACY AID AND ELECTION VIOLENCE

Election observation is often the glamorous public face of international election support. A notable politician serving as chief observer jets into a developing country amid great fanfare and gives highly publicized press statements based on reports by short- and long-term observers; European Union observer teams and their blue emblems roam the capital and parts of the countryside; or the chief observer of another international organization (IO) gravely holds forth at a well-attended press conference on the significance of the election. For many people (the general public and researchers alike), international election support means election observation, and its image is largely positive. Observers work to ensure fair elections, as *The Economist* has put it.[1] Indeed, most studies on this topic indicate that election observation improves governance in host countries. External observers can detect and deter fraud, increase participation of opposition parties, encourage voter turnout, boost confidence in the announced result, and help raise the quality of current and future elections.[2] Public opinion about observation is also positive. As a way of promoting democracy, two thirds of the American public support sending election observers to certify free and fair elections abroad.[3]

However, these commonly held perceptions of international election support are problematic: election observation is not always positive, and it is not the only form of international election support. First, election observation does not only lead to positive outcomes but can also have negative unintended consequences. When observers criticize election results and issue negative verdicts (i.e., condemnations), they inadvertently increase legitimacy and incentives for the electoral loser to challenge and protest the election result, which can turn violent. Negative observer verdicts were followed by outbreaks of violence in, for instance, Panama in 1989, in Cameroon and Mauritania in 1992, in Nigeria in 1999, in Ethiopia in 2005, in Kenya in 2007, in Cote d'Ivoire in 2010, and in Gabon in 2015. In each case, observer groups cast serious doubt on the election result and thereby reduced the credibility of the elections. This observer condemnation increased public support for the loser—more people were willing to go out on the streets—and thus the loser's incentives to challenge the election result. Loser challenges often lead to violence when supporters of opposing camps clash in the streets or with security forces, resulting in fatalities and injuries. In some cases, such post-election violence assumed the dimensions of civil war, as in Kenya in 2007 and in Cote d'Ivoire in 2010, with more than a thousand casualties in each instance. And while the potential of observation to minimize fraud is important, its potential to exacerbate election violence is also important.

Second, the overwhelming scholarly attention given to observation has rendered technical election assistance the neglected stepchild of international election aid. Although leading policy analysts on democracy support such as Thomas Carothers have noted that there are *two main types* of international election support—technical aid for election administration and election monitoring,"[4] research has almost exclusively focused on monitoring/observation. Technical election assistance is grossly understudied, especially compared to the wealth of studies on monitoring/observation and in contrast to the practical use of technical assistance over the last few decades. Such election assistance has been provided by the United Nations (UN) and other organizations in more than a hundred countries since 1990. It seeks to improve election processes by building the capacity and credibility of election administration, often focusing on the national election commission (or, more broadly, election management bodies)[5] and related activities by other actors. Election assistance supports country-tailored reforms and capacity building for election management; this includes fundamental aspects of election organization such as logistics, poll worker training, civic and voter education, voter registration, advice on laws and registration methods, computer applications, and civil society programs.[6] These basic requirements for successful elections often pose significant challenges in many developing countries.

In contrast to observation and its media visibility, technical election assistance tends to have a low profile. Technical election assistance teams do not publicly judge elections or hold press conferences, but they can nonetheless help build public confidence in democratic institutions in fragile environments by improving election quality. This is because election assistance works indirectly, through domestic institutions. For example, post-conflict countries such as Liberia and ethnically divided societies such as Guyana are countries at risk of further violence. However, elections in these countries have been relatively peaceful when technical election assistance was provided. In large part due to extensive UN assistance to Liberia's 1997, 2005, and 2011 elections as well as smaller but continued UN assistance in 2017, all of Liberia's four post-conflict elections were surprisingly peaceful. Similarly, technical support in Guyana's 2006 elections helped overcome the habitual loser challenge after elections, which had previously resulted in violent protests and bloodshed. Despite being all but unknown in the scholarly community, technical election support is, in fact, a rare Cinderella story of international election support.

Thus, international election support consists of more than just observation: technical election assistance can make positive contributions, but it is less visible in the media and has received little academic attention. Further, although election monitoring can have positive effects, it sometimes backfires: my research shows that a critical observer report[7] on election results can embolden the loser to contest the election result—sometimes violently.

Election violence affects about a quarter of national elections worldwide, with even higher rates in the developing world. Election violence is a type of political violence that is aimed at influencing an election's process or outcome and occurs temporally close to an election. Electoral violence is more common before election-day (to influence turnout or vote choice), than after election-day (when it is used to challenge announced results and thus change the outcome). It is directed against people: candidates, voters, election officials, external supporters, and so on. While most analyses—including that contained in this book—focus on the physical use of force, election violence can also include intimidation, threats, verbal abuse, or property damage (to election facilities, party offices, ballots, and the like).

Research to date, however, has largely overlooked both the important role played by technical assistance and the potential negative consequences of election observation. This book explores both of these factors: international technical assistance and election observation. Given decades of practice, this is a critical opportunity to evaluate what we think we already know about election observation and expand our understanding of international election support with an examination of technical assistance and capacity building. The book addresses this gap in knowledge by offering insights into the effect of two prominent support types and their mechanisms and effects across time and space. It provides systematic analyses based on original data to reveal broad patterns across different domestic contexts and international organizations, and it tracks the hypothesized causal links with illustrative cases.

The international community has invested substantial resources in democracy aid and specifically election support in developing countries. Over the last three decades, about 70 percent of national elections in the developing world had international observation, and about 30 percent received technical election assistance.[8] As early as 1948, the UN Declaration of Human Rights recognized "genuine and periodic elections" as critical for participation, and the UN General Assembly resolution on "enhancing the effectiveness of the principle of periodic and genuine elections" (Res. 43/157 in 1988) paved the way for major electoral missions by the UN on a regular basis.[9] Simultaneous with this development, USAID began to fund election assistance, U.S.-based organizations such as the Carter Center, NDI, and IRI began to offer election observation, and the International Foundation for Electoral Systems (IFES) was founded. These efforts accelerated after the Cold War. In particular, the European Union began funding election observation in 1993 and has become an active provider of election support worldwide since then, sending its own observer missions and channeling election assistance through the UNDP. Throughout the 1990s and well into the new millennium, many other groups joined in providing election support, particularly observation. According to official estimates, the amount of official development assistance on government and civil society rose in the years 1990–2015 from 4 to 18 billion dollars annually. Election assistance is one component of this larger budget; it rose to over US$700 million in 2008 and has since hovered around half a billion dollars annually.[10]

This international investment reflects a notion among practitioners and scholars that election support matters. This consensus, however, obscures how little we actually know about the effectiveness of election support. Policymakers and scholars have focused on improving electoral integrity and, for more than a decade, have focused more specifically on the problem of election violence, that is to say, political violence intended to influence the election process or outcome. Funders and implementers of election aid have issued guidelines on how to mitigate election violence, and researchers have undertaken (case) studies on domestic risk factors. Yet over-arching theories of the relationship between international election support and election violence as well as systematic, cross-national evidence are in short supply. As a result, our understanding of this relationship is still quite limited. As one prominent researcher recently put it, "The most basic issues about the impact of election assistance—what it accomplishes, where it succeeds, why it fails, and how it can be improved—remain inconclusive."[11] We need more evidence on what works. More specifically, several critical questions remain unanswered: *When* does election support matter: under what circumstances can such aid influence election violence, and at which points during the electoral cycle? *How* does election support matter: how can it shape the incentives of domestic actors to engage in violence? And does support help reduce violence, increase it, or leave it unchanged? How can unintended consequences be mitigated? Finally, since election support/aid is comprised of both observation and technical election assistance, *which* type of support is better, and when?

This book addresses these questions by providing a theory and detailed cross-national evidence for explaining how international election assistance can influence election violence. I develop the Credible Election Theory (CET) about how democracy aid can influence election violence. The essential arguments of CET are that (1) credible elections are less likely to turn violent and that (2) international election support can make elections more or less credible and thus alter the incentives of domestic actors to engage in election violence. Regarding the first part of the argument, credible elections are less likely to turn violent. Democracy—and in particular peaceful power transitions—requires credible elections. Elections are (ideally) a substitute for violent succession struggles, but when elections are not credible, people tend to express their dissatisfaction with (real or perceived) illegitimate political processes, generating a potential for violence to ensue.

Second, international election support can influence the credibility of elections, which in turn influences the peacefulness of elections. Before elections, external support—particularly observation—can make election manipulation more difficult and more costly and thus less violent. After elections, both types of external support can change the credibility of the announced result and thereby influence the loser's decision of whether and how to challenge the election result. Condemnations by election observers cast doubt on the credibility of election results and can thus contribute to the loser challenging the results. Election challenges can turn violent when the loser initiates violence or when the winner violently represses the loser's peaceful challenge (in court or on the streets). In contrast to observation, technical assistance usually takes more time to implement ahead of elections and is more subtle, but it can improve the credibility of elections, which lowers incentives to challenge and thus helps reduce post-election violence. It can also improve election institutions for dispute resolution and thus provide incentives for the loser to take election disputes (if any) to an institution instead of to the streets.

Virtually all developing-country elections take place in an international context. In some situations, international actors are actively trying to reduce election violence. For instance, "reducing the potential for election-related violence" is one of three key objectives of United Nations election assistance, along with building capable institutions for election administration that have full confidence of the contesting parties and helping member states hold democratic elections.[12] In many cases, though, even when international actors are *not* explicitly trying to affect election-related violence, they still have the potential to alter domestic outcomes in important ways. This book moves past the traditional focus on observers' effect on fraud to focus on election violence and a broader set of election support types, including specifically technical election assistance. Technical assistance and monitoring have been implemented for decades. Yet their impact on election violence has remained an open question, with only a few studies. To what extent, in what ways, and under what conditions does such an effect exist?

The Policy-Research Gap

Policy interest in this question has surged in recent years, yet our understanding of which strategies reduce election violence remains limited. Most importantly, we lack a good deductive theory about the influence of external election support that draws on insights from comparative politics research. Practitioners have long been interested in the effectiveness of democracy assistance. This interest has only grown after three decades of democracy aid, in the face of deeper uncertainties about the status of democracy around the world and at a time of further budget constraints in donor countries. Of course, organizations evaluate their own contributions through monitoring and evaluation programs or broader reviews. For example, the UN Development Programme concluded that it "has contributed to more professional electoral management, more inclusive processes and more credible electoral events than would have been the case without UNDP assistance."[13] While these self-evaluation efforts provide important insights, they often evaluate project implementation rather than effectiveness and can lean more toward success stories than rigorous empirical tests of effectiveness to enable evidence-based evaluation.[14] Some policy-oriented researchers have noted that "international attempts at providing election assistance . . . need to demonstrate that . . . these programs can achieve their stated goals, such as by . . . strengthening the capacity of election management bodies. In a period of belt-tightening for aid budgets, the large-scale investment in programs of election assistance needs justifying."[15]

Some democracy practitioners—such as Thomas Carothers—say it is "time to choose" between limiting democracy aid and continuing it on a stronger evidence base. As one example, he asks, "How can elections be designed and supported in ways that specifically help to reduce the chance of emergent sectarian conflicts?"[16] Election support and conflict management have been important issues in foreign policy research for a long time, but the two strands have only become integrated research areas over the last decade. Several key organizations have issued notes, handbooks, and guidelines that outline the opportunities for and experiences of external actors in addressing electoral security. At the highest level, the United Nations High Commissioner for Human Rights has noted the importance of election violence and potential international remedies.[17] Further, USAID, the European Union, and the UN Development Programme (UNDP) have issued best practice documents.[18] The U.S. Institute of Peace (USIP) has recently published two studies about what works in preventing election violence.[19] The European Commission, UNDP, and USIP have held yearly workshops to train policymakers in electoral security.[20] NGOs, too, have developed substantial expertise. IFES, a Washington-based NGO, has pioneered this effort by developing election violence mitigation tools and integrating them in regular election assistance.[21] Other NGOs, such as International IDEA and ECES, have followed this lead.[22] This impetus is not generated solely by external actors. Regional organizations in Africa and elsewhere have noted the limitations of local remedies and have indicated interest in developing better international preventive and mediation techniques.[23]

Despite this heightened interest, policy evaluations of the effectiveness of democracy aid for election violence have been limited to case studies.[24] While these are insightful and shed light on individual elections, it is unclear whether these examples are representative or generalizable. This is an inferential shortcoming of individual case studies, just as it is a limitation of some research not to account for international context and focus purely on domestic factors when examining the drivers of election violence. Most developing country elections are held in an international context, and it is worth considering the influence of this context on outcomes.

Academia has not yet caught up with policy interest in the link between international election support and electoral violence. Since this link is still somewhat of a blind spot in the democracy promotion literature, current research can offer little guidance for policymakers seeking to reduce election violence.[25] Further, most scholarship on election violence focuses primarily on domestic factors, paying little or no attention to international influences. The comparative politics literature locates the drivers of election violence at the domestic level by focusing predominantly on economics, demographics, and identity issues. This research also highlights how domestic political factors are linked to election violence, such as election rules and institutions, fraud, weak state capacity, and powerful incumbents. However, some of these lines of inquiry are limited in their causal leverage because largely time-invariant factors cannot explain over-time changes in election violence within a country. For example, electoral systems change rarely and economic development changes only slowly. Therefore, these factors are unlikely to systematically explain changes in the level of election violence from one election to the next. Thus it is also important to consider international influences on election violence.

We lack a good deductive theory that integrates findings from comparative politics research while paying attention to the broader international context in which elections are held. I do not argue that it is either domestic or international factors that matter; oftentimes both play a role. However, the effect of international election support on election violence has received little scholarly attention. I build on insights from comparative politics research about common drivers of violence and the importance of election quality. I advance this research by pointing to the importance of international influences on election credibility and how that can help change violence on the ground. When assessing the effect of external support, I include many of the domestic factors noted in current scholarship as control variables in statistical analyses. This allows me to demonstrate that international election support has an additional effect on election violence, controlling for domestic context.

The most prominent argument in the election violence literature revolves around economic development, and virtually all studies of election violence include a variable for development in the empirical analysis. In his book *Wars, Guns, and Votes: Democracy in Dangerous Places*, for example, Paul Collier argues that democracy increases violence in countries with per capita GDP below US$2,700.[26] By implication, then, introducing or holding elections in countries that fall below this poverty threshold increases conflict. Yet the empirical record does not fully support this argument, at least with respect to election violence. Figure I.1 maps election violence—the (logged) number of election-related casualties (people killed or injured) on the Y axis—across levels of economic development on the X axis.[27] Each marker represents a national election between 1990 and 2012 in Africa and Latin America. Larger markers represent a larger number of elections. The proposed development cutoff is marked with a vertical line, and the solid horizontal line represents the smoothed average trend (a locally weighted smoothing or lowess curve). The statistical trend line and visual inspection indicate that violence levels are indeed somewhat lower in richer countries and that elections stay peaceful at the (very) high end of per capita GDP in these regions. In other words, being rich makes it more likely for election casualties to be zero. However, this leaves substantial and interesting violence variation unexplained. Even in relatively richer countries (the right side of the graph), election-related casualties do occur and can be quite substantial. This group includes South Africa, Algeria, and Gabon as well as Venezuela and Colombia, all of which are above the US$2,700 GDP per capita threshold. Further, note that *below* the threshold, higher per capita GDP seems to be associated with more casualties.

Even more interesting is the variation in election violence in poorer countries (the left side of figure I.1). In contrast to Collier's implication, figure I.1 documents that holding elections in poor countries does not lead to violence. In fact, many countries regularly conduct elections peacefully despite being poor. These elections are the many overlapping markers at

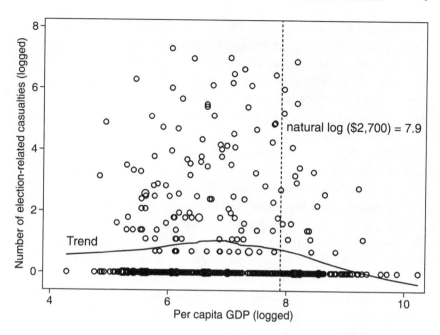

FIGURE I.1. Economic development and election violence (Africa and Latin America 1990–2012, n=476 elections)

the zero line. This group of peaceful elections in poor places includes Benin and Burkina Faso (both with per capita GDP less than US$800), Niger (under US$400), Zambia and Ghana (under US$1,600), and Bolivia (under US$1,800) as well as El Salvador and Ecuador (both under US$2,500 before 2005). This demonstrates that election violence is *not* purely structural; it is caused by context. While structure is important, it is not the whole story. If violence is *not* purely structural but varies widely even within poor countries, this suggests that violence may often be employed as a strategic tool. And if election violence is strategic, it is subject to cost-benefit calculations, which can be influenced.

Another prominent argument—at least for violence *after* voting—revolves around fraud. This line of inquiry is more promising in explaining violence variation within countries, as fraud can vary from one election to the next—unlike slow-moving structural factors like GDP. In their studies of post-election protest (which may or may not be violent), Susan Hyde and her coauthors have noted the importance of fraud as a mobilization mechanism.[28] Africanists have also included fraud allegations in studies of post-election violence.[29] While the focus on fraud is compelling, it misses two important points. First, fraud concerns are substantially more frequent than violence. Focusing again on Africa and Latin

America between 1990 and 2012, there was evidence and significant concerns that an election would not be free and fair in 45 percent of elections.[30] Yet only 13 percent of elections turned violent after election-day.[31] Even if one were to look solely at claims of serious vote fraud made after the election,[32] there is a 9-point discrepancy between elections that were fraudulent and those that turned violent. Specifically, 22 percent of elections were deemed seriously fraudulent, but only 13 percent turned violent after the vote in Africa and Latin America in the 1990–2012 period. This implies that a focus on fraud as a driver of election violence reduces the predictive power of this measure to essentially a coin flip. It also leads to over-prediction: using real or perceived fraud as the predictor of post-election violence would over-predict the actual rate of violence. Discussions of fraud can help us understand why post-vote violence happened (when it did) but it vastly over-predicts its occurrence and thus is not enough to explain this phenomenon. Moreover, fraud is not exogenous; it can itself be influenced. In this book, I argue that election quality can be influenced by international election support, which in turn has consequences for post-election violence. Further, it is often not necessarily fraud itself but "internationally certified fraud" that drives post-vote violence.[33] In this book, I assess the effect of internationally certified fraud on post-vote violence, which is an important contribution for research and policy.

Another alternative explanation for violence after voting—and one closer to the international perspective of this book—concerns the *presence* of observers. The body of work on international election observation has provided many insights. This research has documented observer effects on election fraud and quality,[34] pre-election boycotts,[35] and post-election protests,[36] which may or may not involve violence. With regard to election violence, however, much remains unclear. Two studies show that observer presence at fraudulent elections can increase the number of conflict events.[37] Sometimes it remains unclear whether conflict events are violent and election-related (versus ongoing conflict that happens to occur during an election period).[38] More importantly, while these studies point to the theoretical importance of observer criticism, neither study empirically examines observer assessments or criticism.[39] Observer presence at manipulated elections is not the same as observer condemnation. This is highlighted by the fact that less than half of flawed, observed elections are condemned.[40] Thus, observer *presence* at flawed elections is not a proxy for observer condemnation. This leaves open the important question of whether contestation arose in response to observer criticism, to observer presence, or to the fraud itself.

This book differs from most research on post-vote conflict in its explicit focus on observer *statements* rather than their mere presence. I assess whether negative verdicts—issuing critical statements about election quality—influence election violence. To accomplish this, chapters 3 and 4 disentangle the effect of observer condemnation from observer presence and election fraud.

In the absence of substantial theoretical and empirical work on the broader aid-election violence link, we can only guess which international strategies influence election violence. Economic development explains some of the variation *between* poorer and richer countries (richer countries are more likely to have peaceful elections), but much variation in election violence remains unexplained both among richer countries and among poorer countries. In terms of post-election violence, fraud or observer presence are part of the picture but similarly leave much violence variation unexplained, and prior studies do not address the key issue—arguably of great interest to the policy community—whether it is fraud, observer presence, or observer verdicts that can influence post-election violence.

Indeed, some observer groups seem to be concerned about the potential condemnation-violence link. At least in one instance of election monitoring (Kenya 2007), an organization has noted a link between its negative observer statement and post-election violence.[41] Judith Kelley mentions three other elections—Zimbabwe 2000, Kenya 1992, and Nigeria 1999—in which observer groups may have been less critical of flawed elections because they were worried that observer criticism could lead to violence. She argues that observers may have a stability bias.[42] While all three of these elections were ultimately criticized by at least one observer group[43] the fact that some observers are concerned about this issue is noteworthy. My book provides compelling evidence that such a worry is justified. I show that observer condemnations (rather than their mere presence) can increase post-election violence. Note that if observers' stability bias were pervasive (meaning observers are *less* likely to condemn when they anticipate post-vote violence), it would make it more difficult to find the effect that I find in chapter 3, which is that observer condemnation is associated with an increase in post-election violence.

Moreover, "little is known" about the effect of technical election assistance on election violence and the impact of reforms on election quality and election security,[44] even though technical assistance has been implemented for over three decades. We have information on what technical election assistance is and how it has been implemented in particular elections,[45] but studies of its effects are largely limited to case studies and have found mixed results.[46] For example, Lührmann finds that UN election assistance improved election quality in Nigeria 2011 and Libya 2012 but not in Sudan 2010 because of differences in domestic context (government interference).[47] In a quantitative cross-national study of electoral conflict, Birch and Muchlinski find that UNDP efforts in capacity building and peace messaging lead to one election-related attack less per election cycle.[48] They point out that this research field is still in its infancy and that we need more research to consider the stage of the electoral cycle as well as the conditions under which and the causal mechanisms by which interventions can influence election violence.[49] Similarly, Pippa Norris asserts that assistance to election commissions "deserves more scrutiny."[50] This is particularly important for policy in post-conflict countries, many of which have seen long-term investment through peacekeeping.

Violent elections risk tearing the fragile peace in these environments and forfeiting the investment in prior peacekeeping efforts. Thus, knowing whether, how, and under which conditions technical assistance helps make elections more peaceful is an important issue for research and policy. To fill the policy-research gap, we need better theories and better data. In this book, I develop the Credible Election Theory to explain the interactions between international and domestic politics in the realm of election quality. I explain how international engagement in elections can alter the incentives of domestic actors to resort to violence before and after elections. Before elections, external actors can help reduce manipulation and improve election management, so that concerns about unfair competition are lower and can be addressed through institutions rather than outside of institutions (that is, through violence). Similarly, after the vote has taken place, I propose a rationale for how external actors can change the incentives of electoral losers about whether and how to challenge results by boosting the credibility of the outcome or, alternatively, strengthening the loser's position vis-à-vis the winner. Any peaceful implementation of election results requires the consent of the loser, and the actions of international organizations (IOs) can be critical at that juncture. This book contributes to the debate of how outsiders can make positive political change in fragile democracies.[51]

In addition to the theoretical argument and empirical testing, this book advances our understanding of international election support by addressing the gaps: considering the stage of the electoral cycle and the conditions under which and the mechanisms by which interventions can influence election violence. With regard to empirical value for future research, I contribute to scholarship by providing one of the first global datasets specifically on election violence. The original dataset was collected for this project and improves on existing data on several fronts. This new dataset provides information on election-*related* violence, its intensity and timing. It is based on *Keesing's Record of World Events*, which integrates a wide range of domestic and international news sources and NGO reports. In terms of spatial coverage, it goes beyond many current efforts—which often focus mainly on Africa—by providing data on countries on a global scale. This allows contextualizing violence and comparing across regions and countries to get a sense for the generalizability of the findings. I leverage these data in this introduction and chapter 1 to provide context, guide research design, and then focus the quantitative analyses on two regions in the developing world, which are Africa as well as Latin America and the Caribbean.

In terms of temporal coverage, the original data provide systematic information on election violence before, during, and after polling. Several other datasets offer only aggregate violence indicators for the entire election cycle. However, since the logic of violence differs before vs. after elections, it is important to distinguish between the two empirically. The data also provide details on the extent of violence rather than imposing (arbitrary) thresholds. This allows measuring how many people were killed or injured by election-related violence. The casualty count before (campaigning and election-day) and after elections is a richer measure of violence than binary variables (violent or not violent) and arbitrary cutoffs. For example, coding violence=1 when casualties exceed twenty people could mask much variation: it is a qualitative difference whether violence resulted in two dozen casualties or more than a thousand casualties. As a result, these new original data on casualty counts before and after elections pave the way for further theories and analyses of this important political phenomenon.

Argument: Aid, Credibility, and Violence

This book seeks to fill an important gap in scholarship and ultimately assist policymakers by examining the relationship between international election support and election violence, providing some of the first quantitative data and empirical results pertaining to this issue. I develop and test the Credible Election Theory. As noted above, CET postulates that credible elections are less likely to turn violent and that international support can make elections more or less credible and thus alter the incentives of domestic actors to engage in election violence. In the next few pages, I outline this theory and then discuss it in detail in chapter 1.

What are credible elections? I conceptualize elections as credible when they are competently managed and take place on a level playing field. Credible elections are (perceived as) free of technical glitches and political interference; they are administered smoothly and are not subject to undue political influence. These terms deserve some discussion. Of course, all elections are political, but political interference denotes actions that tilt the electoral playing field, often long before election-day itself. Such actions include restrictions on who can run for office, who is on the voter register (and who is not), limits on expression and association, rules covering campaign spending, and media bias, all of which can hamper fair competition among candidates and parties. Credible elections make it more likely that results accurately reflect public support for opposing factions.

When candidates and parties are more likely to be held accountable for election manipulation, interference becomes more costly and thus less attractive as a strategy. While keeping politicians accountable for their actions is important, mechanisms for this purpose vary widely and tend to be weaker in low-institutionalized contexts like developing countries. When politicians are more constrained, they are less free to use illicit tools of competition.

A level playing field is necessary but not sufficient to make elections credible. Elections free of political interference may still lack credibility if the election commission is unable to manage the process, for example with an outdated voter registry, unclear candidate registration procedures, insufficient ballots in polling stations, lost ballot boxes, or opaque vote-counting practices; few people would believe the announced result of such a process.

In addition to a level playing field, competent election management is important for election credibility. National election commissions are key institutional actors that are responsible for election management, that is, holding elections free of procedural and physical barriers. They are involved in all steps of the electoral cycle, not just on election-day. Election commissions—and in particular their capacity to hold elections under often-difficult conditions in developing countries—are important for election credibility. Technical errors in election administration, such as insufficient ballots, voter registry issues, or vote tabulation problems, can erode public trust and confidence in the announced result. And while actual and perceived election quality are strongly related,[52] perception often matters more than objective measures.

Credibility is fundamentally about beliefs by the public and opposing political elites. What matters is often less an objective measure of accountability and capacity and more the public *perceptions* of capacity and accountability. This is perhaps most visible in election management, where technical shortcomings can be interpreted as unintended errors or deliberate manipulation. Such distinctions—important as they are conceptually—are in practice often difficult to judge by people outside the election commission and easy to exploit by politicians who have incentives to raise doubt about election quality. Thus commission competence, in the form of resources, transparency, efficiency, and fairness, is key for election management. To illustrate some of these dynamics, chapter 4 uses measures of both (objective) commission capacity and (subjective) public trust in the commission.

Yet competent election management alone does not make elections credible, since technically clean elections can still be accompanied by political interference, such as vote buying, media bias, or unlawful detention or intimidation. Both aspects—capable commissions and a level playing field—are important components of election credibility. If an election was relatively free of technical errors and undue political interference, it is more likely to reflect the will of the people and thus be credible in the eyes of the public and contestants.

This conceptualization of credible elections is similar to some terms used in previous work[53] but departs from the idea of election integrity, which has gained prominence in the last few years. According to Pippa Norris, election integrity is "an all-encompassing" notion of whether elections meet a long list of international standards of election quality. This list includes aspects of a level playing field (presence or absence of vote buying, candidate restrictions, media bias, campaign spending) and aspects of capable election management (vote counting) but also aspects of violence (coercion, intimidation, harassment).[54] By promoting this term, Norris has raised the importance of election quality in popular and academic attention, has unified some previously scattered research strands, and has generated a fruitful research agenda.[55] The notion of election integrity has started to replace the contested but commonly used term of "free and fair" elections.[56] However, the umbrella term of integrity also has some drawbacks. For the purpose of this book—examining the links connecting external support, election credibility, and election violence—it is important to distinguish between credibility and violence. Subsuming both in a single term (like integrity) would be tautological for the purpose of this book and render it analytically impossible to examine how one influences the other.

I argue that the election support provided by international organizations can influence election credibility and thus election violence.[57] Technical assistance can improve election management (making election commissions more capable), and election observation can improve the accountability of candidates/ parties for manipulation (making the playing field more level).[58] Both contribute to election credibility and influence election violence. International observation can act as an external accountability mechanism, while technical assistance can increase election quality by boosting election administration, so that the process and announced result are more credible. The effect of international election aid on violence depends on the electoral stage (before or after election-day) and the type of international support (technical assistance or observation). External support usually helps reduce violence, but under certain circumstances it can contribute to unrest and instability.

IOs and Pre-Election Violence

Before elections, violence is often used to influence vote choice and turnout. In the run-up to election-day, international election support can alter the political environment in which elections are being held by reducing manipulation. In particular, external support can increase accountability and capacity, thus making the whole process more credible and less susceptible to violence.

Election observation can act as a constraint on potential perpetrators of violence and fraud in the pre-election period by increasing the risk that such manipulation will be exposed.[59] Using violence is essentially a cost-benefit calculation; in environments where accountability is low, the cost of perpetrating violence can be negligible or null. Observer groups can act as an external accountability mechanism by making it more likely that violence and its perpetrators are detected and punished. Manipulation is more likely to be detected and reported upon with observation than without observation. In the run-up to elections, credible observer groups send pre-assessment missions and issue statements about the possibility of a fair election. These statements detail institutional shortcomings and malpractice by contestants, including violent and nonviolent manipulation (for instance, attacks, forced displacement, misuse of state resources, failure to update the voter register). The anticipated public exposure of manipulation generates incentives for domestic actors to limit manipulation or at least to adopt less overt strategies.

The second major type of international election support, technical election assistance, can increase the capacity of the national election commission to run a smooth and clean election, remove potential conflict triggers, and prevent violence from escalating. Technical assistance can facilitate coordination between the election commission, police, parties, and civil society. It often provides a platform for stakeholders to come together in regular meetings prior to the election. These meetings can be used to help monitor local tensions and mediate them before they escalate into larger violence. Technical assistance can also directly remove some triggers of violence, for instance by changing procedures so that opposing parties' candidates register on different days and thus do not physically meet at the election office when tensions are high. Overall, election support can increase election credibility, help calm tensions, and lower election violence in the run-up to elections.

IOs and Post-Election Violence

In the wake of elections, violence often erupts if electoral losers challenge election results that they deem not credible. At this point, IO support can have divergent effects on losers' incentives to reject the results: technical assistance can increase election credibility, thus lowering incentives to challenge results, and—if results are challenged—encourage peaceful protest in court rather than in the streets, thus reducing violence. In contrast, observer verdicts about election credibility can contribute to violence.

Long before elections are held, technical assistance often focuses on raising institutional capacity and credibility to better manage elections. Besides institutional reforms, election assistance also encourages contestants to stay calm; it aims to socialize citizens and parties to acknowledge that losing is just part of the democratic game, one that they may win in future competitions. Taken together, these efforts increase citizens' knowledge of and respect for the national election commission as well as for the result that it announces. This in turn should reduce domestic agents' incentives to challenge the results or challenge peacefully, thereby reducing post-election violence.

For preliminary evidence that the capacity of the national election commission (NEC) plays a role in post-election violence, consider figure I.2. This shows post-election casualties—the (logged) number of people killed or injured in post-vote violence—across levels of NEC capacity. On the x-axis, election commission capacity ranges from 0 (no capacity; glaring deficits in staff, funding, or other resources) to 4 (high capacity; adequate staff and other resources needed to administer a well-run election).[60] Again, markers represent national elections, with larger markers representing proportionately more elections. The solid horizontal line is the average linear trend.

Figure I.2 documents two facts. First, the intensity of election violence drops sharply with more capable election commissions. That is, the most violent

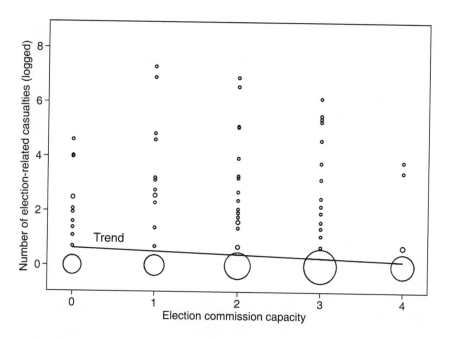

FIGURE I.2. Election commission capacity and post-election violence (Africa and Latin America 1990–2012, n=476 elections)

election (highest point on the y-axis) involves fewer and fewer casualties as election commissions go from low to moderate to high capacity. At high NEC capacity the most violent election resulted in forty-five post-election casualties.[61] In contrast, at low NEC capacity a highly violent election resulted in about a thousand post-election casualties, plunging the country into civil war.[62] Second, the number of peaceful elections increases with election commission capacity. When elections took place in countries with high-capacity NECs, only 6 percent of elections turned violent whereas 18 percent of elections turned violent at low NEC capacity. As the capacity of election commissions increases, post-election periods tend to be more peaceful and—if elections do turn violent—they tend to result in fewer casualties. This provides some preliminary evidence for the argument that election commissions' capacity—and thus the credibility of the result they announce—play an important role in post-election violence.

Unlike technical assistance (which builds institutional capacity and credibility), observation provides an independent validation of the election result. When observers cast doubt on the credibility of the result by issuing a negative report, they may unintentionally encourage losers to challenge the outcome. International condemnations can strengthen the loser's incentives to challenge by increasing the number of people who are willing to support, mobilize, and potentially fight for the loser. Negative reports strengthen the loser's relative power by serving as focal points for mobilization and by indicating that the loser has more popular support than the official (potentially biased) vote shares suggest. When losers are more likely to win a potential post-election contest, they are also more likely to challenge the result, which can lead to violence. Because a negative IO report increases losers' incentives to challenge the result, it can have the unintended consequence of contributing to violence. Election challenges can turn violent when the loser initiates violence or when the winner violently represses the loser's peaceful challenge.

Empirical Strategy

To test the argument and its observable implications empirically, this book uses both quantitative and qualitative methods. For the quantitative analyses, this book focuses on two world regions: Africa and Latin America.[63] The statistical analyses include more than 470 national elections in seventy countries in these two regions from 1990 to 2012. The analysis begins in 1990 as this marks the end of the Cold War and the effective beginning of international election support. While election support existed before 1990, it used to be sporadic and has expanded greatly since then. Further, the end of the Cold War marks a change

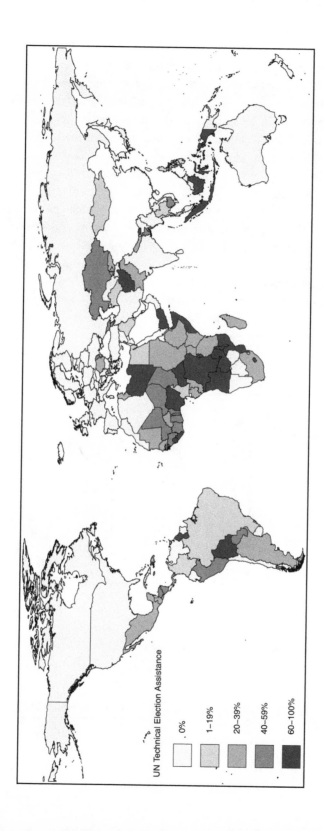

FIGURE I.3. Percent of elections with United Nations technical election assistance (worldwide 1990–2012, n=1,169 elections)

in both underlying conditions and international democracy promotion, which would make it difficult to infer which of these two (conditions or promotion) changed violence in a pre- vs. post-1990 comparison. The analysis ends in 2012 because information on international election observation (Nelda dataset) is only available until 2012. Testing the argument in Latin America and Africa is a significant advance over most existing work on election violence, which tends to focus on individual elections, individual countries, or—if cross-national— overwhelmingly on Africa.[64]

Africa and Latin America are chosen because these two regions have been the focus of international election support and have experienced substantial election violence.[65] Selecting regions with sufficient variation on these key variables is important for identifying which factors (election support, country-level characteristics, and so on) are associated with changes in violence. First, variation in the independent variables of interest (election support types) is important.

Technical election assistance has been prevalent in Africa and Latin America but less so in other regions. Figure I.3 shows the percentage of national elections that received UN technical election assistance; darker shades indicate that a

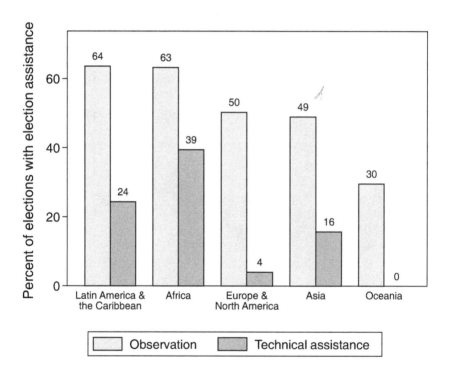

FIGURE I.4. Rates of election support across regions (worldwide 1990–2012, n=1,107 elections)

higher proportion of a country's elections were supported.[66] Africa stands out as the primary focus region of UN activity: about 39 percent of African elections have received UN technical election assistance for their national elections between 1990 and 2012. Africa has wide variation in election assistance across countries. Some countries have received UN technical assistance before most or all of their national elections (Somalia, Angola, Democratic Republic of the Congo, Mozambique), others less often (South Africa, Benin, Ghana), and some never (Namibia). Beyond Africa, Latin American countries frequently receive technical election assistance. UN technical election assistance has accompanied about 80 percent of elections in Guyana and Haiti; about 40 percent of elections in Mexico, Paraguay, Peru, and Honduras; and no elections in Cuba, Chile, and Surinam.

Technical election assistance is more common in Africa and Latin America than other regions. This is shown in figure I.4.[67] In terms of regional aggregates, almost 40 percent of African elections and a quarter of Latin American elections have received such assistance. In the other regions, rates of technical election assistance are significantly lower, at 16, 4, and 0 percent respectively. Technical election assistance is sporadic in Asia and rare in Europe, North America, and Oceania. For the purpose of studying election aid and particularly technical assistance, that means that issues of selection and non-random treatment loom even larger in Asia, posing greater challenges to inference about effects. Further, in terms of case studies exploiting within-country variation, countries that regularly have election violence but no election support (such as India) make it difficult to investigate the effect of election aid on election violence.

The relative prevalence of election observation across regions follows similar trends: it is more common in Latin America and Africa than other regions. About two thirds of elections in Latin America and Africa have been monitored by reputable observer groups.[68] This contrasts with less than half in Europe and Asia and only a third in Oceania: election observation is less common in these regions than in Latin America and Africa. Overall, both observation and technical election assistance are most common in Africa and Latin America.

Second, Africa and Latin America have high rates of election violence in their region as well as wide variation across and within countries. Figure I.5 shows that these two regions have among the highest rates of election violence in the world. For the 1990–2012 time period, electoral violence before or after election-day accompanied around 30 percent of elections in Africa and Latin America and Asia. In contrast, in Oceania only about 19 percent of elections were accompanied by electoral violence and 10 percent of elections in Europe and North America, which provides less leverage for distinguishing the relative impact of a range of potential influences.

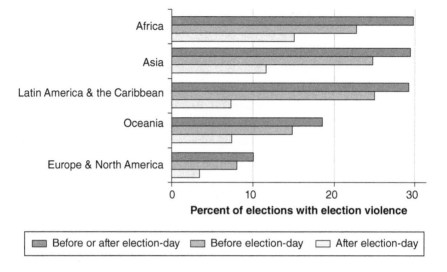

FIGURE I.5.   Rates of electoral violence across regions (worldwide 1990–2012, n=1,169 elections)

Additionally, Africa and Latin America are chosen because they are roughly comparable in levels of democracy. While both regions have some staunch autocracies (Cuba, Zimbabwe, Uganda) and hybrid regimes (Venezuela, Mozambique), they also have a number of democracies (Brazil, Bolivia, Benin, Botswana). This stands in contrast to other regions like Asia and the Middle East, which have quite a number of closed autocracies (North Korea, Vietnam, Saudi Arabia, Oman) and where the move toward democratization has been less consistent in the region. Therefore empirical chapters (2, 3, 4) focus on two regions that have been the focus of international election support: a higher share of elections in Africa and Latin America received both observation and technical election assistance than other regions (see figure I.4). Focusing on regions with sufficient variation in international election support allows for a better assessment of whether changes in support are associated with changes in election violence. In contrast, when election support is rarer—such as technical election assistance in Asia—issues of non-random treatment loom larger, which generates a higher risk that one or two cases are driving findings. To mitigate these risks, this book focuses on Africa and Latin America, and employs statistical models addressing non-random treatment alongside other estimations.

Looking at Africa and Latin America of course does not mean that elections in these two regions are exactly the same. There are differences in election contexts and dynamics, which re-surface in the empirical analyses and findings.

One important difference between the regions is that countries in Latin America democratized earlier and have had more time to develop democratic institutions, such as national election commissions. In Latin America, transitions to democracy began in what Huntington calls the second and third waves of democratization.[69] Even before the start of the third wave with Portugal's revolution in 1974, several countries in Latin America transitioned to multiparty elections. Chile, Colombia, Costa Rica, Uruguay, and Venezuela became and remained fairly democratic, although some have experienced reversions in recent years.[70]

In contrast to the democratic transitions in Latin America beginning long before and during the 1980s, African democratization (and re-democratization after short-lived post-colonial openings) largely set in after 1990. With the exception of early transitions such as in Botswana and Mauritius, most African countries (re-)introduced multiparty elections and transitioned from one-party or military regimes to more competitive electoral regimes after the end of the Cold War.[71] A few countries in North Africa—notably Tunisia, Egypt, and Libya—experienced regime changes even later, during the Arab Spring in the 2010s, leading to debates over a potential fourth wave of democratization.[72]

In addition to the timing of democratization, regional support for democracy and elections also emerged first in Latin America and then in Africa. These developments are reflected in the respective regional organizations: the Organization of American States (OAS) and the African Union (AU). While both regional organizations had internal struggles over the relative importance of sovereignty/non-interference and democracy/elections, democratic principles won out earlier in the OAS than in the AU. While the OAS adopted a democracy clause first in its charter of 1948 and reinforced it in 1997 and 2001, the AU only established its charter on democracy in 2001.[73] Similarly, the OAS engaged in some early forms of election observation first in the 1960s and then more extensively and professionally after the 1980s, while the African Union began only in 1989.[74]

The differential timing of democratization and regional democracy support—starting earlier in Latin America than Africa—has had implications for institutional development. On average, Latin American countries tend to be somewhat more democratic and more developed than African countries, particularly when it comes to national election commissions. Figure I.6 shows the distribution of election commission capacity across regions, with higher values indicating more capable institutions.[75] The grey boxes encompass the 25th to 75th percentile of values, and hollow circles mark outliers.[76] Black diamonds indicate median capacity. The median capacity of national election commissions clearly varies across regions: from serious deficiencies (coded 2) in Africa, to partial deficiencies (coded 3) in Latin America and Asia, to adequate resources (coded 4) in Oceania, North America, and Europe.

Latin American countries tend to have more capable election commissions than African countries, giving rise to a ceiling effect. When election support is deployed, the maximum impact it can have is likely smaller in Latin America than Africa because election commissions are already more developed, elections more credible, and election violence less frequent. In contrast, where election commissions have lower capacity levels (Africa), election support can induce larger changes in election credibility and electoral violence.

Thus, the effects of election aid on election violence should be stronger in Africa than Latin America. This is indeed what empirical analyses in subsequent chapters show. Rather than cutting out the region with smaller effects and focusing only on stronger and consistently statistically significant results, though, Latin America is included precisely to test and illustrate some of the scope conditions of the argument and to get a better idea about the type of countries in which election support is impactful. This gives us a better sense of the circumstances under which arguments holds. Analyses on both regions also allow us to put in context much of the previous work on election violence, which has largely focused on Africa. As with research on any phenomenon, it is important to not just examine the cases where the it happens but also where it does not happen.

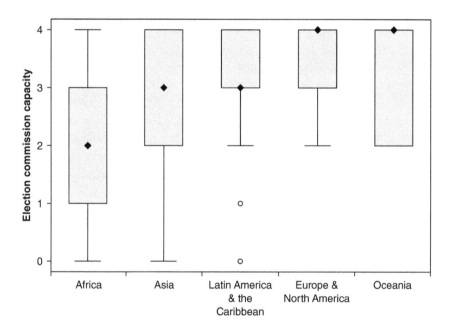

FIGURE I.6. Election commission capacity across regions (worldwide 1990–2012, n=1,165 elections)

In addition to the quantitative evidence, I provide qualitative case material from a number of elections. These are intended to illustrate the argument and deepen the analyses and are thus mostly chosen as representative cases. The qualitative case material, too, is drawn from Africa and Latin America. However, there are certainly elections outside these two focus regions in which my argument also applies. To show that the argument has traction in other parts of the world as well, the empirical chapters also note cases from other regions, such as Asia and the former Soviet Union. For example, chapter 3 mentions Georgia as a case of observer criticism and reduced election credibility, and chapter 4 draws on Bangladesh—whose election commission also had capacity issues and where the voter register had been a conflict point—to illustrate the role of technical assistance for election commission capacity and reduced loser challenges beyond Latin America and Africa.

Is Election Violence Undesirable?

Before previewing the book chapters, it is worthwhile to step back for a moment and elaborate on the hitherto implicit assumption that election violence is undesirable. While this might seem obvious to many, some may argue that there are cases where post-vote violence has led incumbents to stand down, resulting in leadership change. Some of the color revolutions in Eastern Europe come to mind, such as the Tulip Revolution in Kyrgyzstan. In Kyrgyzstan's 2005 parliamentary election, the candidates affiliated with the autocratic incumbent, Askar Akayev, did unsurprisingly well, but international election observers criticized the election. The day after the election, observers from the Organization for Security and Cooperation in Europe (OSCE) issued a preliminary statement saying that the election "fell short of . . . standards for democratic elections in a number of important areas" and that it "was undermined throughout the country by widespread vote buying, deregistration of candidates, interference with independent media, and a low level of confidence in electoral and judicial institutions on the part of candidates and voters."[77] Condemnation by reputable election observers prompted mass protests, which soon clashed with riot police. In the end, three people were killed and hundreds injured. However, in the heat of unrest, Akayev fled to Russia for exile and resigned. The condemned elections were nullified and new elections were held four months later, giving rise to new leadership. So isn't election violence worth the cost? I contend that it is not, for three reasons: rare positive outcomes, democratic theory, and detrimental consequences.

First, for every "good" post-election instance of violence like Kyrgyzstan, there are many other examples where post-vote violence did not lead to leadership change or, perhaps more importantly, democratization. It remains an open empirical question whether post-election violence on average leads to positive, negative, or no political changes. To my knowledge, the link between post-vote violence and democratization has not been put to systematic empirical tests. If post-vote violence were associated with democratization, proponents of the argument would still have to weigh positive outcomes against the scale of casualties. Further, pre-election violence is more common than post-election violence, and—from a review of cases—seems even less linked to leadership change or democratization.

Second, basic democratic theory precludes election violence. The fundamental premise of the theoretical concept of "democracy" is that it provides a nonviolent, peaceful solution to succession struggles. Peaceful elections are a cornerstone of democracy. In Robert Dahl's classic definition of polyarchy, it is a key requirement that "elected officials are chosen in frequent and fairly conducted elections in which *coercion is comparatively uncommon*."[78] While the importance of elections relative to other institutions and freedoms has been debated,[79] elections are a necessary component of democracy. As Michael Bratton put it, "while you can have elections without democracy, you cannot have democracy without elections."[80] Further, few people would disagree with Dahl's argument that peaceful transitions of power are a minimal requirement of democracy as well as a key advantage over other systems of government. This is not just high political theory but a practical reality for citizens' perception of governance. As one government official remarked about Afghanistan's 2014 relatively peaceful election: "Whenever there has been a new king or president [in our past], it has been accompanied by death and violence. For the first time, we are experiencing democracy."[81] While elections are not a panacea, peaceful and credible elections are minimum requirements of democracy.

Third, violent elections have detrimental consequences for democracy, development, and conflict. In terms of democracy, election violence can have negative effects on democratic attitudes and behavior, such as voter turnout and candidate participation. When elections trigger conflict rather than serving as a peaceful means of selecting leaders, citizens may justifiably shift to prefer stability over political rights. Public support for democracy decreases when elections become associated with violence,[82] such as harassment, intimidation, unrest, and destruction. Specifically, fear of campaign violence is associated with reduced support for multiple parties, competitive elections, satisfaction with democracy, and a small increase in support for returning to the previous autocratic form of government.[83] Further, election violence may also lower the legitimacy of the resulting government because it came to power in a flawed process that may not have reflected the will of voters. Case studies suggest that election violence can also generate frustration with politicians and the police because they failed to protect citizens from violence,[84] or worse, deliberately allowed violence to unfold.[85] Citizens' frustration with politics can linger for years after violence occurs and shape expectations about what elections mean. As one Zimbabwean citizen put it: "It will never be different with the same spirit of killing. I know that when these coming elections are coming, I know many people are going to die."[86] Overall, then, election violence may give electoral competition and democracy more broadly a bad name, making alternative forms of governance relatively more attractive.

Apart from impairing democratic attitudes, election violence can also change behavior and in particular turnout. Most research indicates that campaign violence reduces turnout,[87] although in some elections it also seems to have been used to forcefully mobilize voters and increase the vote of the violence-perpetrating parties.[88] Usually, fearing campaign violence lowers turnout because it reduces the ability and willingness of citizens to cast their votes.[89] That is, turnout is lower when election violence increases the costs of voting. Voting is always costly, requiring informational and physical effort, and as costs increase and benefits remain constant, the rational voter should be less likely to vote.[90] These costs are substantially higher if the act of voting risks one's physical safety. Targets of campaign violence may "choose" to abstain on election-day due to earlier intimidation, often abandoning their right to vote not just in the current but also in future elections.[91] For example, Nigerians' odds of voting decreased by 52 percent if they or someone they knew was threatened with violence for a certain vote choice.[92] There are more extreme cases. In Sri Lanka, only 1 percent of voters voted in the Tamil-dominated district of Jaffna, "partly due to intimidation and pressures" from the Tamil Tigers/LTTE.[93]

Finally, citizens may be less willing or interested in voting when their vote choice has been restricted. Violence in the run-up to elections can also cause candidates to withdraw or not register in the first place, which limits candidates' political rights as well as voters' choice. For example, in the Ethiopian elections of 1992, 2000, and 2001, the opposition withdrew its participation due to intimidation and harassment by the ruling party.[94] Similarly, in Zimbabwe's 2008 presidential election, the opposition candidate withdrew when the ruling party and associated security forces systematically targeted and killed opposition supporters after the first round. Overall, about a hundred opposition activists were killed and thousands more were tortured and raped. This violence was effective: the main challenger (Tsvangirai) withdrew, resulting in an unopposed victory for President Robert Mugabe.[95] Election violence can also impair citizens' ability to turn out on election-day by interfering with voter registration, physical access to polling stations, and physical displacement.[96] For instance, in Kenya thousands of people left Mombasa before the 1997 and 2007 elections because of ethnic cleansing in the campaigning period.[97]

In addition to undermining democracy, violent elections can also dent economic development, and the human cost can be staggering. While they were extreme cases, post-vote violence after three African elections led to about two thousand people killed, hundreds injured, and 250,000 people displaced (Kenya 2007, Cote d'Ivoire 2010, and Nigeria 2011). Indirect human costs arise when periods of election violence limit individuals' access to medicine and health facilities, resulting in treatment interruption.[98] Human costs have implications for human capital and labor force. Property damage to houses and shops deprives citizens of their livelihoods, often with no or little government compensation. Even agriculture and tourism, in some countries the main sources of national income, can take a significant hit.[99] Similar to civil wars, high levels of election violence can also result in "development in reverse as incidents of violence undermine government legitimacy, scare away domestic foreign investors, and result in low levels of social trust."[100]

Moreover, election violence may trigger larger conflict. For example, after the 1992 elections in Angola, the country plunged back into civil war, and the 1999 independence referendum in East Timor resulted in 1,400 civilian casualties due to violent attacks by anti-independence militias. Even when large-scale conflict does not erupt, subnational regions or entire countries can fall into a conflict trap, a vicious cycle in which conflicts aggravate existing poverty and other societal cleavages, which increases the risk of future conflict.[101] The relapse into conflict is particularly unfortunate when elections have been part of peace-building strategies.

In short, the consequences of election violence are detrimental and can be severe for democratic attitudes and behavior, development, and larger conflict risks. Although there are a few cases where post-vote violence has resulted in leadership change or democratization, a review of existing work and cases indicate that the vast majority of violent elections have not resulted in positive consequences. While future research is needed to answer this question definitively, the weight of the evidence supports the notion that election violence is undesirable.

Chapter Outline

In chapter 1, I present my argument in detail. First, I distinguish the logic of violence before vs. after elections and outline frequent causes and triggers, highlighting those that can be influenced by external election support. Then I detail how the effect of international election support on election violence depends on the type of support (observation or technical assistance) and the election period (before/after voting). I specify testable hypotheses and contrast them with alternative approaches, emphasizing strictly domestic factors. I also introduce the main empirical measures used in subsequent chapters.

In chapters 2 through 4, I test the argument proposed in chapter 1 and its observable implications. Chapter 2 empirically tests the pre-election argument. I leverage cross-national data on technical election assistance, observation, and election violence for Africa and Latin America since 1990. I show that election support significantly reduces campaign violence. I substantiate the causal mechanism about limiting manipulation and removing conflict triggers with a test of alternative explanations and illustrative case material, including data from elections in Sierra Leone, Liberia, and several other countries.

Chapters 3 and 4 shift the focus to the post-election period. Electoral losers are important for the dynamics of violence unfolding after elections, since the peaceful implementation of any election outcome requires their consent to an adverse result. Chapter 3 examines the effect of observer verdicts on post-election violence. I document how election observers' negative verdict about an election's credibility can exacerbate violence by strengthening electoral losers. I show that international condemnations increase post-election violence and that this works through loser challenges. I also show that this observer effect is not due to fraud alone or reverse causation. I then flesh out the large-N results and illustrate these dynamics with case material from Kenya, Sierra Leone, Cote d'Ivoire, and short examples from other regions. This chapter contributes to research on election monitoring by highlighting its effects on violence, whereas much prior research has underlined effects on related phenomena, such as fraud, boycotts, and protests. It also contributes to research on the negative unintended effects of international organizations.

In chapter 4, I show that technical assistance can reduce post-election violence. Using data on UN technical election assistance, I present quantitative evidence that such assistance has reduced violence in Africa, and I document that this effect works through increasing the capacity and credibility of the election commission and the cleaner election process. Importantly, these analyses account for the previous quality of the national election commission. The mechanism—increased capacity and credibility of the election commission—is further illustrated with case material from elections in Guyana and Bangladesh. Since technical assistance has received virtually no scholarly attention, chapters 2 and 4 provide some of the first quantitative empirical results about its effects.

The concluding chapter summarizes the book's arguments and findings and outlines implications for research and policymaking. The international community has invested considerable resources in democracy aid, often with the aim of influencing and assessing the credibility of elections and reducing conflict around elections. Yet, as the chapters demonstrate, these efforts have had mixed results. Here, I suggest that international election support could focus more on strengthening domestic election commissions to help them hold more credible—and thus more peaceful—elections. I also outline ways to conduct election observation that might mitigate the risk of post-election violence.

1

CREDIBLE ELECTION THEORY

How does international democracy aid influence election violence? In this chapter, I explain how external election support can alter the incentives of domestic actors to engage in violence by shaping election credibility. First, I conceptualize election violence and explain the different logics of violence pre- and post-election. I then outline the frequent causes and triggers of violence and highlight which of these can be influenced by election support. This yields a baseline model of election violence, which I use in the empirical analyses of chapters 2, 3, and 4.

Second, I describe how international election support can influence electoral violence by changing the election's credibility. I explain how the effect of democracy aid on violence depends on the type of support (monitoring or technical assistance) and the election period (before/after voting). Technical assistance has the potential to reduce violence before and after elections by strengthening the credibility of election management and thus the credibility of the announced result. Observation can also reduce pre-election violence by monitoring the behavior of the participants and making misconduct costly. After elections, however, observation can exacerbate post-election violence by lowering election credibility. I derive testable hypotheses from the argument and contrast them with alternative approaches emphasizing strictly domestic factors.

Election Violence: Concept, Logic, and Drivers

Conceptualizing Election Violence

Election violence is a type of political violence aimed at influencing the election process or outcome and occurs temporally close to elections. More specifically, election violence is physical force intended to hurt or kill someone in order to influence an election. Electoral violence differs from other forms of political violence in terms of its timing, target, and motive/purpose.[1] I address each of those three aspects in turn.

First, election violence differs from other forms of political violence in its timing, as it occurs temporally close to election events. While many people tend to think of elections as events occurring on a specific day, it is more useful to conceptualize elections as processes involving a period before and after election-day. Conceptualizing elections as a process rather than an event is useful because even though voting is restricted to election-day(s), many activities related to the election take place both before and after voting. Although the number of months associated with an election varies somewhat by country (the length of campaigning periods differs, for instance), scholars most frequently define the election timeframe as the six-month period before an election and the three-month period after the election has passed.[2] This is the definition that I use in this book as well. This period of time is usually appropriate because most election-related fatalities and incidents occur within this timeframe. Hence, the unit of analysis in this book is the national election and within that, the relevant election period—either violence before polling (six months before and including election-day) or violence in the three months after polling.

Second, electoral violence differs from other forms of political violence in terms of its target: it is directed against people and stakeholders involved in the electoral process. These include candidates, their supporters, voters, and election officials. Physical harm against such stakeholders manifests itself in targeted assassinations, killings, injuries, arrests, and sometimes kidnappings. While this book focuses on the physical use of force against people (as measured by election-related casualties), broader definitions of election violence used elsewhere also include property damage directed against campaign signs or posters and election facilities, such as the national election commission, voter registration centers, polling places, and party offices. Some other definitions of election violence also include intimidation, threats, or verbal abuse. These manifestations often present empirical challenges for research because they require more subjective choices for measurement. When does a verbal threat constitute election violence or ethnic conflict? Further, how can we know how many people were impacted by a verbal threat? Were only two bystanders intimidated or a much larger group of people, assuming that victims shared their experience with family, friends, and their broader community? When is graffiti or broken windows election violence rather than vandalism? We also know that women tend to fear election violence more than men—so the same act of intimidation can be perceived quite differently. Thus it often remains unclear how many people were present or affected by intimidation and threats, which makes these aspects more difficult to measure consistently.

Even if we exclude more difficult-to-quantify aspects like intimidation, election violence has been rather pervasive. If we focus on whether people were killed or injured as a result of electoral violence, we find that many countries in the developing world have had more than half of their national elections since 1990 affected by violence. Figure 1.1 visualizes each country's proportion of elections that were violent, with darker shades indicating that a higher percentage of elections have been associated with violence.[3] Figure 1.1 documents that election violence is a global phenomenon: even in industrialized, advanced democracies, it is not unheard of.[4] Yet it disproportionately affects Africa, Latin America, and Asia. Violence varies widely even within the most conflict-prone continent, Africa. Data indicate that some African countries have not experienced election violence between 1990 and 2012 (such as Namibia, Botswana, Mozambique, Zambia); many other countries have experienced violence at some of their elections; and in a third set of countries, violence accompanied more than 60 percent of elections (such as Zimbabwe, DR Congo, Kenya, Nigeria, Cote d'Ivoire, Algeria, and Sudan).[5]

For the empirical analyses of this book, I have restricted election violence to the more clear-cut, objective, and replicable measure of casualties. Unlike low-level harassment or psychological pressure (intimidation), the (attempted) termination of life in the form of killings and injuries is more difficult for either side to dispute and more consistently and reliably documented. Casualty counts, too, are not perfect measures but lend themselves better to large-scale data collection and analysis for the reasons outlined above. Thus the measure used in the empirical analyses is casualties: the number of people killed or injured in election-related conflict.

Third, election violence differs from other forms of political violence in its motive. As is usually the case, motive is often the trickiest of these three aspects to properly examine. Some forms of politically motivated violence are relatively easy to distinguish from election violence. For example, terrorism, civil war, secession movements, or violence related to drug trafficking occur throughout the year; while they may also happen during election times, they are usually not aimed directly at the election process. For example, the Taliban have been active in Afghanistan for many years and carry out attacks on a near-daily basis.

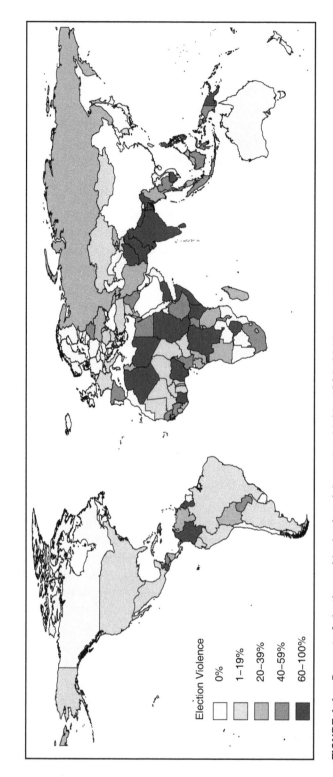

FIGURE 1.1. Percent of elections with election violence (worldwide 1990–2012, n=1,169 elections/162 countries)

Since the stream of Taliban attacks is almost daily, some of these attacks also occur during election campaigns and on election-day; but only some of these attacks are actually aimed at disrupting the election. Taliban attacks would occur whether or not an election happened to be held. Thus, while Taliban attacks on outposts or markets are likely "regular" political violence, attacks on polling stations or against election officials, candidates, and voters are more likely to be election-related. Since violence is an illegal strategy, perpetrators rarely if ever give a detailed account of their motivation behind particular incidents or attacks. While an actor's reasoning often remains unobservable, it is still possible to make inferences from observed behavior, such as the target or location (e.g. candidate, polling station).

That said, it is important not to mistake all political violence that happens to occur during election periods as election-related violence. When in doubt, it is advisable to err on the side of caution when measuring election violence. If political violence during an election period is not clearly related to election targets or motives and its electoral nature cannot be established, it should not be considered or counted as election violence.

Finally, it is important to understand that, for perpetrators, election violence is a strategic tool, used to influence political processes. It is a tool of political competition employed to maximize the chances of winning the election. It should therefore come as no surprise that election violence is usually orchestrated by politicians, particularly incumbent politicians or their affiliates. According to data collected on election violence in sub-Saharan Africa, about 80 percent of pre-election violence and 70 percent of post-election violence is orchestrated by incumbents.[6] The remaining share of violence is organized by opposition forces or both/multiple camps. While opposition forces seem to be responsible for a smaller share of violence, they at times engage in nonviolent actions that increase the risk of clashing with police (government forces) or prompting violent reactions. Further, election violence can be—or at least can appear to be—spontaneous,[7] such as when supporters of rivaling candidates/parties did not expect to meet but then clashed. More often, however, election violence is organized, planned, and directed by political elites. It is strategic. While elites are responsible for planning election violence, they are rarely associated with the implementation of violence. Case studies in comparative politics research document that politicians often implement violence through party militias, youth wings, or unemployed thugs for hire, exploiting particularly vulnerable sections of society.[8]

While some early work has conceptualized violence as the ultimate form of fraud,[9] much subsequent research—and this book—examines these two phenomena as distinct forms of manipulation (nonviolent fraud vs. violence).[10]

Related research has begun to theorize and examine how politicians choose between fraud (ballot stuffing, vote buying, media bias) and intimidation/ violence as alternative means of manipulating elections.[11] Outside the election context, other research has addressed why actors choose violent or nonviolent means[12] as well as the relationship between dissent and repression.[13]

The Logic of Election Violence

It is important to distinguish the logic of election violence before and after election-day. Pre-election violence has different motivations than post-election violence. Pre-vote violence is used by political actors (the government or opposition forces) to influence vote choice and turnout. In contrast, post-vote violence usually erupts in reaction to the announced result, as the loser violently challenges the election outcome or the winner violently represses a peaceful loser challenge.

These distinct theoretical motivations for violence before vs. after voting imply that patterns of election violence should differ over time. Figure 1.2 supports this observable implication by showing that even within individual countries, political violence is not constant within election cycles. Figure 1.2 illustrates the distribution of election violence (whether election-related casualties occurred) in African countries before and after election-day for national elections 1990–2012.[14] For each country, it shows the proportion of elections experiencing electoral violence, with darker shading indicating a higher percentage of violent elections.

Figure 1.2 demonstrates that pre- and post-election violence are not the same; this suggests that there are different dynamics motivating election violence over the course of an election cycle. It is not just general political violence that consistently pervades the election period. Violence varies with stages in the electoral cycle. For instance, in some countries, pre-election violence is a regular phenomenon but post-election violence is not. This group includes South Africa, Sierra Leone, Algeria, Tunisia, and Libya. Other countries tend to experience post- but not pre-election violence, such as Tanzania, Guinea-Bissau, and Somalia.

While election violence is most commonly deployed when it is used to influence vote choice or turnout before elections, and less so when results are challenged after elections, there are also rare cases in which violence is used to disrupt and reject the election itself. In other words, sometimes violence is not a means of influencing the outcome but rather a means of preventing the election from happening. This was the Taliban's strategy in Afghanistan when it targeted election facilities and stakeholders to disrupt Afghanistan's elections in 2014 and 2018.[15] This was also the goal of terrorist group Boko Haram, which disrupted Nigeria's

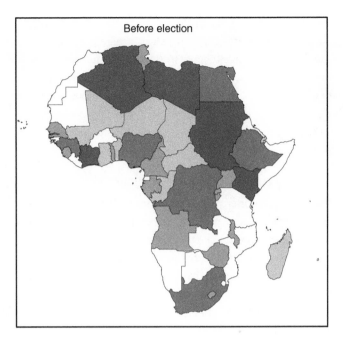

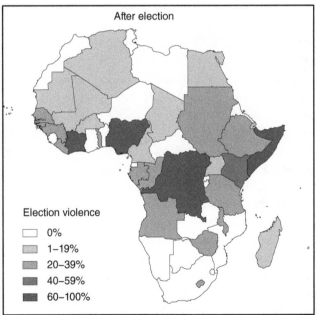

FIGURE 1.2. Election violence in Africa before and after election-day (1990–2012, n=312 election/49 countries)

2015 presidential elections by attacking polling stations, killing voters and a politician, arguing that authority comes from a spiritual figure rather than from the people.[16] While these examples demonstrate that violence can be used to prevent voting from taking place at all, violence is more commonly used to influence the results of elections. Violence is frequently used to coerce certain voters to cast ballots in favor of a particular candidate, to prevent certain segments of the population from participating in the election, or to contest the announced election result.

INCENTIVES FOR PRE-ELECTION VIOLENCE

Pre-election violence is often employed to shape turnout and vote choice and thus ultimately election outcomes.[17] It is a tool of political competition during the campaigning period used primarily to keep the opponents' supporters from voting, but it is also used to mobilize one's own supporters or influence partisan choice. One mechanism of doing that is raising the salience of particular identities and thus voting blocs, as Wilkinson argues in his work on election-related riots.[18] Note that the logic of violence is identical on election-day and in the campaigning period before election-day: perpetrators are still trying to influence vote choice and turnout until the polls close. A reading of cases confirms this. For example, in Ghana 2004, "political parties have accused one another of encouraging their supporters to vote early and then disrupt the process in the afternoon to prevent the opposing party supporters from casting their ballots."[19] Thus, the logic of violence up to and including election-day is consistent: to change the election result by influencing mobilization and/or partisanship.

Campaign violence can limit both the ability and willingness of citizens to vote, thus reducing turnout. Election violence can impair citizens' ability to turn out on election-day by interfering with voter registration, blocking polling stations, and achieving the physical displacement of potential voters so that they cannot reach polling places.[20] Citizens can lose their willingness to vote when their preferred candidate has withdrawn or failed to register because the candidate experienced violence and intimidation.[21] Campaign violence is often used to keep an opponent's supporters from turning out on election-day, but it can also be used to mobilize one's own supporters. Pre-election violence can be used to increase party discipline and to boost identity politics and the stakes surrounding an election; it can be used to convert a passive supporter into a rabid voter fearful of the consequences of not voting or of what happens if "others" should prevail. In Burundi 2010, Kenya 2007, and India more regularly, campaign violence has been used to boost the support of the parties initiating the violence.[22]

In addition to changing turnout, campaign violence can also be used to change vote choice by threatening citizens to vote for a certain candidate/party or—even earlier in the game—by keeping potential candidates from running in the election at all. Recent work has noted that violence can be used early in the campaigning period as intra-party "nomination violence" when candidates of the same party vie for a spot on the general election ballot.[23] Pre-vote violence can cause candidates to withdraw or not register in the first place, which limits candidates' political rights as well as voters' choice.

INCENTIVES FOR POST-ELECTION VIOLENCE

In contrast to pre-election violence, which is intended to influence vote choice and turnout, post-election violence usually erupts if losers challenge the announced result. After elections, the main actors are not necessarily incumbent and opposition forces but rather the electoral loser and winner. During this time, losers have incentives to challenge the announced result if the election was not credible.[24] The loser's consent is more likely when the election result is credible, and this credibility can be shaped by external support. A loser challenge can occur in various ways: it can be verbal, legal, or physical and can be itself violent or generate violent repression by the winner.

Election losers are key actors in the post-election context because they have both motive and opportunity to challenge announced results. Losers have incentives to withhold their consent because they have the most to gain from a change in the status quo of future political leadership. In contrast, election winners usually have few incentives to resort to force without a provocation. Election losers are also critical because they "decide whether to fight on" or comply with adverse results.[25] For the election outcome to be implemented, displeased losers and their supporters must consent to the adverse result rather than challenge it.[26] In many nascent democracies, losers constitute a "weak link in the chain of stable democratic governments."[27] While winners and losers always tend to perceive an election's legitimacy differently, the usual winner-loser gap in these perceptions is substantially wider in countries with less democratic experience.[28] This attitude translates into behavior. Compared to election winners, losers are more willing to denounce flawed elections, to defend institutions against manipulation, and are less inclined to consent to government authority, particularly in African countries.[29] In short, the consent of election losers is critical for post-election peace and democratic stability.

The loser's decision to challenge or consent to the result is part of the strategic interaction between loser and winner after an election. The interaction between loser and winner can be seen as steps in a strategic game and is illustrated as such in appendix figure 1B.1. The basic intuition of this game is fairly straightforward, so I describe it here and relegate formal details to appendix 1B. I concentrate on the two key players: the winner (W) and the loser (L).[30]

After election results are announced, the loser either consents to the election result or challenges it. The loser's consent ends the post-election game and allows the winner to accept his or her office smoothly and peacefully. Alternatively, the loser can decide to challenge the result, for example through a verbal announcement, legal proceeding, or street protests, which all involve some marginal cost of challenging. If the loser challenges the result, the winner must decide whether to resist that challenge or concede. If the winner concedes to the loser, the game ends.[31] If the winner resists—through a verbal act or violent repression—then the loser chooses whether to back down or fight. At this point, a decision by the loser to fight will likely lead to violence used by both sides and sometimes even civil war.

That is, post-election violence can be initiated by either actor and erupt at any of three stages: (1) if the loser challenges violently rather than through legal means or peaceful demonstrations; (2) if the winner violently represses the loser's peaceful protests; or (3) if the loser resorts to violence after the winner's resistance. My argument is not about *who* initiates violence but that loser challenges heighten post-vote violence.

What makes the loser decide whether to consent to or to challenge the election result? The relative support for the loser vis-a-vis the winner is critical. The basic insight—supported by the model—is that a balance of power (symmetry) increases conflict and a dominance of power (asymmetry) diminishes conflict.[32] Greater support for the electoral loser has a conflict-increasing effect. Anything that boosts the loser's chance of winning a potential post-election fight encourages conflict and loser challenges. This intuition is in line with related research on the link between elections and civil war. This research has noted the link between vote shares as proxies for the mobilization potential of each camp: "although the probability of winning an election increases with the size of a group, so does the probability of winning an armed conflict."[33] Voting and fighting are complements rather than substitutes.[34] Some argue that casting a ballot and fighting are linked "in the sense that people who vote for a party are also likely to fight for the same party."[35] Election results are a proxy for the distribution of underlying support and the potential to mobilize a sufficiently large portion of the population against another candidate or party. If the loser is more powerful—due to domestic popular support or external legitimation, as I outline below—he or she has greater incentives to challenge the announced result.

Loser challenges of election results can occur in various ways: verbal, legal, or physical. The loser may announce that he or she does not respect the outcome of the election, may file a legal challenge to the court, or may mobilize support-ers to pour into the streets for protests, demonstrations, or violent riots.[36] When institutions to address election disputes are weak or nonexistent, contestants are more likely to express their disputes with extra-institutional means such as vio-lence. Violence—physical force and harm—then occurs when either the initial challenge by the loser is violent or when the winner violently represses a peaceful loser challenge.

In contrast to the loser, the winner has little or no incentives to wield violence after elections uninitiated. While the loser has incentives to challenge outcomes in an effort to change the status quo or voice dissatisfaction, the winner has few incentives to use violence against the loser, simply because he or she has already won. Doing "nothing" until inauguration is the rational choice. Thus it should not come as a surprise that it is rare for the winner to initiate post-election violence without any prior loser challenge. When it happens, it is an effort to punish the losing camp for "wrong" behavior. The winning camp at times uses post-election violence to punish the losing camp for making the "wrong" choices—either not participating or participating in favor of the opposition. Armed with information from election results about the location of candidates' support bases, it becomes rather easy to target repression in the "correct" locations. For example, in the 1991 presidential election in Burkina Faso, the opposition refused to participate and voter turnout was only 25 percent, denying the incumbent, President Blaise Compoare, a strong mandate. After the election, two opposition candidates were attacked: one grenade attack killed opposition activist Clement Ouedraogo, and another attack seriously injured opposition member Moctar Tall. Many people in Burkina Faso believed the government—the winning candidate's camp—was responsible for these attacks.[37]

To conclude, it is important to recognize the different logics of violence before and after elections. Pre- and post-vote violence has different data-generating processes underlying it. Pre-election violence is used to influence vote choice and turnout, whereas post-election violence often erupts after the losing camp challenges the announced result. The next section outlines the main drivers of election violence generally as well as a few specific to each period (before vs. after elections).

The Drivers of Election Violence

Understanding the logic of violence outlined in the preceding pages is important for understanding the next step: the drivers of election violence, that is to say, factors that can increase or reduce election violence by altering the incentives of potential perpetrators. In this section, I propose a baseline model of election violence containing several factors and then explain which of these factors can be influenced by international democracy promotion. The baseline model of election violence presented here includes the most common factors highlighted in existing research[38] and practitioner handbooks.[39] The model that emerges from those sources is then used as a baseline model for empirical analyses in chapters 2, 3, and 4. In those chapters, I add the key explanatory variables (technical election assistance and observation) to the baseline model in order to empirically demonstrate how democracy aid influences election violence above and beyond domestic factors currently identified in the literature.

The baseline model of election violence proposed here includes several drivers which can be divided into two groups: country-level root causes and election-specific triggers. These drivers are listed in table 1.1. Underlying root causes of election violence are contextual country factors. Oftentimes such root causes are deep-seated and slow-changing. These factors include democratic constraints on political elites, post-conflict (civil war history), economic development, natural resources, population size, and ethnic fractionalization. Since elections are high-stakes events with a significant impact on political power, underlying tensions or conflict risk factors can erupt during elections. Some election-specific triggers of violence include fraud (for post-vote violence), competition (incumbent running for pre-election violence, or the loser's vote share for post-election violence), poll type (legislative, executive, or general election), and previous election violence. I explain each group of factors in turn. In table 1.1, concepts followed by an asterisk differ slightly in their empirical measures between the pre- and post-election models.

Underlying root causes are contextual and can generate discontent (incentivizing violence) or leave potential perpetrators relatively unconstrained (lowering the costs of violence). For example, low accountability (few democratic checks and balances on political elites, a powerful incumbent) is perhaps the most important factor influencing election violence.[40] When the perpetrators of fraud and violence go unpunished, this can generate incentives for (more) violence in two ways. First, impunity for election manipulation signals that the election commission and other democratic institutions are weak, so that the costs for committing election crimes are low. This encourages (more) illicit political activity during elections. Second, when election manipulation is not addressed by formal institutions, contestants may take matters into their own hands and resort to extra-institutional means to call attention to what they see as unfairness. The expected level of accountability—that is, the cost for manipulation—often depends on institutional constraints on the executive/political elites and conflict history. In advanced democracies, there are many institutional checks on the executive (especially the judiciary and the legislature) and also informal checks such as independent media and civil society. In contrast, electoral autocracies feature few if any checks on the incumbent: the opposition is constrained, media and civil society are curtailed, and the judiciary is often staffed by incumbent partisans. In this context, incumbents face few if any consequences if they direct party loyalists or state security forces to attack political opponents.

It also matters whether elections are held in a post-conflict environment because previous experience of civil war may lower accountability costs and increase the means of violence, which increase incentives to engage in election violence. A large body of work has noted how elections in post-conflict settings are different in terms of their context and purpose.[41] Post-conflict elections often occur after peace agreements to resolve who governs, and those peace agreements often give the international community a large role in assisting the electoral process through funding, logistics, security, and monitoring.

Post-conflict elections serve additional purposes beyond "just" choosing a government: they are meant to facilitate or symbolize an end to intra-state conflict, re-conciliate former combatants, consolidate peace agreements, and further democratization.[42] Such elections are supposed to be a conflict-resolution mechanism short of war and to replace bullets with ballots. Yet these high aspirations often hit the hard reality of the most challenging domestic contexts to hold elections, as years of civil war have left their mark: deep political polarization, grievances, weak institutions of all kinds (parties, judiciary, government bureaucracy, media, civil society, roads/infrastructure), and a large group of people with recent combat experience, subject to usually imperfect demobilization and re-integration. These impediments are deepened by refugees, internally displaced people, and a voter register that is likely out of touch with reality. Holding an election under such circumstances would be challenging for any election commission but especially so for commissions destroyed by war, with few

TABLE 1.1 Which election violence drivers can be influenced by international election support

	DRIVERS WHICH CAN BE INFLUENCED	DRIVERS WHICH CANNOT BE INFLUENCED
country-level root causes	democratic constraints	post-conflict economic development natural resources population size ethnic fractionalization
election-specific triggers	(real or perceived) fraud*	competition* poll type past election violence*

professional staff and strained budgets. In post-conflict contexts, international election support is critical to help overcome these obstacles, to lift elections off the ground, and to make them more credible. Based on detailed case studies of post-conflict elections, Kumar summarizes: "International electoral assistance is essential . . . without substantial international assistance, elections would not have materialized in Angola, Cambodia, Haiti, Liberia, and Mozambique, and they would have been less credible in El Salvador and Nicaragua. The Ethiopian elections, which saw the lowest level of international involvement, were also the least credible of the postconflict elections covered in this volume."[43] International election support can help compensate for the lack of administrative and financial capacity to organize elections, improve the voter register, and otherwise improve the prospects of credible elections.

With regard to influencing election violence, countries recovering from civil war often have weak institutions that lack sufficient capacity to enforce the rules and apply the necessary tools to hold credible elections (party registration, voter register, voter education, and the like). Weak capacity to enforce rules and ensure security is of great consequence for post-conflict elections where past experience with violence has normalized violent behavior such that individual incidents go un-reported or un-punished. Lower accountability means lower costs for violence. Further, unresolved grievances from a recent civil war can provide a motive for violent competition, particularly if the politically opposed sides were also combatants in the civil war. Old grievances may generate differing expectations about who should be in power and may lower the bar at which violence is seen as beneficial. Thus, if political elites have incentives to organize election violence, they are more willing to do so if accountability is low: when they face fewer constraints or act in an environment where violence is normal.

In addition to low accountability, lower levels of economic development—which often result from conflict—can lessen the costs for violence and thus increase incentives for engaging in election violence. Lower economic development makes it easier and cheaper for political elites to hire (oftentimes) unemployed young men to engage in violence, for instance.[44] If individuals have little to lose, they are more likely to engage in risky activities. It is worth noting, however, that even countries with a history of civil war vary in election violence. That is, past civil war does not explain all country-level variation in election violence. It still leaves variation un-explained: some post-conflict countries tend to have violent elections (Angola, DRC, Haiti), whereas others tend to have relatively peaceful elections (Mozambique, Liberia, Sierra Leone, El Salvador).

While some factors lower the cost of violence, others can increase the benefit of using violence. For instance, the prevalence of natural resources can increase the stakes of elections, since the winner will be able to distribute more goods among his or her supporters—natural resources heighten the stakes because there is more to distribute. Here, the difference between being in and out of power can have substantial implications for supporters of political camps. Hence rivalries over natural resources and conflicts over their distribution can increase the benefits of engaging in election violence. Further, domestic ethnic arrangements—high fractionalization or salient ethnic identities that are split along party lines—can also increase the benefit of using violence because political elites can use violence against the "other" to increase ethnic identification in their own camp.[45] In a range of countries, winning elections is a numbers game of calculating the relative size of ethnic support groups, and polarization along ethnic lines then raises conflict risk along the same lines. Lastly, population size is included in many models because larger countries tend to experience more election violence.

While these underlying root causes of election violence are compelling in some cases, they provide limited leverage in explaining variation in levels of election violence in a single country over the course of several election cycles. That is, many of these lines of inquiry are limited in their causal leverage because largely time-invariant factors—things that change very slowly over the years—cannot explain changes in election violence within a single country across a series of elections. This is especially true of factors like economic development and conflict history, which change only slowly. Since the level of per capita income stays largely constant over five- and ten-year periods, it is difficult to use (largely constant) income as an explanation for violence variation, i.e. why one election remained peaceful and another turned violent, given similar levels of economic development. In addition, most political institutions are usually slow to change, perhaps with one exception: electoral institutions can be strengthened in the short term through democracy support provided by international organizations (discussed further below).

To explain variation across elections within individual countries—as illustrated in figure 1.2—election-level factors provide more leverage than country-level factors. The three most relevant election-level factors for election violence are fraud (for post-election violence), competition, poll type, and past election violence. All four factors can change from one election to the next.

Election fraud is one of the key correlates of post-election violence. After elections, contestation is often triggered by fraud or the exposure of fraud. Perceived or real unfairness is one of the key motivators for contestation.[46] Election-day fraud can serve as a focal point for collective action as it makes it easier for political elites to rally their troops. The exposure of fraud can change individuals' calculus about participating in protest and rebellions.[47] However, relative to the large share of elections where at least one party claimed fraud, the incidence of post-election violence is relatively small. This implies that variation in fraud (or fraud claims) alone cannot explain variation in post-vote violence. Below, I explain how fraud and the external exposure of fraud can be influenced by international election support. Specifically, I argue that it is not fraud itself but rather the exposure of that fraud by credible external actors—in other words, internationally certified fraud—that often facilitates post-election challenges and violence. Following this logic and much of the literature, fraud concerns are included in the post-election models but not the pre-election models.[48]

Further, electoral competition can influence election violence. Before elections, competition is often closely linked to whether the incumbent is running. When the incumbent is running, he or she usually commands a much larger share of resources than opposition candidates; this has the result of tilting the playing field or disproportionately favoring the incumbent in the electoral process. Yet the implications about how competition affects pre-election violence often remain unclear. While the incumbent has access to a large state apparatus to wield coercive power, opponents—who have less access to state coffers and thus less leverage through vote buying and fraud—may use campaign violence as a weapon of the weak. In contrast, the effect of competition on post-election violence is rather clear in that more competitive elections are more prone to violence. This means that when two parties or candidates enjoy similar popular support and election results are close, with a small margin of victory, then incentives are high for the loser to challenge the election. This is because close election results are more likely to be overturned through re-counts or re-votes than when one candidate or party wins in a landslide. In cases where the loser enjoys almost as much popular support as the winner, the large percentage of the population who voted for the losing candidate could be more strongly motivated by perceptions of fraud to protest against the announced result. Thus competition is operationalized as incumbent running for the pre-election models and as loser vote share in the post-election models. Competition is listed as a driver that cannot be influenced by international support because of the way in which it is measured here. The decision of the incumbent to run and the national election result are rarely influenced directly from the outside.[49]

Additionally, poll type—whether the election is for the legislature, the executive, or both—also has the potential to influence election violence because it heightens the stakes and can therefore impact the usefulness of electoral violence as a political tool. While electoral system design seems to matter in some cases,[50] the nature of the election at stake can be particularly important. Executive elections tend to be perceived as more prone to violence because the executive in many countries is more powerful; this is particularly true in sub-Saharan Africa and Latin America, which are predominantly presidential or semi-presidential systems. Given this logic, legislative elections should be less prone to violence than executive elections, which should in turn be less prone to violence than general elections because those combine the stakes—and administrative challenge—of both contests on a single day.

Lastly, many studies of election violence control for whether the country's previous election was violent. That is, studies of campaign violence usually include an indicator of whether the previous election was violent. And studies of post-vote violence usually control for whether pre-election violence occurred. Results about the correlation between pre- and post-vote violence vary. Some have found a correlation between pre- and post-election violence or protest,[51] but others have found no relationship.[52]

This book focuses on the international influences on election violence—particularly those that can increase constraints on political elites or reduce fraud—but I include all of the domestic factors discussed above as control variables for the statistical analyses undertaken in chapters 2, 3, and 4. That is, the baseline model of election violence includes constraints on the executive, conflict history, economic development, natural resources, population size, ethnic fractionalization, as well as competition (incumbent running, loser vote share), poll type, and past election violence. In addition, post-election models also include fraud as a control. Appendix 1C details the data sources and measurement.

The Argument: Election Support, Credibility, and Violence

This section introduces the theoretical argument of how international election support can affect election violence by altering election credibility. As detailed in the introduction, I conceptualize elections as credible when they are competently managed and on a level playing field. For an election to be seen as credible, the process needs to be managed well (usually but not exclusively through the election commission) and political elites need to be held accountable for their actions during the process, so that they can expect to pay costs for tilting the playing field. This is a matter of degree, and countries vary widely in election credibility. Credible Election Theory has two parts: international support can influence election credibility, and more credible elections are less likely to turn violent.

International election support can change the credibility of an election by increasing the accountability of contestants for manipulation and by improving election management. Elections are more credible when potential perpetrators of manipulation (fraud and violence) are held responsible for their actions. If political elites are more likely to be identified and publicly denounced, they are more likely to be deterred from manipulation. This, in turn, means that it is more likely that citizens will vote freely, that citizens will be confident that their votes will be counted, and that the announced result accurately reflects preferences in the population. Yet accountability can also backfire after election-day: when election observers draw attention to manipulation and declare that the election did not meet democratic standards, it can fuel conflict. Such a negative observer verdict reduces the election's credibility and can increase the loser's incentives to challenge the result, potentially leading to violence.

The effectiveness of international election support depends on the reputation of international actors. In particular, the effect of international election observation on election violence hinges on how well observer groups act as an external accountability device. This is why I focus on reputable observer groups throughout this book. Observer groups vary widely in their reputation, which is a function of costly effort, willingness to criticize, and independence.[53] Costly effort involves larger missions, spending more time in the host country (particularly with a smaller, advance group of long-term observers), making a systematic effort to observe, and issuing more detailed reports that outline the reasoning behind their assessment. Willingness to criticize in past elections influences observer reputation: groups that get it wrong and fail to condemn clearly fraudulent elections risk reputation loss. Observer reputation is earned over time (as groups attend and assess elections) and is never fixed or certain, even for experienced groups. For instance, several reputable observer groups did not condemn Kenya's 2017 election, which was subsequently nullified by Kenya's Supreme Court, and this generated a wave of criticism and doubt over the accuracy of even established observer groups.

Reputation has to be earned and preserved time and again. Independence from the host country government or organizations and, to some degree, from single-country external donor funding also boosts reputation. This is one reason why some domestic observer groups and some regional observer groups are seen as less credible: because they sometimes share funding and potential interest in the election outcome rather than the electoral process. Reputable observer groups prioritize and evaluate the electoral process, not the election result. Based on seminal research by Susan Hyde, reputable observer groups include—but are not limited to—the European Union (EU), the Carter Center, the Organization of American States (OAS), and the Commonwealth Secretariat.[54] The National Democratic Institute (NDI), International Republican Institute (IRI), and International Foundation for Electoral Systems (IFES) are also reputable groups because they exert costly effort and are willing to criticize, although host countries have tried to discredit them over questions of independence (partial U.S. government funding).[55] Still other observer organizations are not reputable, as they exert little effort, are rarely or never critical, and have questionable independence; these include the Commonwealth of Independent States and the Shanghai Cooperation Organization. These groups are not the subject of this book. This book focuses on reputable observer groups (and criticism by such reputable groups) as defined here and captured in the Nelda dataset.[56] Only reputable groups are in a position to increase the accountability of contestants for manipulation. Groups that do not criticize do not pose a deterrent threat on potential perpetrators.

Further, elections are more credible when the key election institution—the national election commission (NEC) or another election management body—has a higher capacity to organize and conduct elections. When the NEC is more competent, independent, and able to conduct a clean and smooth electoral process, then there is less room for real or perceived unfairness. The risk of election fraud can be diminished when elections are planned well in advance, when potential shortcomings are identified and addressed, and when technical glitches are avoided. Recent research has highlighted the large role that election commissions play, for both real and perceived election quality: election commissions' performance is the most important driver of citizens' attitudes about election quality in Africa.[57]

Since election fraud and manipulation are key motivators behind election contestation, elections that are perceived to be well conducted should also be less likely to result in electoral violence after voting. Proper tabulation of the votes and accurate aggregation of local to national results generates fewer motives for challenges and thus higher costs of political elites to rally their supporters for contestation. The risk of perceived election fraud can be further reduced with voter education: there is less room for ignorance to be exploited, for propaganda about unfairness to be seen as legitimate, and for rumors to spread if political elites and voters are informed about their rights and responsibilities, the process of voting and tabulation, and institutional channels for dispute resolution. When it is more difficult to mobilize supporters for unrest, political elites who still wish to contest the election and engage in political violence will find it more costly to do so. Violence becomes a less politically viable alternative. In other words, competent election management can reduce the amount of fuel available to feed the fire of election violence.

In a conceptual and qualitative study, Höglund, Jarstad, and Kovacs point to election institutions, and in particular election commissions, as one of the key factors for election violence in war-torn countries.[58] My argument builds on these insights and extends them in two ways: (1) election commissions can improve election quality and help reduce violence also in the campaigning period by providing transparent administration and a venue to manage mistrust and disputes; and (2) election commission capacity can be boosted by technical election assistance. That is, while domestic political will is necessary for reforming election management,[59] international technical assistance helps enhance the logistics and fill capacity gaps that otherwise might remain unaddressed.

With reference to table 1.1, reputable election observers can serve as an external accountability mechanism, acting as an external constraint that helps deter political elites from manipulation and helps level the playing field. Observation and its anticipated report on election quality can serve as an external accountability mechanism by holding political elites accountable for illegitimate practices, deterring manipulation, and thus heightening costs for violence. Also with reference to table 1.1, technical election assistance can increase election management capacity to hold smoother elections, handle disputes better, reduce (real or perceived) fraud, and thus lower incentives for violence. Taken together, more credible elections are less prone to election violence because the costs for using violence are higher and there is less reason to use violence in clean and smooth electoral processes. The other side of the coin is that publicizing manipulation when it happens can reduce election credibility in the short run and thus make contestation and violence more likely. Notably, when international election observers allege that voting or counting were fraudulent, they raise doubt that the election result accurately reflects preferences in the population, suggesting that the credibility of the election is low. In other words, observer condemnation can undermine the legitimacy of the election result. While observer groups largely follow their mandate of publicly judging elections and do not intend to raise tension, a condemnation provides the losing camp a stamp of approval for potential challenges to the election result.

Before proceeding, it is worth addressing two reasonable questions. Some may wonder whether IOs are strategic actors and why IOs are needed in the first place. IOs are often needed in elections in developing countries because they provide authoritative information and resources that would not have been available otherwise. The added value of monitors is providing information on election quality. Hyde argues that international observer groups have several credibility advantages over domestic organizations, such as independent funding and usually an interest in the process rather than in the election outcome.[60] Further, international support is often needed because developing countries tend to encounter resource shortages, and organizing an election can be a daunting task.

Consider Liberia's recent 2017 election, which was the first time in decades that the national election commission was primarily responsible for managing the elections. Two civil wars and the 2014 Ebola crisis have damaged domestic infrastructure and resources: only about half of adults are literate and roads are often in desolate conditions outside the capital Monrovia. While the country is recovering, the physical act of holding an election under these conditions is challenging. This is perhaps most apparent when it comes to the transportation of ballot boxes and staffing of polling stations. Five staff members were to be present in every polling station, but only two of them were required to be literate because otherwise these positions would have been difficult or impossible to fill across the country.

Even with the best domestic efforts, technical glitches or deviations from procedures can be perceived as intentional, potentially raising fears of manipulation. A return to violence could potentially lose years of investment in peacekeeping and reconstruction. In such fragile contexts—and others—external support for the planning, training, staffing, and logistical effort that an election entails is important for election success, that is, for being seen as a credible democratic exercise. In the case of Liberia 2017, the UN provided expertise to the NEC, with the UNDP Chief Technical Advisor physically located in the NEC building for close collaboration. When election disputes and tensions did arise after the first round of presidential elections, the UN helped organize a refresher training on electoral dispute resolution for hearing officers and clerks to better handle complaints.[61] The run-off proceeded peacefully. It is often difficult to see the dog that did not bark, but individual cases such as this show that external support is meaningful and can boost domestic capacity.

Another issue is whether international organizations are strategic in where they go and what they do. For both types of support examined here, host country governments must invite or accept external support. It is an interaction between two actors (and often three, if donors are separate from implementing organizations). Accepting technical assistance often involves intense scrutiny and reforms, which is one reason why governments are less open to assistance than to observation. As I show elsewhere,[62] the demand and supply of technical assistance has systematic components: on the host country side, governments are less likely to request technical assistance when the political costs are high (when they are autocratic) or when the benefits are low (when they already have strong electoral institutions). On the provider side, international organizations are less likely to provide such technical assistance when the government appears to lack the political will for reform and when full project implementation is unlikely. Since we lack consistent data on government requests (demand) for observation, similar studies of demand and supply have not been conducted for observation. Although we are unable to systematically assess demand separately (or whether governments invited a range of organizations but were turned down by some of them), research has identified what drives the eventual outcome (supply or whether elections are observed).[63] In this book, I incorporate this knowledge of strategic selection and draw on these previous studies to model the process of non-random assignment (where IOs go), which is explained at the end of this chapter.

Further, in terms of IOs being strategic in what they say, some may reasonably point to observers perhaps withholding criticism if they do anticipate the condemnation-violence link. In fact, Kelley has argued that there is evidence for the notion that observers withhold criticism in fear of triggering or worsening violence.[64] Note that, if true, it lends support to the argument in this book in two ways. One, it provides evidence that the statistical result uncovered in this book (condemned elections have more post-vote violence) is indeed supported by experiences on the ground. Second, if observer groups are indeed strategically issuing more positive reports when they fear generating violence, it makes it *more* difficult to uncover the condemnation-violence link in the statistical analysis. That is, strategic adaptation of observer statements would make it more difficult to find the effect that I find in chapter 3.

Support and Pre-Election Violence

In the pre-election period, international support can change the electoral environment, reduce manipulation, and thus shape the political arena by making the electoral process more credible. First, reputable international observers can increase the accountability of potential perpetrators of fraud and violence because external scrutiny increases the likelihood that the perpetrators are detected and publicized. Given increased accountability, perpetrators have incentives to reduce manipulation or abstain from it entirely; they are more likely to play by the official rules. Second, technical election assistance can increase the capacity of election management (often working with the national election commission) to run a smooth and clean election, to remove potential conflict triggers, and to keep conflict from escalating. While election observers can increase accountability through their presence (and the anticipated public reports of their findings), technical assistance can boost election quality, which should change contestants'

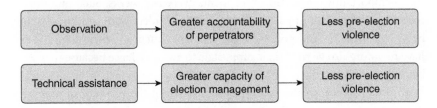

FIGURE 1.3. International election support, credibility, and pre-election violence

experience of the election and the perceived credibility of the election overall. This is illustrated in figure 1.3.

OBSERVATION: INCREASING ACCOUNTABILITY

International election observers can increase the accountability for potential perpetrators of fraud and violence by increasing the likelihood that perpetrators are caught. While actors may prefer to influence vote choice and turnout and at times even resort to campaign violence for this purpose, they also face constraints. These constraints come in the form of democratic constraints on political elites. When potential perpetrators face a higher risk of being held responsible for their actions, they are less likely to pursue their preferences for influencing vote choice and turnout with violence. Greater accountability should lower violence, and may instead reduce manipulation or abstain from it entirely. Yet developing countries vary widely in the robustness of those institutional constraints on political elites. Particularly when these domestic constraints are lacking or not well developed, international election support can supplement weak institutions.

Reputable election observation can increase accountability by making it more likely that manipulation will be detected and publicized. IO monitors can detect election fraud by being physically present throughout the voting process and the campaigning period. Beyond polling and vote aggregation, many observers also evaluate the legal framework, media bias, and campaign spending, all of which can significantly tilt the playing field.[65] Such evaluations, which often come when the electoral process is already fully underway, provide information about the quality of the election. Anticipating that the observer's findings will be published, domestic political stakeholders can be deterred from engaging in manipulation.[66]

It is rare but noteworthy to get political leaders publicly stating that external monitoring changed their manipulation. One such occasion came to light during IFES' involvement in the 2006–2007 election in Bangladesh, where monitors were observing manipulation and specifically electoral violence, and then—importantly—reported on incidents every two weeks. Such monitoring seems to have had an impact as "local political leaders were concerned about being 'watched' . . . and political leaders in constituencies where IFES did *not* have monitors also warned their supporters to avoid violence because they were being monitored!"[67]

In principle, the greater cost of manipulation in the presence of observers can have two effects: it can deter would-be cheaters entirely or cause them to use more subtle means that are less likely to be caught and condemned.[68] For example, less overt manipulation like changes to the law or election management body far ahead of the election (instead of overt ballot stuffing) are less likely to be criticized because it often remains unclear whether it is caused by malicious intent or maladministration. However, either type of manipulation (overt or covert) is relatively more likely to be discovered in the presence of observers than in their absence.[69]

In terms of building accountability, I extend existing arguments about observer effects on fraud to the issue of violence because the logic of the causal mechanism should apply equally. If IO monitors can detect and deter fraud (nonviolent manipulation),[70] they should also be able to detect and deter pre-election violence (violent manipulation). Similar to fraud, international monitoring also increases the risk that election violence is revealed as well as the risk that its perpetrators are publicly condemned. For example, the European Union mission condemned campaign violence in Guyana in 2001: "Last night, Wednesday 28 February, international observers witnessed an incident of violence at a political meeting in Tucville, Georgetown, involving stone throwing. We strongly condemn any acts of violence and urge all Parties to call on their supporters to act with restraint."[71] Assuming that domestic actors anticipate critical observer reports, they should also be deterred from using violence as a campaign tool. Violence before and on election-day is more costly in the presence of observers, implying that election violence should be reduced in the presence of observers.

Manipulation is costly because it usually results in negative observer reports, which cast serious doubt on the credibility of the election. Such negative reports by reputable observer groups—what I call condemnations—can generate costs in the domestic and international realm. On the domestic side, condemnations cast doubt on the legitimacy of the election winner and strengthen the electoral loser; this increases the risk of challenges to the election result and increases the chances of violence in the aftermath of the election. In several documented cases, condemnations have contributed to unrest and regime changes,[72] thus diminishing the winner's chance of actually ruling. From the perspective of the incumbent, the fundamental challenge is in maximizing all levers of winning while not overstepping the boundaries of political competition so far as to trigger observer condemnation or a loser challenge to their victory. Whoever wins wants the loser(s) to accept the election result so that gaining and holding power can progress smoothly. Thus manipulation, including violence, should be lower when international observers attend elections.

Criticism by international observers can result in punishment in the form of reduced foreign aid, trade, and diplomacy. When observers issue a negative verdict, international organizations are more likely to impose material or reputational costs on the government. In particular, IOs are more likely to suspend member states or impose economic sanctions when elections have gone bad.[73] Regional organizations where countries risk losing membership benefits are particularly active in this regard,[74] but external sanctions (such as by the EU against African countries) are also often imposed after democratic transgressions.[75] In addition, observer verdicts can trigger cuts in aid and trade,[76] depriving countries of democracy-contingent benefits until their return to good standards. One prominent example is Togo: its failure to hold plausibly democratic elections led to the near-total suspension of foreign aid for over a decade.[77] The European Union and bilateral donors suspended their aid in response to Togo's lack of democracy and its worsening human rights record. The international community made credible elections a condition for resuming its aid to Togo, but subsequent elections failed to reach that threshold. The EU partially resumed aid when the government committed to initial reforms in 2005. The EU opened up more development funds after the 2007 election, which its observers deemed fairly credible. In short, international observation can help hold political elites accountable for manipulation. Hence, election observation should help make the campaigning period more credible and less violent.

TECHNICAL ELECTION ASSISTANCE: INCREASING CAPACITY

Technical assistance is aimed at improving processes of election management that fall short of domestic and international standards or otherwise cause disruptions. This includes improvements in voter registration and education, an increase in the resources for election management and the number and training of election staff, complaints adjudication, legal regulations, communication, and cooperation between the election commission and other stakeholders around the election, including security forces and media.[78] It is often—but not exclusively—focused on increasing the capacity of the election commission, as that is the central player in the electoral process, one that is involved in all phases and aspects of the electoral cycle. Technical election assistance efforts usually begin months (and sometimes years) before the election and involve working with both institutions and civil society. As technical assistance is focused on increasing the capacity and credibility of election management, it should increase the credibility of the process and ultimately the announced result. That is, technical assistance should boost election quality, which changes contestants' experience of the election. This, in turn, can have meaningful effects on post-vote violence, as it makes it more likely that the loser consents or at least channels a dispute through institutions instead of taking it to the streets.

In the pre-election period, technical assistance can remove conflict triggers through institutional reforms and can keep violence from escalating through security reforms. When a country has particular conflict triggers in the electoral process which have led to tensions or violence in past elections, these can often be addressed through technical assistance. For example, procedural changes in how and when candidate registration or voter registration is done can ease tensions. In some countries, voter registration has been done fairly close to the actual election date which overlaps with political campaigns. This can make voter registration drives seem political, rather than an administrative necessity. Technical assistance can consult with the election commission to move up the schedule of pre-election events and assist in holding or even completing voter registration before political party campaigns commence. Similarly, political party/candidate registration can become conflictual at times, and procedural changes to the timing of their registration can also lower the conflict potential.

Technical assistance can also help keep tensions from escalating by raising election security. This is done before, on, and after election-day, if more police are hired and trained to provide security to campaign rallies, individual polling stations, and ballot boxes. Security interventions can also influence pre-election dynamics through increased coordination between the election commission, political parties, civil society, and the police; this can help detect local tensions earlier, discuss incidents, address rumors, and resolve problems in a joint forum. Regular meetings of such joint committees can act as mediation forums to detect local hotspots and address them before tensions spiral into violence.

Technical assistance can also help make voting on election-day more smooth and less conflict-prone by increasing the capacity of the election commission in terms of its staff and material and in terms of its voter education efforts. Assistance to the NEC often includes material support such as hiring and training more polling station officials; purchasing ballots, ink, and ballot boxes; and helping with the logistical challenge of transportation on and after election-day. Further, technical assistance to the election commission often includes voter education, which can inform more citizens about how voting works, such as which polling station to go to and which identification documents to bring. When potential voters know what to expect, polling staff are well trained, and sufficient supplies arrive in time, then voters should become less likely to be turned away at polling stations or be disenfranchised. More effective election-day management makes it less likely that tensions erupt on election-day, such as scuffles between polling station staff and voters or property damage when potential voters express their dissatisfaction with long wait times. This leads to the first set of hypotheses:

Hypothesis 1a. *International election observation should reduce pre-election violence.*

Hypothesis 1b. *International technical election assistance should reduce pre-election violence.*

Support and Post-Election Violence

I now turn to violence after elections. As explained above, violence after elections often emerges when the electoral loser deems the results to be not credible and challenges them, leading to clashes between contestants. International election support can influence post-election violence by increasing or diminishing the credibility of the result; this in turn influences the loser's willingness to consent to the election result.

Election observers can reduce the credibility of the election result by publicizing the misbehavior of contestants. As noted for the pre-election period, election observation can increase the accountability of potential perpetrators of manipulation by increasing the risk that perpetrators are identified and called out. After election-day, domestic and international actors await the announcement of this observer verdict. When observer teams issue their verdict on the election's quality and that verdict is negative, they publicly cast doubt on the credibility of the election. In negative reports, observers allege significant manipulation and declare that the election process fell short of democratic standards, usually due to actions of political elites. Those actions can relate to voting and counting (ballot stuffing, questionable tabulation, or unrealistically high turnout) or to the pre-election period if the playing field was significantly tilted at that time. Casting doubt on the credibility of results can heighten the loser's incentives to challenge. Since electoral losers tend to be dissatisfied with election results, they have incentives to take any doubt on the result's credibility as a legitimate motive for mobilizing their supporters.

In contrast, technical assistance should improve the credibility of the result by increasing the capacity of the election commission to conduct a smoother and cleaner election, thus diminishing the loser's incentives to challenge it. It can also improve processes to adjudicate and resolve election disputes and thus encourage the loser to work through institutions rather than taking disputes to the streets if a challenge does take place.

Election assistance can increase the capacity of the national election commission to reduce delays and technical difficulties in the counting and tabulation process; it also helps ensure that there are sufficient ballots, ink, and ballot boxes delivered on time, so that voters have a chance to vote rather than being denied this opportunity and being turned away at the polling station. Technical assistance can also support the commission's effort at voter education, activities that include setting expectations about election-day (which documents to bring, where to go) and counting/tabulation. For example, voter education can clarify that the initial results often change as more regions submit their local results. While one candidate or party is leading in initial results, the leading candidate can change as results from different locations trickle in during subsequent hours and days, and these changes are not necessarily due to manipulation. When elections run smoothly, expectations are clear, and results are verified in a timely manner, this works against rumors and speculation of result tampering that might otherwise arise in the post-election period. While even technically smooth elections are no panacea for violence, improving the capacity of the election commission should help build the credibility of the process and of the announced result. This diminishes the loser's incentives for a challenge and thus increases the probability of the loser's consent and post-election peace. This is illustrated in figure 1.4. In the remainder of this chapter, I introduce these arguments in more detail.

OBSERVATION: INCREASING ACCOUNTABILITY THROUGH (POTENTIALLY NEGATIVE) OBSERVER VERDICTS

Election observers can increase the accountability for manipulation by publishing authoritative statements about election quality. Shortly after election-day, observer organizations issue press statements and accompanying reports about the credibility of the electoral process and, by implication, its result.[79] Observer verdicts are often eagerly awaited and are widely disseminated through the domestic and international media. Observer verdicts can be either positive or negative.

When election observers issue their verdict on the election's quality and that verdict is negative, they publicly cast doubt on the credibility of the election. Neg-

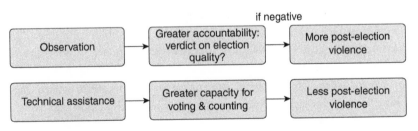

FIGURE 1.4. International election support, credibility, and post-election violence

ative verdicts ("condemnations") allege significant fraud and usually state one of the following: "elections have fallen short of key international and regional standards for democratic elections," "there was significant manipulation," or "there was evidence of widespread manipulation."

An election is condemned when at least one reputable observer group criticizes the election, as "criticism by one internationally reputable group is usually sufficient to cast doubt on the quality of the process and potentially arm post-election protesters with greater legitimacy."[80] The shortcomings noted are usually intentional malpractice: when ballots are late or missing predominantly in opposition strongholds; when ballot boxes are stuffed in front of observers; ballots are marked identically; or when ballot boxes disappear and re-emerge with additional ballots inside them, making it unclear which ballots should be legitimately counted toward the result. Observer groups also place particular emphasis on transparency in the counting process: they note when they have been physically excluded from the room where counting took place and when the aggregation of local results does not match national estimates. An observer group's decision to condemn an election usually requires substantial evidence that egregious manipulation has occurred.[81] Consequently, when reputable groups *do* condemn elections, this public statement is a strong indication of manipulated results. Drawing attention to manipulation and casting doubt on the accuracy of the announced election result reduces the credibility of results, which strengthens the loser.

Since electoral losers tend to be dissatisfied with election results, they have incentives to take any doubt on the result's credibility as a legitimate motive for mobilizing their supporters. Observer condemnation makes electoral losers more likely to *believe* that the election result was not credible.[82] These attitudinal changes can translate into behavioral changes and generate violence. Condemnations strengthen the loser—and thus increase the risk of a challenge and violence—in two ways: by revealing that the true level of the loser's popular support is likely higher than the official election result suggests; and by serving as a focal point for mobilization among the loser's supporters. First, an international condemnation indicates that the result is likely biased in favor of the winner and that the loser likely performed stronger than the official vote share suggests. Since manipulation is usually in favor of the winner, this suggests that the losing candidate's actual vote share and support are higher than the official results.[83] For example, this may indicate that instead of 40 percent of the popular vote, the loser actually enjoys the support of 45 or 50 percent of voters. As discussed above, popular strength at the ballot box and in the street are closely linked, so the loser has ways to infer her or his mobilization potential.

Second, a condemnation also serves as a focal point for coordination and helps crystallize support behind the loser in favor of overturning the result. While the condemnation indicates that the loser is likely stronger than expected, the decision to challenge is often contingent upon a decision at the individual and group levels: Should we mobilize and go out on the streets to rebel or should we stay home and thereby consent? Although supporters prefer standing by their candidate, their individual cost of rebellion potentially involves violence and state repression, which need to be weighed against the probability of success. Thus, from the supporters' perspective, judging the legitimacy of the potential challenge is critical. However, claims of fraud are easily and often made—especially by electoral losers.

An international verdict can help supporters distinguish between political cheap talk and claims substantiated by evidence. Observer verdicts have higher informational value than domestic allegations of fraud because observers have fewer ties to domestic contestants and issue allegations of fraud much less often than domestic actors. The exposure of fraud can change an individual's calculus about participating in rebellions.[84] In particular, exposure of fraud can facilitate mobilization by lowering individuals' cost of punishment and increasing the likelihood of success.[85] Once a sufficient number of supporters gather on the streets, "informational cascades" can set in where the size of the masses keeps swelling,[86] further reducing an individual's likelihood of being targeted for punishment. As such, the exposure of fraud can serve as a focal point for solving collective action problems by changing an individual's calculus about participating in rebellions.[87] In short, the IO report serves as a coordination mechanism to decide between two equilibria: all stay home or go out into the streets. The latter is the focal point if an election is condemned. Thus a negative IO report shifts the candidate's probability of winning a post-election fight in favor of the loser by increasing the number of people who are willing to fight for the loser.

Overall, condemnations can increase the risk of post-vote violence because electoral losers can draw on these international verdicts to legitimize their challenge and facilitate mobilization among their supporters. If the loser is more likely to win a potential fight, s/he is more likely to risk a fight by challenging the result. Challenges can trigger violence either when the challenge itself starts out violent, when it provokes reactionary violence by the winner, or when the loser decides to use force after the winner resists. Thus one should be able to observe increased election violence after negative observer reports. This leads to the second set of hypotheses, the first of which runs as follows:

Hypothesis 2a. *Observer condemnation should increase post-election violence. That is, conditional on having observers, condemned elections should experience more post-election violence than non-condemned elections.*

TECHNICAL ELECTION ASSISTANCE: INCREASING CAPACITY

Technical election assistance can boost the credibility of the election commission and the result that it announces. In fact, building the NEC's capacity for voting and counting processes gets to the core of what technical election assistance is all about. There is some evidence that this is successful: UN technical election assistance increases the NEC's capacity and raises the quality of election management.[88] Importantly, better-managed elections have direct implications for election violence. When the election commission is more credible, the result that it announces is also more credible, which should diminish the loser's incentives to challenge it. While even technically smooth elections are not a guarantee against violence, improving the capacity of the election commission helps raise the credibility of the process and announced result, thus leading to less post-vote violence.

However, election assistance may *not* have a measurable effect on loser challenges because of a countervailing dynamic: making elections more credible should reduce challenges, but making legal dispute resolution more promising should increase (institutional) challenges. Election assistance also informs contestants about their legal recourse options in case they want to challenge results and helps improve electoral dispute resolution. If election assistance successfully strengthens dispute resolution procedures, losers are more likely to challenge peacefully through institutions rather than through street demonstration. International assistance often includes this element and has several strategies to improve the processing and fairness of complaint adjudication.[89]

Strengthening the relevant institutions (usually election commissions or electoral courts) to investigate and adjudicate election disputes should make these institutions more capable and trustworthy arbiters of disagreements. Disputes are more likely to be channeled through institutions when dispute resolution procedures are stronger. In contrast, when dispute resolution mechanisms are weak or not trusted, challengers are more likely to take their complaint into the streets rather than to the court or to the election commission hearing officer. Overall then, election assistance may increase information about and the quality of dispute resolution mechanisms, which would increase election challenges. Although that might strike some as an increase in conflict, peaceful protests channeled through institutions, as a legitimate way of expressing dissent in a democratic system, are a preferred alternative to street demonstrations, because they follow democratic procedures and are less likely to spiral into violence than street protests. Street protests may be violent or peaceful but even peaceful demonstrations may provoke clashes or repression by the winner or government/security forces.

Regardless of the effect of election assistance on *challenges*, their expected effect on violence is clear: it should be negative. Assistance should lower violence because the election commission is more capable and the election result is more credible than otherwise; *if* challenges occur, losers should be more likely to challenge peacefully (through institutions).

Again, research in comparative politics underscores the importance of strong election commissions here. This research suggests that it is commission capacity, rather than independence, that matters. Sarah Birch shows that formal commission independence has no effect on election manipulation or contestation.[90] Similarly, Pippa Norris argues that some earlier research had unduly emphasized legal status and shows that commission independence does not influence election integrity.[91] That might be because *de jure* and *de facto* independence are different things but also because capacity—staff, resources, technical knowledge—is an important aspect, or at any rate a more important aspect. Norris suggests that "elections are flawed . . . where officials struggle with limited organizational capacity, poor technical expertise, inexperienced and poorly trained temporary staff, and/or inadequate financial resources."[92] Moreover, Opitz, Fjelde, and Höglund have shown that NEC capacity is important for violence: if results have been protested by opposition actors, election commissions can help reduce post-election violence.[93] They find that what matters for post-election violence is not the legal independence (autonomy) but the ability of election commissions to address opposition concerns (capacity).

To reiterate and expand on the previous explanation of what technical election assistance does, relevant activities include: (1) reforming the voter registry (purging ghost voters to reduce multiple voting and registering new voters to increase participation); (2) improving the quantity and quality of election material (ballots, ink, ballot boxes) and processing; (3) training election officials, such as officers and security forces, about their proper role; (4) improving mechanisms of dispute resolution and complaints processing; and (5) improving internal and external communication. The latter includes greater transparency about registration requirements and the location of polling places, which can decrease tensions on election-day and beyond because potential voters are not turned away from polling stations and therefore do not feel disenfranchised, especially after long commutes and waits at the polling station.

Apart from institutional capacity and compliance, citizen knowledge is also key: if people understand the institution and its function, "it will motivate their support for the institution and their compliance with its rules."[94] Strategies to reduce a credibility deficit can be either top-down (improving administrative capacity) or bottom-up (improving citizens' knowledge and respect for institutions).[95] Thus, technical support can be effective from both directions because it aims to affect institutions themselves as well as citizens' perceptions about these institutions. At the most basic level, voter education informs citizens about their rights and responsibilities. Such activities include education about the voting process (polling booth procedures and locations, ID requirements) and the counting process (expectations about tabulation). As already mentioned, voter education can also clarify that initial results may change significantly as more regions submit their local results. While one candidate or party may lead in initial results, the leading candidate can change as results from different locations come in during subsequent hours and days, and these changes are not necessarily due to manipulation. In certain situations, voter education can detail recent reforms and explain how difficult manipulation has become.

Youth and first-time voters are especially important to reach through civic education programs because young people are often hired as perpetrators for violence.[96] One initiative in Guinea to bring the "peaceful consent" message to young voters entailed multiple soccer matches between party youths. In iterated tournaments, winning, losing, and (mostly) peaceful competition are part of the normal game.[97] While one team may lose today, it may win in the future. This expectation underlines many sporting competitions, and in East Timor technical assistance organized iterative matches in the hopes that this message would transfer from competition in sports to politics.[98] Playing and losing against different "teams" is not the end of the day but just a temporary state of affairs until the next competition. That is, voter education also encourages contestants to stay calm and often reminds citizens and parties that losing is just part of the democratic game, which they may win in future competitions.

These efforts are aimed at increasing citizens' trust in election management and in the announced result, so that questioning results becomes less viable. How does NEC credibility matter for post-vote violence? Administrative competence is critical because technical problems can be seen as politically motivated.[99] For example, Kenya has long struggled with trust in its national election commission (currently called IEBC) because of capacity and credibility issues. When the lack of trust is coupled with irregular institutional behavior, greater distrust can lead to violence. Even though institutional reforms took place before the 2013 election, past actions of the commission made citizens wary of trusting the institution. After polling for the 2013 election, some people felt that "technical glitches have opened up the space for doubt. And that's a problem in an environment where the perception of integrity is as important as the reality."[100] In other words, trust—the *perception* of electoral quality—is important to keep political competition peaceful. When elections and thus the resulting government are perceived as illegitimate, election results are more likely to spur popular protests[101] and violence.

In most advanced democracies, election institutions are perceived to have high integrity because they have a positive track record from past elections. That positive record generates trust and keeps violent contestation low; citizens regard these institutions as reliable. This reliability is lacking in many developing countries. If post-election violence breaks out because the election result is not perceived to be generated by a trustworthy institution, then one way to reduce violence is to increase the integrity of electoral institutions. This is the major purpose of technical assistance. Technical assistance should be associated with less post-election violence because such assistance can increase the capacity and credibility of the election commission, the credibility of the announced result, and thus loser's consent. This leads to the final hypothesis:

Hypothesis 2b. *Technical election assistance should reduce post-election violence.*

The key point is that technical assistance works through a different mechanism than observation. Technical assistance activities do not provide information about fraud (and popular strength) but rather build the credibility of election commission and the result that it announces. Technical assistance may decrease or increase challenges, while observer condemnation should only increase challenges and violence.

Research Design

To assess the influence of international election support on election violence intensity, I analyze national elections in Africa and Latin America from 1990 to 2012, as outlined at the end of the introduction. The sample consists of over 470 elections in seventy-four countries.[102] The unit of analysis is the national election.[103] The discussion in the introduction and chapter 1 has a number of implications for research design and the empirical analyses in subsequent chapters. It tells us something about which control variables should be included and which types of statistical models are appropriate.

First, the description of the logic of violence and common drivers suggest which factors should be controlled for in the quantitative analyses. While the main interest is in assessing the influence of international election support on election violence, we need to account for differences between countries and elections. Context factors include country-level root causes and election-specific triggers, which are summarized in table 1.1. Building on this tabular summary and recalling the earlier discussion, the baseline model of election violence includes measures of democratic constraints (the number of institutional constraints on executive authority); a binary indicator for whether the country experienced a civil war in the previous ten years; economic development in the form of (logged) GDP per capita; natural resources in the form of (logged) oil and gas income per capita; (logged) population size in millions; ethnic fractionalization to measure the degree of heterogeneity; poll type indicating legislative, executive, or general election; and past election violence (casualties during the previous election or pre-election period). Competition is proxied with incumbent running for the pre-election models and loser vote share in the post-election models.

The post-vote models also include suspected election fraud, which—following most previous research—is a binary variable that indicates whether there were "significant concerns that elections will not be free and fair."[104] This measure, which has been widely used, relates to "domestic or international concern" about the quality of the election, including whether "elections were widely perceived to lack basic criteria for competitive elections."[105] The main advantage of this measure over others is that it is clearly pre-treatment to the observer assessment and post-election violence, as concerns need to be documented in sources prior to the election. Virtually all other measures in the literature are either based on information from election-day or explicitly include observer statements in the fraud measure. For example, fraud measures based on U.S. State Department Human Rights reports are not pre-treatment because the reports explicitly incorporate observer verdicts and are written up to a year after the election date.[106]

This list of factors is not exhaustive of every reason any country has ever experienced electoral violence. Building such a model could easily result in a much longer list, throwing in "everything but the kitchen sink," which risks overfitting and multicollinearity. Instead, the goal is to account for the main alternative explanations and to avoid omitting variables that are important for the hypothesized relationship. An overview of the coding, data sources, and descriptive statistics for the variables can be found in appendix tables 1C.1 and 1C.2. I also use alternative measures for robustness tests, particularly for fraud and for ethnic fractionalization/excluded population.

Second, the patterns of election violence and international support suggest certain types of statistical models. The outcome of interest in this book is election violence intensity. To measure this, I leverage original data, which disaggregate how many people were affected (killed or injured) and in which stage of the election. I collected these original data because available data were not suitable for the analyses in this book; this is detailed in appendix 1C. To collect original data on election violence—the number of people killed, injured, and so on—I used the printed version of *Keesing's Record of World Events*. *Keesing's* provides an objective monthly digest of political, economic, and diplomatic affairs around the world, written mostly by academics and journalists. It relies on a large variety of sources from around the world, including international media outlets, regional news outlets, country-specific news providers, radio broadcasts, and election-related sources.[107] *Keesing's* was chosen over alternative information sources because it draws on many in-country sources and NGO reports in addition to media outlets, provides consistent coverage over time, is reasonably detailed, and has been used in other prominent data collection efforts for election research[108] and conflict research.[109]

Data were collected through human coding. Importantly, human coding (as opposed to machine coding) allows more clearly identifying whether violence was in fact election-related or not. Determining whether conflict had an electoral dimension is critical; otherwise data would pick up other types of ongoing conflict that just happen to also occur during an election cycle. For example, persistent terrorist violence perpetrated by the Tuareg in Mali was excluded from the coding unless it was clearly election-related. Casualties from a bombing occurring at polling centers are coded as election violence while those from bombing at market places are not. Comparing the new GEVD to other commonly used datasets reveals a high rate of agreement on both aggregate violence rates and on individual elections, which strengthens confidence in data reliability. These are detailed in appendix 1C. The advantage of the GEVD data over other sources is that GEVD provides additional information, not just *whether* violence happened but how *intense* it was. Empirically, this measure ranges from 0 to more than a thousand casualties, with about 24 percent of elections experiencing pre-election violence and about 13 percent experiencing post-election violence in Africa and Latin America.

Since the outcome of interest or dependent variable in this book is violence intensity, measured by casualty counts, I use a count model. For count data, standard linear regression (OLS) tends to produce inefficient and biased estimates, so OLS models are not appropriate.[110] Instead, count data should be analyzed with count models.[111] Further, election-related casualty counts are not normally distributed (with equal deviation around the mean, like a bell curve). Instead, they are skewed to the right, with a long tail of larger outbreaks of violence with higher casualties. As figure 2.1 and the discussion of cases show, elections vary widely in their casualty counts: many stay peaceful (zero casualties) while violent elections often have casualties in the tens and lower hundreds, and some violent elections resulted in several hundred and at times over a thousand casualties. Indeed, descriptive statistics of the casualty count—detailed in appendix table 1C.2—show that both pre- and post-election casualties have a mean of about 14 casualties, while their standard deviations are much higher. Their variance exceeds the mean, indicating overdispersion. To handle the overdispersion in the dependent variable, the appropriate model choice is a negative binomial rather than a Poisson.

Further, in terms of the specific count model, theory and statistical estimations indicate that zero-inflated negative binomial models are more appropriate than a standard negative binomial model. Zero-inflated models assume that there are two data-generating processes, one process or set of factors generating peaceful elections and a second process for violence-prone elections generating violence intensity. Figures 1.1 and 1.2 show that some countries' elections are always peaceful, while many countries experience variation in election violence over time. Context matters: elections in highly developed countries without a history of civil war are likely to stay peaceful (violence=0). In less developed countries with a legacy of civil war, elections have some nonzero risk of turning violent, and violence intensity is influenced by a number of factors. As discussed earlier in this chapter, more economic development can make countries less prone to violence (although high development does not assure peaceful elections in all cases and leaves violence variation in poor countries unexplained). In addition to development, case studies indicate that a history of civil war shapes a country's risk of turmoil during elections.[112] For example, elections in a number of Latin American countries tend to be peaceful—including Cuba, Chile, Costa Rica, Ecuador, Panama, Suriname, Trinidad and Tobago, and Uruguay—and these are also countries without a civil war history. In contrast, Colombia and Guatemala, which have a legacy of civil war, were more prone to election violence. The same trend holds for African countries such as Namibia, Botswana, Mauritius, Morocco (no civil war legacy, less election violence) on the one hand and Algeria, Ethiopia, the DRC, Senegal, Somalia, Uganda (civil war history, more prone to election violence) on the other hand. These two factors—development and conflict legacies—are also in line with recent work on the democratizing power of elections, which points to conflict history and economic development as important conditioning variables.[113] Thus, peaceful elections (the zero inflation) are modeled as a function of development and conflict history. All context variables (domestic drivers listed in table 1.1) are included to model violence intensity. In addition to theory and empirical knowledge, the statistical estimations in subsequent chapters indicate that the chosen model is more appropriate than any of the alternatives. However, I use alternative models in robustness checks. All analyses account for the non-independence between elections within a country by clustering standard errors on the country level.

It is also important to deal with selection or the non-random assignment of "treatment" (international support) to elections in these observational data.[114] In an ideal world of causal inference, we would randomly assign elections to treatment or control (international support or not) to isolate the effect of the treatment on outcomes. In such an experimental design, we could be sure that there are no confounding factors—factors that influence both treatment and outcome. However, randomly assigning international support across a large number of elections is neither feasible nor ethical, as it would involve tremendous coordination across international organizations and countries and would also likely conflict with real-world policy pressures.[115] Since we cannot conduct a field experiment for such a cross-country analysis, we must rely on observational data. Observational data have the drawback that subjects (countries) can self-select into treatment (international support). Such non-random assignment of treatment seems to be the case here because technical assistance tends to cluster in some regions and some countries, as shown in figures I.3 and I.4 and discussed in the introduction. Some countries receive the "treatment" of election support never, some always, and many countries every now and then. In fact, technical assistance and observation are not randomly distributed but are the result of interaction between the recipient country and implementing or donor organization.

In earlier work[116] I have shown that the provision of technical election assistance depends on the strategic interaction between donors and host countries and also that technical assistance is more likely in countries that are poor, have low capacity for election management, allow some competition (compared to autocracies), and show some domestic political will for reform. The UN provides technical election assistance in challenging contexts rather than in countries where elections are likely to be clean, credible, or peaceful. Such non-random assignment of subjects to treatment groups complicates our analysis because there might be confounding factors (unobserved components) that influence both treatment assignment (whether international support was provided) and outcome (violence intensity). Any empirical investigation about the influence of such interventions needs to take this non-random assignment into account.

I address non-random treatment assignment in two ways: (1) testing for selection to assess which drivers make "treatment" (observation or technical assistance) more likely;[117] and (2) using endogenous treatment effects models to account for these drivers of treatment and potential unobserved confounders. Endogenous treatment effects models estimate experimental-type causal effects from observational data in a potential outcomes framework.[118] The idea here is that "treatment" is endogenous to certain observable factors and that there are possibly additional unobservables that affect both treatment and outcome, leading to spuriousness (a type of endogeneity). Endogenous treatment effects models allow treatment assignment to be endogenously correlated with the potential outcomes and thus relax the assumption of conditional independence.

The models used here are two-stage models that estimate an average treatment effect of a binary endogenous treatment variable.[119] The first stage models the treatment (international support) and the second stage models the outcome (violence intensity) while including residuals from the treatment model in the outcome model. This estimation accounts for non-random treatment assignment and gets us closer to recovering a causal effect from observational data.

Finally, a word is in order about the main explanatory variables used for observation and technical election assistance. The observation variables—observer presence and condemnation—are binary indicators drawn from the Nelda dataset,[120] which is the most prominent dataset on this issue and has been frequently used in other studies, allowing for comparability. The variable on UN technical election assistance is also a binary indicator and is drawn from both previous work and original data collection. Data on such assistance from 1990 to 2003 comes from von Borzyskowski (2016), which itself relies on the UN-internal compilation of assistance projects published in Ludwig (2004a). These data are supplemented—mainly for 2004–2012—with original data on UN technical election assistance projects. These additional data were compiled from the UN Secretary General's biennial reports on election assistance and the UN's websites for election assistance.[121] Comparing these original data to a similar data collection effort by Anna Lührmann shows high rates of agreement, which increases confidence in the reliability of this measure.[122] The appendix to this chapter provides more information on the data sources, coding procedures, and reliability. Although it would be desirable to use more fine-grained data on the budget or size of observer groups and technical election assistance missions, such data is not consistently available.[123] This is why cross-national work so far has relied on binary indicators.

The measure of technical assistance provision is focused on the UN because the UN has a "near monopoly in the area," making it the "central player" and the "largest multinational provider" of technical election assistance worldwide.[124] While many bilateral and multilateral donors include a component of election assistance in their portfolios, many donors' projects are channeled through or implemented by the UN. For example, the EU channels much of its assistance through the UNDP but conducts its own observer missions. In addition to the number of elections assisted, the UN also exceeds any other provider in terms of the budget and scope of its assistance activities. For example, paying for a substantial portion of a country's national election budget to increase capacity or setting up an entirely new voter register to increase transparency are activities that are usually outside the realm of possibilities of other providers. That is, the UN is the major provider both in terms of the number and the nature of technical election assistance projects. In principle it would be desirable to also account for the many smaller (in terms of budget, staff, projects) implementing organizations (such as IFES) that have been active in the field, but that is precluded by lack of systematic reporting. This is not for lack of data collection effort, as other experts in the field have run into the same data limitations.[125]

Currently available budget measures of "election aid" (from USAID, OECD, AidData, among others) do not consistently distinguish between technical assistance and election observation. Further, they often lump both of these together with other potential election-related projects for such things as political party support (as in the USAID measure). Using such aggregate budget figures would make it impossible to distinguish the proposed effect of observation from the effect of technical assistance (and from other aid effects) or to examine whether different types of support may point in different directions. Further, none of the budget measures include the full set of UN assistance projects documented on the UN websites. Using binary variables on the key providers is in line with virtually all previous cross-national research and thus allows comparability.

SHAPING THE ELECTORAL ENVIRONMENT

International Support and Pre-Election Violence

Elections are meant to ensure a peaceful and meaningful transfer of power, but in many countries campaign violence is a "strategic option in the competition for elected office."[1] Pre-election violence is used as a tool to influence vote choice and turnout, thereby shaping the election outcome. In particular, political elites use campaign violence to shape the behavior of potential candidates and voters. Pre-election violence is more frequent than post-election violence. Campaign violence has accompanied 23 percent of elections, whereas post-election violence has accompanied "only" 13 percent of elections in Latin America and Africa since 1990, as shown in chapter 1. Why are some election campaigns more violent than others?

This chapter empirically tests the argument detailed in chapter 1: that external election support can reduce violence before elections. Two forms of IO election support—observation and technical assistance—can shape the electoral environment by increasing election credibility. In particular, observation can raise the accountability of potential perpetrators by making it more likely that manipulation is detected and publicized. This externally generated, additional cost for using violence can change the cost-benefit calculation of perpetrators and help deter them from using violence in the campaigning period. Technical assistance can increase the election commission's capacity to run a smooth election and manage violence by removing triggers of conflict and mitigating tensions where they occur. The argument tested here is whether election support reduces pre-election violence (Hypotheses 1a and 1b).

Quantitative Tests

I test the argument about campaign violence in a statistical analysis of more than four hundred elections in seventy countries in Latin America and Africa from 1990 to 2012. The unit of analysis is the national election. For the statistical analyses in this chapter, the outcome of interest is campaign violence, measured as *Pre-election casualties* in the six months up to and including election-day. This variable is sourced from an original data collection, the Global Election Violence Dataset, which is detailed in chapter 1 and appendix 1C. The variable ranges from 0 to 980 people harmed per election. The average number of casualties per election is 14, with a standard deviation of 74. The standard deviation far exceeds the mean, indicating that this variable is overdispersed. Figure 2.1 illustrates wide variation in violence intensity. In about half of the elections with campaign violence, 1 to 10 people were killed or injured, with a long skew with

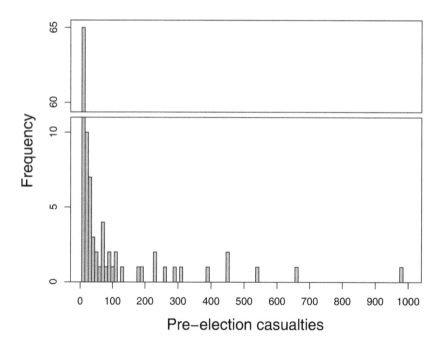

FIGURE 2.1. Distribution of campaign violence (omitting elections with zero casualties)

many elections that are much more violent. On the high end, as many as 980 people were killed or injured in South Africa 1994; other high-end cases include Malawi 1992 and Colombia 1990.

Since the dependent variable—*Pre-election casualties*—is a count of casualties, I use a count model. To handle the overdispersion in the dependent variable (variance exceeds the mean), the appropriate model choice is a negative binomial rather than a Poisson. Theory and statistical estimations indicate that a zero-inflated negative binomial model is appropriate. As outlined at the end of chapter 1, some countries and elections have essentially zero chance of turning violent, and a country's risk of turmoil during elections is shaped by economic development and conflict history.[2]

Context matters: elections in highly developed countries without a history of civil war are likely to stay peaceful (violence=0). In more conflict-prone contexts, elections have some nonzero risk of turning violent, and violence intensity is influenced by several factors as detailed in chapter 1. In addition to theory and empirical knowledge, the statistical estimations below indicate that the chosen model is more appropriate than any of the alternatives. I return to this issue in the result discussion below.[3]

To evaluate whether international election support can reduce campaign violence, I use three independent variable measures. The variable *Observation* indicates whether any reputable election observer organization was present. The variable *Technical election assistance* indicates whether the United Nations provided technical assistance. Of the national elections in this sample, 65 percent had observation and 34 percent had technical assistance. This difference in the prevalence of observation and technical support is fairly comparable to other regions and times.[4] The third variable, *Observation and/or technical assistance*, indicates whether neither was provided (0), either observation or technical assistance was provided (1), or both were present (2). In this sample, 43 percent of elections had one form of election support and 25 percent of elections had both forms of election support.

I also include a number of control variables to account for potential confounders and other drivers of pre-election violence. Control variables follow the baseline model of election violence as introduced in chapter 1, specifically table 1.1. To reiterate, this baseline model of election violence includes country-level root causes and election-specific characteristics. For pre-election violence, the control variables are *Executive constraints, Post-conflict, Economic development, Natural resources, Population size, Ethnic fractionalization, Incumbent running, Poll type,* and *Past election violence*. To mitigate endogeneity, all control variables are lagged by one year except for the election-specific variables (*Poll type, Incumbent running*). Descriptive statistics of all variables and their data sources are detailed

TABLE 2.1 Effect of international election support on pre-election violence

	LATIN AMERICA AND AFRICA				AFRICA			
	(1)	(2)	(3)	(4)	(5)	(6)	(7)	(8)
Predicting violence intensity (count)								
Observation	-1.178***		-1.168***		-1.238**		-1.225**	
	(0.367)		(0.369)		(0.497)		(0.497)	
Technical election assistance		-0.052	-0.308			-0.575	-0.703	
		(0.552)	(0.539)			(0.598)	(0.597)	
Observation and/or technical assistance				-0.819***				-0.976**
				(0.303)				(0.392)
Executive constraints	-0.434***	-0.458***	-0.427***	-0.433***	-0.525***	-0.531***	-0.483***	-0.470***
	(0.136)	(0.157)	(0.136)	(0.131)	(0.135)	(0.137)	(0.144)	(0.132)
Post-conflict	-1.066	0.011	-1.159	-1.297	-1.741**	-1.871**	-1.974**	-2.113***
	(0.738)	(0.818)	(0.799)	(0.817)	(0.724)	(0.788)	(0.786)	(0.740)
Economic development	0.390	0.443	0.360	0.318	0.689	0.642	0.598	0.555
	(0.476)	(0.396)	(0.447)	(0.400)	(0.563)	(0.536)	(0.530)	(0.516)
Natural resources	-0.000	-0.020	0.000	-0.002	-0.017	-0.014	-0.008	-0.007
	(0.059)	(0.061)	(0.058)	(0.057)	(0.063)	(0.060)	(0.060)	(0.059)
Ethnic fractionalization	-1.733	-0.745	-1.848	-2.068	-2.593*	-2.630*	-2.713*	-2.860**
	(1.263)	(1.757)	(1.276)	(1.315)	(1.375)	(1.191)	(1.322)	(1.278)
Population size	1.088***	1.115***	1.084***	1.083***	1.107***	1.078***	1.102***	1.100***
	(0.182)	(0.199)	(0.180)	(0.176)	(0.204)	(0.205)	(0.194)	(0.190)
Poll type	-0.051	-0.354	-0.018	-0.033	-0.039	-0.418	0.103	0.072
	(0.320)	(0.359)	(0.333)	(0.322)	(0.441)	(0.424)	(0.459)	(0.463)
Incumbent running	0.056	0.022	0.169	0.392	0.360	0.888	0.520	0.679
	(0.416)	(0.489)	(0.418)	(0.430)	(0.692)	(0.697)	(0.684)	(0.646)
Past election violence	0.454*	0.508	0.351	0.133	0.382	-0.283	0.169	0.019
	(0.255)	(0.483)	(0.324)	(0.285)	(0.307)	(0.360)	(0.341)	(0.311)

Predicting zero violence

	(1)	(2)	(3)	(4)	(5)	(6)	(7)	(8)
Post-conflict	-1.887	0.162	-1.855*	-1.865*	-2.576	-32.925***	-2.328	-2.464
	(1.196)	(1.983)	(1.055)	(0.984)	(2.796)	(2.918)	(2.198)	(2.420)
Economic development	0.496	2.901*	0.467	0.430	0.434	0.509	0.386	0.373
	(0.468)	(1.584)	(0.406)	(0.339)	(0.346)	(0.351)	(0.335)	(0.318)
Log α	2.216***	2.648***	2.169***	2.135***	2.183***	2.293***	2.060***	2.057***
	(0.259)	(0.169)	(0.297)	(0.288)	(0.395)	(0.180)	(0.517)	(0.502)
Observations	403	436	403	403	260	278	260	260
Clusters	72	72	72	72	48	48	48	48
AIC	1181.93	1305.23	1183.64	1182.93	760.21	835.69	761.22	759.52
BIC	1241.91	1366.40	1247.63	1242.92	813.62	890.10	818.19	812.93
LL	-575.96	-637.62	-575.82	-576.47	-365.10	-402.84	-364.61	-364.76

Notes: The table reports estimates from count models (zero-inflated negative binomial models). The dependent variable is the count of election-related casualties in the six months before and including election-day. The unit of observation is the national election. Robust standard errors are clustered on country. ***, **, and * indicate significance at the 1%, 5%, and 10% levels.

in appendix tables 1C.1 and 1C.2. The standard errors are clustered by country to account for the lack of independence between elections within states.

STATISTICAL RESULTS

The results provide strong support for the argument that international election support can reduce campaign violence. Table 2.1 presents the coefficient estimates from zero-inflated negative binomial models predicting pre-election violence. Each column shows the baseline model to predict violence intensity, along with a parsimonious model to predict zero violence. Columns 1 through 4 use data on Latin America and Africa, and columns 5 through 8 use data on Africa only. Columns 1 and 5 show the estimated effect of observation, columns 2 and 6 show the estimated effect of technical assistance, columns 3 and 7 include both explanatory variables and essentially set up a horse race between them, and columns 4 and 8 show the effect of having none, either, or both support types.[5]

As expected, the estimated coefficients on the election support variables are negative in all models of table 2.1. This indicates that election support and violence intensity are negatively correlated. Moreover, the coefficients on observation are highly statistically significant ($p < 0.05$), indicating that these relationships are unlikely to be due to chance alone. Observed elections tend to experience less campaign violence.

The substantive change is also meaningful. The magnitude of the observer effect is estimated from model 3 for a typical case in the data, setting all other variables to their means. For the more than four hundred elections included in this analysis, the predicted number of casualties is about twelve when election observation is absent and about four when it is present. International election observation is associated with approximately eight fewer people killed or injured, all else being equal. To put this in perspective, recall that the average number of people harmed is fourteen in the full set of elections. Expressed differently, the effect is approximately a 11 percent change in the standard deviation of campaign violence. The exact substantive magnitude should not be overemphasized, as statistical estimates are accompanied by uncertainty and can vary by estimation method and model specification. What is important to note is that the number of casualties tends to be lower when observer groups are present than when they are absent. The results in table 2.1 provide strong evidence in favor of Hypothesis 1a: internationally observed elections tend to have less campaign violence.

Technical assistance is also negatively associated with campaign violence, but this correlation does not reach statistical significance in this analysis. While there might be cases in which technical support has helped reduce campaign violence, the average effect across elections does not appear sufficiently large to be certain of this relationship based on this analysis. It is, of course, possible that the conflict-reducing effect is "hidden" because the analysis in table 2.1 does not account for selection, which is the issue of non-random treatment where more problematic elections are more likely to receive technical election assistance. I return to the importance of technical assistance in the selection models below and in the case studies.

There seems to be some added value in having both types of election support. Column 4 in table 2.1 shows that campaign violence is significantly reduced when both support types are provided. With both types of election support, campaign violence is significantly lower than when only one or neither is provided. In terms of the substantive magnitude, the presence of both support types is associated with ten fewer casualties during the campaigning period. The predicted number of casualties is twelve without any international election support; it is six casualties with either observation or technical assistance, and two casualties with both types of international election support.

To test the robustness of this violence-reducing effect of election support, I run several follow-on analyses. First, I check that this effect also exists for Africa alone. I do this because one previous study on observation and campaign violence found the opposite effect. Ursula Daxecker finds that observation increases the number of conflict events from 0.3 to 0.9 in the three-month campaigning period excluding election-day, which is an increase of about half a conflict event per election.[6] This previous study finds no significant correlation between observation and conflict incidents on election-day itself. Thus, in that study, observation is found to be positively related to pre-election violence, in contrast to the findings here. The difference in our findings—increase of half a conflict event vs. reduction by eight casualties—may be due to a difference in sample, estimation, model specification, or measure. In the prior study, the timeframe is shorter (a three- instead of a six-month window, and until 2009 instead of until 2012) and the number of countries is smaller, pertaining to Africa alone. I thus re-run the analysis (models 1–4) but restrict the sample to Africa. The results are shown in columns 5–8. Note that restricting the analysis to a single region reduces the number of observations from over 400 elections for both Africa and Latin America to 260 elections in Africa. However, the results are highly consistent. The coefficient on observation is again negative, statistically significant, and of similar substantive magnitude (eight fewer casualties). The reinforcing effect of having both types of support also holds when we focus on African elections. The observation and joint support effects are also robust to using the same estimator as in the previous study (negative binomial), although the substantive magnitude is somewhat smaller (five and four casualties, respectively). The consistency suggests that the difference in our findings might be due to the different outcome measures: event counts vs. casualty counts.[7] The event counts are weighted equally, regardless of casualties. That is, one event of intimidation counts the same as several fatalities. The substantive interest in this book, however, is the number of people directly affected by violence.

The second robustness check is about model choice. These follow-on analyses confirm that the chosen model is appropriate. The estimate of the overdispersion coefficient, α, is significantly different from zero in all models. This indicates that a negative binomial model is indeed more appropriate than a Poisson model. Further, diagnostic tests comparing ordinary and zero-inflated negative binomial models indicate that the zero-inflated negative binomial models are preferred. I have replicated each of the eight models in table 2.1 with negative binomial models, comparing the model fit statistic (AIC) between the two estimation methods, resulting in eight test statistic comparisons.[8] In all of the eight AIC comparisons, the zero-inflated estimation is preferred over the alternative (regular negative binomial). Thus diagnostic tests confirm that the chosen statistical model is indeed appropriate and preferred over alternatives.[9] The results are also robust to using hurdle models, that is, logit models paired with negative binomial models. In fact, the negative coefficient of technical assistance is weakly significant in one of the hurdle models. Further, I replaced the ethnic fractionalization measure with the percentage of the excluded population, which yields similar results.[10]

Alternative explanations based on domestic drivers of election violence are accounted for in the main analysis. Table 2.1 accounts for other common drivers of campaign violence. Even controlling for these domestic characteristics, election support has an additional effect on campaign violence. Among those control variables, most are in line with expectations. For example, peaceful elections (violence=0) are somewhat less likely when the country has experienced a civil war in the previous ten years. Violence intensity is significantly higher in more populous countries and lower in countries with more constraints on political elites, which is in line with expectations and the base model of violence proposed in chapter 1.

Perhaps surprisingly, the coefficients on economic development are insignificant in almost all models. Only in one model is the coefficient weakly significant, suggesting that more developed countries are more likely to have nonviolent election campaigns. This null result for economic development casts some doubt on arguments made by Paul Collier that elections in poor countries cause violence.[11] This aligns with the visual impression from figure I.1 in the introduction, which shows wide variation in casualty numbers below Collier's threshold of US$2,700 and a portion of violent elections in more developed countries.

Alternative Explanation: Selection?

The results indicate that international election support is associated with USS pre-election violence. Arguably the most important alternative explanation for lower violence is selection. Observer groups and UN technical election assistance might simply go to the easy, more peaceful elections. If this were the case, we would find an association between election support and less campaign violence, but the result would be due to selection rather than an independent effect. If the UN or observer groups attended elections where peace is likely to last, then these elections would be peaceful anyway, regardless of international involvement. At its core, this involves the issue of non-random treatment.

Among the two major election support types, the selection issue might be less pronounced for observation than for UN assistance. Election observation has become a norm, meaning that a large majority of countries in the developing world have election observation during their elections.[12] In Latin America and Africa since 1990, two-thirds of elections have been observed but only one-third of elections have received technical election assistance. While it has become a norm for election observers to be invited and to attend, as Hyde shows in her seminal study, this is not the case for UN technical assistance.[13] As noted in the previous chapter and detailed elsewhere,[14] selection issues—demand and supply—are critical in international election support and more pervasive for technical election assistance. Some governments clearly resist technical election assistance and request it never or rarely, and the UN itself does not supply assistance to every requesting government, taking into account the domestic political will as well as its own budget constraints. Most countries have had observers at most of their elections. The same is not true for technical assistance. Countries that have not received technical election assistance before 2012 include Botswana, Cape Verde, Costa Rica, Cuba, Ecuador, Equatorial Guinea, Morocco, Namibia, Trinidad and Tobago, Uruguay, and Venezuela. Further, countries that have had technical assistance at all elections (1990–2012) are not exactly exemplars of stability. To the contrary, regular recipients of technical election assistance include Somalia, the Democratic Republic of the Congo (DRC), Rwanda, Angola, and Burundi. Countries with technical assistance at many elections include Haiti, Mozambique, and Guyana. It stands to reason that the two groups of countries—those that have assistance rarely/never or frequently/always—differ in some respects. If the countries with frequent UN election assistance would be generally more peaceful, then we would wrongly attribute the lack of violence to UN actions. Yet many of the frequent recipients—such as Haiti, the DRC, and Somalia—are not generally peaceful places. While this speaks against selection concerns and for the validity of the argument, the selection dynamics warrant a deeper and more systematic analysis.

To investigate more systematically whether observation or technical assistance selects into less violent elections, I analyze where international election support is deployed. These models follow prior research on the selection of observation and technical assistance. Hyde models the presence of observation as a function of *Opposition competition, Uncertain election, Economic development* (pc GDP) and *Economic wealth* (GDP), *Year,* and whether any *Previous election was observed.*[15] *Opposition competition* is coded 1 when all of the following hold: opposition parties are legal, allowed, and there is a choice of candidates on the ballot. Almost all elections have opposition competition, except for Cuba and Tanzania in 1990. *Uncertain election* is coded 1 when any of the following apply: it is the first multi-party election, the previous election was suspended, or the country is ruled by a transitional government. About one quarter of the elections are uncertain. Based on my prior research,[16] the presence of UN technical election assistance is modeled as a function of *Regime type* (autocracy, hybrid, advanced democracy), *Post-conflict, Poll type, UN peacekeeping,* as well as *Opposition competition, Uncertain election,* and *Economic development.* As before, I cluster standard errors on country to account for non-independence of elections within the same country. Since the dependent variable—presence of election assistance—is binary, I use logit models.

Table 2.2 reports results from the analysis of selection of observation and technical election assistance. Columns 1 through 4 show models of observation and columns 5 through 8 show models of technical election assistance. Odd-numbered columns (1, 3, 5, 7) show parsimonious models based on prior research as described above. Even-numbered columns (2, 4, 6, 8) show fully saturated models that include the variables from the other estimation. The fully saturated models of observation (columns 2 and 4) also include the variables from the technical assistance models, and the fully saturated models of technical assistance (columns 6 and 8) also include variables from observation. These more comprehensive models ensure that all major drivers are accounted for. On top of these base models predicting international election support, I add the variable of interest: *Pre-election casualties,* which is the (logged) number of election-related casualties in the six months before and including election-day. I also include a binary variable for *Any election casualties,* which indicates whether any election-related casualties occurred for six months before and three months after the election. This variable is included because aid might select into elections based on overall expected violence rather than violence specific to the campaigning period.

Before proceeding with the interpretation of results, note that the predictors from the baseline model all point in the expected direction, which increases confidence in the results. Election support is more likely to be provided when elections are uncertain, that is, when the elections are the first multi-party elections, were previously suspended, or are organized by a transitional government. In addition, election support is more likely to be provided when elections are presidential or general elections, are more recent, or held in less developed or poorer countries. Election support is less likely to be provided in autocracies than in hybrid/middling regimes that fall short of consolidated democracy. Further, UN peacekeeping is an important predictor for both types of support. This is an important side finding for researchers interested in modeling where observers go and indicates that current models of observation should be supplemented with whether peacekeepers were in the country. Whether previous elections have been observed in this country also drives current observation but not technical assistance. All of these relationships are in line with previous research. To those, the analysis adds two alternative measures of election violence as predictors of election support in order to test for selection.

The results in table 2.2 do *not* provide empirical support for the concern that aid selects into less violent elections. To the contrary: if anything, there is some indication that support—specifically UN technical assistance—tends to go to more violent elections. The coefficient on *Pre-election casualties* is statistically insignificant throughout all models, indicating that there is not a strong relationship between the intensity of pre-vote violence and where support is provided. The coefficient on *Any election casualties* is also insignificant for observation but positive and weakly significant for technical assistance in column 8 of table 2.2. This means that elections with UN election assistance are somewhat more prone to violence. In theory, this could be the result of two processes: either the UN selects into more violent elections (the argument here) or the UN makes elections more violent. The latter would be a damning finding for foreign election aid and would contradict much of what we think we know about the kinds of places where the UN is likely to go.

In fact, the UN provides technical assistance to those countries where it is needed—countries that lack strong election commissions and civil society, and at times they even enter a country in order to curb expected violence.[17] It is more plausible that technical election assistance missions are sent to the places where they are most needed. Therefore, the positive correlation between UN election assistance and election violence is likely due to selection into violent places. Borrowing an analogy from Page Fortna's work on UN peacekeeping, "crime rates are probably highest in neighborhoods with the most cops on the street." This is not because police cause crime but because police "are put in place in response to the likelihood of crime."[18] In any event, selection needs to be taken into account when modeling the effect of technical support on campaign violence. These circumstances lead me to develop a more sophisticated statistical strategy that accounts for potential selection directly.

TABLE 2.2 Testing for selection of international election support into less violent elections

	OUTCOME: ELECTION OBSERVATION				OUTCOME: TECHNICAL ELECTION ASSISTANCE			
	(1)	(2)	(3)	(4)	(5)	(6)	(7)	(8)
Pre-election casualties (logged)	-0.049	-0.002			-0.036	0.105		
	(0.086)	(0.083)			(0.086)	(0.095)		
Any election casualties			0.167	0.219			0.145	0.491*
			(0.255)	(0.259)			(0.244)	(0.282)
Opposition competition	1.631	1.043	1.563	0.978	-0.159	-0.058	-0.229	-0.128
	(1.012)	(0.899)	(1.005)	(0.888)	(1.038)	(0.863)	(1.034)	(0.860)
Uncertain election	0.990***	1.036***	0.957***	1.010**	0.635**	0.816**	0.626**	0.764**
	(0.357)	(0.393)	(0.361)	(0.395)	(0.302)	(0.317)	(0.302)	(0.311)
Previously observed	1.155***	1.077***	1.122***	1.051***		-0.523		-0.562
	(0.352)	(0.373)	(0.342)	(0.366)		(0.346)		(0.346)
Economic wealth	-0.031	-0.145*	-0.050	-0.159**		-0.197**		-0.210**
	(0.076)	(0.079)	(0.076)	(0.078)		(0.096)		(0.090)
Economic development	-0.306**	-0.166	-0.287**	-0.154	-0.553***	-0.568***	-0.558***	-0.551***
	(0.138)	(0.139)	(0.139)	(0.141)	(0.125)	(0.136)	(0.128)	(0.130)
Year	0.036	0.027	0.040*	0.030		0.128***		0.129***
	(0.022)	(0.024)	(0.022)	(0.024)		(0.029)		(0.029)
Poll type		0.575***		0.581***	0.204	0.236*	0.205	0.235*
		(0.134)		(0.132)	(0.126)	(0.121)	(0.126)	(0.121)
Regime Type: Autocracy		-0.626*		-0.621*	-1.627***	-1.228**	-1.636***	-1.226**
		(0.352)		(0.348)	(0.494)	(0.527)	(0.487)	(0.534)
Regime Type: Advanced democracy		0.058		0.080	0.035	0.293	0.057	0.306
		(0.319)		(0.323)	(0.250)	(0.250)	(0.255)	(0.249)
Post-conflict		0.413*		0.417*	-0.277	-0.027	-0.288	-0.008

	(1)	(2)	(3)	(4)	(5)	(6)	(7)	(8)
UN peacekeeping		1.116**		1.127**	1.528***	1.180**	1.490***	1.103**
		(0.233)		(0.231)	(0.246)	(0.249)	(0.253)	(0.254)
		(0.531)		(0.531)	(0.444)	(0.474)	(0.449)	(0.472)
Observations	429	429	429	429	467	460	467	460
Clusters	71	71	71	71	72	71	72	71
LL	−248.75	−235.26	−248.72	−234.92	−258.68	−235.13	−258.59	−233.99

Notes: The table reports estimates from logit models. The dependent variable is the presence of observation (models 1–4) and the presence of technical election assistance (models 5–8). For regime type, the excluded baseline category is hybrid regimes. The unit of observation is the national election. Robust standard errors are clustered on country. ***, **, and * indicate significance at the 1%, 5%, and 10% levels.

To more thoroughly account for non-random treatment—which seems to apply for technical assistance—I replicate the main analysis (models 1 through 3 in table 2.1) in a two-stage setup. The first stage predicts election support, and the second stage predicts pre-election violence but accounts for non-random treatment. As detailed toward the end of the previous chapter, I use treatment effect models to estimate an average treatment effect in a linear regression augmented with a binary endogenous treatment variable (*Observation* and *Technical assistance*, respectively).[19] The results of this analysis are in table 2.3. Columns 1 and 2 examine observation with a parsimonious and a fully saturated model; columns 3 and 4 examine technical support with a parsimonious and a fully saturated model. Column 5 further adds observation as a control variable.[20] The results of the selection stage of table 2.3 are in line with table 2.2: uncertain elections in poorer and less developed countries and with peacekeepers are significantly more likely to receive both types of election support; autocracies are significantly less likely to request and receive technical election assistance.

The results in table 2.3 highlight two important findings. First, in terms of modeling pre-election violence, there is no selection for observation but there is selection for technical assistance. The relevant test is the Wald test of independent equations ($\rho = 0$) at the bottom of table 2.3, meaning whether the two processes—modeling (1) election support and (2) the effect of this support on campaign violence—are linked. In the case of observation, the relevant test statistic indicates that these two processes are independent; the probability of χ^2 is far from statistical significance, as indicated by the large p-values (0.94, 0.56). These large p-values mean that we cannot reject the null hypotheses that these are independent processes. Thus for observation, the straightforward (single-stage) models in table 2.1 are appropriate. Interpretation about the effect of observation should be based on table 2.1.

Second, the provision of technical assistance and its effect on campaign violence *are* linked, so interpretation about the effect of technical assistance should be based on table 2.3 instead of table 2.1. In columns 4 and 5 of table 2.3, the relevant test (the Wald test of independent equations) yields a statistically significant result, with the probability of the chi-square test statistic estimated at 0.00.[21] This means we reject the null hypothesis that these two processes are independent of each other. This is in line with the finding from table 2.2: UN assistance tends to select into more conflict-prone environments rather than smooth and peaceful elections.

This selection of the UN into more conflict-prone environments suggests two things. First, it biases against finding a violence-reducing effect of the UN. Estimations of the effect of technical assistance on campaign violence should account for the selection of technical assistance into more conflict-prone elections. Table 2.3 does that and provides evidence that technical support has a violence-reducing effect once we account for selection. In models 4 and 5 of table 2.3, technical assistance is significantly associated with less campaign violence. Substantively, these analyses support the argument that UN technical election assistance has a violence-reducing effect. This supports Hypothesis 1b. This effect exists even though the UN tends to operate under difficult conditions (selecting into more violence-prone elections). That is, despite going to violence-prone places, technical assistance still manages to reduce campaign violence. Second, it means that an analysis of violence as a binary outcome (instead of violence intensity as used here) would likely indicate that the UN is associated with more violence, leaving unclear whether that is due to selection or an actual effect.

In sum, the quantitative analyses provide strong support for the argument that international election support can reduce campaign violence (Hypotheses 1a and 1b from chapter 1). Observer groups do not select into more or less violent elections, and the practice of observing elections has become widespread. Observed elections tend to have lower pre-election violence. UN technical assistance is non-random; it tends to select into more conflict-prone elections. Once we account for that selection into certain types of elections, technical assistance is associated with reduced campaign violence. These indications remain somewhat tentative, as there is no perfect statistical model to estimate these relationships. To strengthen the evidence and trace the processes underlying these relationships in more detail, the remainder of this chapter turns to case material.

Illustrative Cases

The quantitative evidence presented above supports the argument that international election support (observation and technical assistance) can reduce campaign violence. This section shifts to qualitative evidence for two purposes. First, I illustrate that these relationships are not just artifacts of broad cross-country analyses but also hold within individual countries over time. Second, I detail some of the specific activities undertaken by international actors, how these increase accountability and capacity and thus help contribute to less campaign violence. This sheds light on causal mechanisms that are often difficult to trace in statistical studies.

Before proceeding, a word of caution is in order. Fraud and violence are illicit activities. Hence, political elites seldom go on public record to explain *why* they attacked or killed someone. We can infer the underlying motivation from the

TABLE 2.3 Effect of international election support on campaign violence, accounting for potential selection

	ENDOGENOUS TREATMENT: OBSERVATION		ENDOGENOUS TREATMENT: TECHNICAL ELECTION ASSISTANCE		
	(1)	(2)	(3)	(4)	(5)
Main model predicting violence					
Observation	-0.042	-0.327			-0.007
	(0.407)	(0.506)			(0.130)
Technical election assistance			-0.656	-1.093***	-0.944***
			(0.416)	(0.348)	(0.323)
Executive constraints	-0.055	-0.050	-0.033	-0.024	-0.031
	(0.039)	(0.041)	(0.043)	(0.042)	(0.039)
Post-conflict	0.122	0.152	0.145	0.161	0.121
	(0.149)	(0.175)	(0.141)	(0.152)	(0.145)
Economic development	-0.027	-0.055	-0.139	-0.179*	-0.138*
	(0.073)	(0.079)	(0.103)	(0.093)	(0.082)
Natural resources	0.003	0.004	0.011	0.009	0.004
	(0.014)	(0.014)	(0.014)	(0.014)	(0.014)
Ethnic fractionalization	-0.417	-0.402	-0.382	-0.340	-0.382
	(0.303)	(0.307)	(0.278)	(0.272)	(0.293)
Population size	0.170***	0.161***	0.173***	0.158***	0.152***
	(0.057)	(0.058)	(0.058)	(0.060)	(0.059)
Poll type	-0.091	-0.059	-0.053	-0.040	-0.054
	(0.078)	(0.093)	(0.077)	(0.083)	(0.082)
Incumbent running	0.076	0.067	0.038	0.065	0.107
	(0.159)	(0.159)	(0.149)	(0.151)	(0.153)
Past election violence	0.355**	0.348**	0.328**	0.261	0.286**
	(0.138)	(0.138)	(0.166)	(0.166)	(0.141)
Selection model predicting international election support					
Opposition competition	0.785	0.385	-0.371	-0.287	-0.268
	(0.579)	(0.523)	(0.592)	(0.390)	(0.417)
Uncertain election	0.684***	0.706**	0.458**	0.415**	0.423**
	(0.259)	(0.284)	(0.216)	(0.200)	(0.215)

	(1)	(2)	(3)	(4)	(5)
Economic development	-0.178**	-0.111	-0.347***	-0.341***	-0.314***
	(0.089)	(0.090)	(0.080)	(0.085)	(0.082)
Economic wealth	-0.021	-0.089*		-0.127**	-0.130**
	(0.046)	(0.046)		(0.056)	(0.053)
Previously observed	0.846***	0.774***		-0.449**	-0.412**
	(0.248)	(0.273)		(0.183)	(0.196)
Year	0.020	0.019		0.079***	0.072***
	(0.018)	(0.020)		(0.015)	(0.015)
Poll type		0.352***	0.094	0.129	0.157*
		(0.082)	(0.084)	(0.079)	(0.081)
Regime Type: Autocracy		-0.400*	-1.034***	-0.747***	-0.719**
		(0.210)	(0.277)	(0.277)	(0.291)
Regime Type: Advanced democracy		0.027	0.061	0.241	0.199
		(0.198)	(0.157)	(0.149)	(0.151)
Post-conflict		0.267*	-0.192	-0.002	0.006
		(0.146)	(0.166)	(0.162)	(0.160)
UN peacekeeping		0.986***	0.948***	0.762**	0.759**
		(0.239)	(0.313)	(0.305)	(0.310)
Rho	-0.01	0.14	0.26	0.50	0.47
Wald test of independent equations ($\rho = 0$), $\Pr(\chi^2)$	0.94	0.56	0.11	0.00	0.00
Observations	397	397	432	426	397
Clusters	71	71	72	71	71
LL	-881.36	-868.00	-950.62	-915.63	-850.79

Notes: The table reports estimates from treatment effects models, which are linear regressions with an endogenous binary treatment variable in the first stage. The endogenous treatment variables are observation (in models 1–2) and technical assistance (in models 3–5). The dependent variable is pre-election violence, i.e., the logged number of election-related casualties in the six months before and including election-day. For regime type, the excluded baseline category is hybrid regimes. The unit of observation is the national election. Robust standard errors are clustered on country. ***, **, and * indicate significance at the 1%, 5%, and 10% levels.

target, timing, and location of events as well as accounts from witnesses, but it is rare for a political candidate to readily admit to sending thugs to attack an opponent or an opponent's supporters. It is even more challenging to document the causal link between the absence of violent actions and the deterrent power of interventions. That is because political elites rarely publicly admit that they were deterred from illicit actions by the domestic or international constraints placed upon them. As Thomas Carothers, an expert on democracy support, noted:

> Out of fear of being caught by foreign observers, political authorities may abandon plans to rig elections. Of course, few foreign officials would readily acknowledge having had such plans, making it hard to measure precisely the deterrent effect of electoral observation. Yet that effect should not be underestimated.[22]

Political elites rarely acknowledge manipulation or—more importantly—the fact of being deterred from manipulation. Conclusively proving changes in intention or motivation is difficult when subjects have strong reasons not to reveal or misrepresent their intentions. We can, however, still make inferences based on observed behavior and circumstantial evidence. In the remainder of this chapter, I document the observation-violence link across elections within single countries and then turn to specific support activities and how they have helped reduce campaign violence.

TRACING THE OBSERVATION-VIOLENCE LINK WITHIN COUNTRIES

While the quantitative results above uncover general patterns and support the violence-reducing effect of observation and technical assistance in a broad range of countries, this section illustrates that individual countries experience this variation over time. Focusing on one individual country allows us to hold many contextual factors constant, including the root causes of violence.

Several countries have experienced campaign violence in one or more elections that were not observed but experienced substantially reduced or even no campaign violence in subsequent elections that were observed; examples include Benin, Malawi, and Ghana. In each country, elections without international observation were marred by substantial pre-election violence. In Benin, one person was killed and fifteen more were injured during voting at the unobserved 1991 presidential election.[23] In Malawi, forty people were killed and several hundred more were injured during the unobserved 1992 election when security forces opened fire on anti-government, pro-democracy protesters in the campaigning period. Similarly, in Ghana's unobserved 2000 election, eleven people were killed on election-day. In each of these countries, the next election and, indeed, the next several elections were observed and experienced no pre-election violence. As one political scientist from Benin notes, "International observers played a major role in preventing incumbent leaders from unleashing violence on the opposition and stealing the vote."[24] An exception is Benin's 2007 election, which was observed and resulted in five people injured—yet even that was a decline from the more than a dozen wounded and a death in the unobserved 1991 election. In Malawi, the presence of technical assistance may have also played a role in reducing violence, as each of its subsequent elections received technical assistance from the United Nations and was either peaceful or had only limited violence (as in the 2004 election). Undoubtedly, there are several factors at play in these circumstances, but the influence of international election support—and particularly observation—cannot be dismissed.

In addition to variation within individual countries over time, subnational studies also support the argument. For example, one recent field experiment during Ghana's 2012 elections finds evidence that observation can reduce the number of physical attacks on election-day.[25] These dynamics are unlikely to be due to selection because observers were randomly assigned to subnational polling stations. Random assignment is the polar opposite of strategic selection. Thus variation across elections within single countries provides support for the argument that election observation can reduce campaign violence.

Another piece of evidence is that the opposition often fears more government crackdown during campaigning periods if no international observers are present. For instance, in Guinea, the opposition parties have regularly requested that President Lansana Conte allow foreign election observers. Conte came to power in a military coup in 1984 and ruled until his death in 2008, introducing multi-party elections in 1993. President Conte allowed international observers for the 1995 election, which remained peaceful. In contrast, Conte refused observation during the 1993 and 1998 elections, which were both marred by campaign violence. During campaigning for the unobserved 1993 election, more than 200 people were killed and wounded. Three months before the 1993 election, opposition forces staged a demonstration calling for an independent electoral commission and a transitional government; the police used excessive force to disperse the crowds, leading to fatalities and injuries, which then spiraled into more violence.

By the time of Guinea's 1998 election, the link between foreign observers and reduced violence had become evident. As a prominent BBC Africa correspondent noted: "The government has refused to allow foreign election monitors into the country and local rights monitors have expressed fears about the escalation of campaign violence."[26] The opposition's expectations of government violence in the absence of observers were proven right. During campaigning for the unobserved 1998 election, more than a hundred people were harmed.[27] There were reports of security forces killing and injuring opposition supporters.[28] There were also reports of clashes between supporters of the incumbent and the opposition.

These examples illustrate that reputable international observers can increase the accountability of potential perpetrators of fraud and violence. Observation increases the probability that perpetrators are identified and exposed. While the deterrent power of observation is difficult to trace in firsthand accounts of perpetrators, the victims' reports, the temporal variation across elections within single countries, and similar evidence from subnational studies support the argument that observation can reduce campaign violence. Given increased accountability for their actions, perpetrators have incentives to reduce manipulation or abstain from it entirely, leading to a reduction in campaign violence.

VIOLENCE-REDUCING ASSISTANCE ACTIVITIES: SIERRA LEONE

In addition to tracing the observation-violence link across elections, a review of prominent cases of technical assistance also supports the argument about its violence-reducing potential. As argued in chapter 1, technical election assistance can increase the capacity of the national election commission to run a smooth and peaceful election through removing potential conflict triggers, and keeping conflict from escalating.

One such case of violence-reducing technical support is Sierra Leone. Sierra Leone's 2007 election provides a good example because it illustrates both the breadth of initiatives and their impact on conflict management. Presidential and parliamentary elections were held on 11 August 2007, with a presidential run-off on 8 September. The elections were contested by seven political parties with their own presidential and vice presidential candidates as well as over 500 parliamentary candidates across 112 electoral constituencies.

Sierra Leone's 2007 election is arguably a hard case for reducing campaign violence because this election context had many of the domestic drivers of violence. Perhaps most importantly, Sierra Leone's 2007 election was the first election after a decade-long civil war (1991–2002). After the war, most political violence was between the two main political parties, which were themselves aligned with former factions in the civil war: the Sierra Leone People's Party (SLPP) and All People's Congress (APC). This inter-party violence was expected to be further intensified by the upcoming elections. In addition to persistent conflict lines (which provide a motive), means of violence were easy to come by: small arms and light weapons were still widespread, as disarmament programs had been imperfect. Further, the withdrawal of UN peacekeepers in 2005 meant that election security was no longer being provided by UN peacekeepers. The 2007 election received UN technical assistance, but peacekeeping troops had left the country.[29]

As one country expert put it, Sierra Leone's 2007 election was a "perfect candidate for election violence, and many feared such violence would occur."[30] In addition to the post-conflict environment, conditions for election violence were ripe due to low economic development; the country had ranked lowest on the UN human development index for several years. High youth unemployment, a culture of immunity, and a lack of prosecution all contributed to the pool of hirable thugs, which tends to facilitate electoral violence. Moreover, the country featured few constraints on the executive, a history of ethnic conflict, and past election violence. In the run-up to the 1996 election, 27 people were killed during election-related violence.[31]

In terms of election support, both technical assistance and observation were implemented in the run-up to the 2007 elections. In particular, technical assistance was provided by the United Nations and IFES starting in December 2006, eight months before the election.[32] Observation was implemented by the National Democratic Institute (NDI) and the European Union (EU); these observer missions arrived in July and August 2007, respectively. With regard to observation, there is some evidence that observers raised accountability. They pointed out vote buying and tensions and named the main perpetrators. For example, the EU observer team noted that all parties engaged in "the distribution of money, food and other incentives" and that "both major political parties employed groups of youths and ex-combatants to travel around their strongholds."[33] This created accountability with the incumbent party but also identified the main opposition party for questionable activities.

Technical assistance also played a role in reducing violence. Sierra Leone's national election commission (NEC) received external assistance for institutional reform. This included (1) procuring a permanent building for the NEC headquarters; (2) hiring and training staff for competence in electoral laws, internal procedures, planning and budgeting, timelines, hardware and software; and (3) creating a durable voter registration system.[34] These changes were aimed at creating more competent election management, so that the election could proceed more smoothly, with sufficient resources, fewer technical glitches, and in a calmer manner.

Capacity-building support also included procedural changes to remove some conflict triggers and prevent potential violence from escalating. Two examples of this are changes in party registration and the strengthening of district monitoring committees. During the campaigning periods for Sierra Leone's 2002 national and 2004 local elections, the process of candidate nominations had been particularly conflict-prone. For the 2007 election, the UN and IFES helped the NEC design new procedures. To help avoid personal confrontations in the nomination process, each political party was allocated time slots for registration. This greatly reduced occasions in which candidates from competing parties were sharing the same space at a high-stakes event (registration) and thereby reduced the potential for confrontations and personal conflicts. As a result, the nomination proceeded peacefully, and "political parties expressed satisfaction in the nomination process," which stands in contrast to the two previous elections.[35]

Besides conflict prevention, technical assistance also supported mitigation once conflict arose. To promote peaceful campaigning, the major innovation was the creation and training for the District Code of Conduct Monitoring Committees (DMC). While a code of conduct for political parties was created in late 2006 and a national monitoring committee in Freetown, the capital, was established in January 2007, these initiatives were largely paper tigers with little impact on behavior. As a solution, regional units were established in all of the fourteen districts and were active from May to October 2007. All of these units were comprised of stakeholders from political parties, civil society, and the police, which was crucial for its enforcement function. This design allowed the DMCs to identify areas of conflict and to mitigate tensions.

Further, the UN financially supported rapid response actions for conflict mitigation. In the campaigning period, these included interventions such as a mediation meeting settling a dispute between the two main parties on 3 August 2007. The EU observers praised the DMC for having become "an efficient forum for addressing contentious issues. Their regular meetings acted as an efficient conflict mediation tool during the campaign period and successfully promoted reconciliation among political parties after clashes between their supporters."[36] Thus external assistance for reforms can increase institutional capacity to minimize conflict triggers and mitigate conflict before it escalates into violence.

In addition to conflict prevention and mitigation, technical assistance was also provided for voter education. Voter education increased knowledge about how, when, and why to vote and what behavior is appropriate. This related both to the importance of peaceful campaigning and the reduction of perceived unfairness. Technical assistance helped the NEC design and produce voter education materials, which informed citizens about the electoral process as well as the need for *peaceful* participation. Given an 80 percent illiteracy rate, many of these messages were implemented through the radio, which reaches the vast majority of the population. Other channels included pictorial illustrations on posters, stickers, leaflets, and T-shirts. A total of ten thousand posters, eight hundred T-shirts, and four thousand stickers and leaflets were produced by IFES for voter education purposes. As an important part of this voter education, IFES and the Independent Youth Forum developed a "citizens' peace pledge" which was printed on T-shirts that were widely distributed. Moreover, radio programs spreading the message of nonviolence reached an estimated 250,000 Sierra Leoneans. Primarily aimed at first-time and young voters, these messages were also aired in the form of jingles and video clips before soccer games and public cinema performances.[37] As a result, election officials, voters, and security actors were more informed about their role in the process, the role others would play, the definition of legitimate behavior, and acceptable reactions to transgressions. When citizens are informed about these things and have reasonable avenues of complaint, it becomes more difficult for political actors to manipulate the election.

The case of Sierra Leone illustrates how technical assistance can remove conflict triggers, keep conflict from escalating, and help the NEC run nonviolent elections. Even though the average effect across countries might not be large, effects are certainly noticeable in such cases. In Sierra Leone the election campaign stayed peaceful despite significant concerns about impending violence in this post-conflict environment. Campaign violence did not occur, contrary to expectations, and this was in no small part due to international election support. Along these lines, the head of the IFES technical assistance mission stated that this election exemplifies how "election violence can be prevented or mitigated even in the most difficult environments through effective international support."[38] Likewise, the UN stated that "the remarkably peaceful elections were the result of well-designed and -managed election support processes that saw all stakeholders make peaceful elections a major priority."[39] The UNDP also singled out "the significant reduction of political and election-related violence" as a key achievement in that election.[40] While skeptics might discount these statements as self-congratulation, this election had all the trappings for campaign violence but nonetheless stayed peaceful.

Sierra Leone also provides evidence that observation can hold perpetrators accountable for dubious activities and thus potentially deter them from using violence. Overall, this provides qualitative support for the proposed causal link between international election support and reduced campaign violence, complementing the statistical analysis. The final part of this chapter turns to Liberia as a similarly conflict-prone environment in which both types of election aid have jointly contributed to reduced election violence.

THE JOINT EFFECT OF OBSERVATION AND TECHNICAL SUPPORT: LIBERIA

Sierra Leone's neighbor Liberia has been struggling with a similar post-conflict environment. Liberia has been at high risk of election violence for all four of its elections since the first civil war ended in 1996 (1997, 2005, 2011, 2017 elections)—yet the country has experienced surprisingly little election violence. One important reason for Liberia's surprisingly peaceful elections was extensive international election support. The United Nations first administered the elections and then helped build a national election commission (NEC), which allowed more credible election processes and outcomes. In addition to such technical election assistance, several international election observer groups have attended and endorsed Liberia's elections and thus supplemented accountability and provided a seal of approval for sensitive processes in a fragile political and security environment. At all four of its post-conflict elections, observation and technical assistance were provided. All four elections had fairly peaceful campaigning periods. Together, these forms of international election support—technical assistance and observation—have helped make Liberia's elections more credible and have thus lowered the incentives of political contestants to resort to election violence.

Like Sierra Leone, Liberia is a post-conflict country. Post-conflict environments are notoriously prone to recurring conflict, and elections are often trigger events for violence. Tensions underlying the prior civil war are seldom fully resolved, disarmament and reintegration of former combatants is imperfect, and internally displaced people are often widespread. Dismal infrastructure, low economic development, and high unemployment and illiteracy also contribute to instability. Furthermore, post-conflict domestic institutions usually lack the capacity and credibility to organize smooth elections processes (and keep contestants in check), so that technical problems in the election administration readily fuel conspiracy rumors about misconduct, irregularities, and fraud. These circumstances provide motive for violent contestation and opportunities for mobilizing, leading supporters of opposing camps to fill the streets and clash with each other or the police/security forces, resulting in fatalities and injuries.

From 1989 to 2003, two brutal civil wars wrecked Liberia. Cumulatively, these horrific wars resulted in hundreds of thousands of deaths in a country of only four million inhabitants, leaving deep scars on the population. The first civil war (1989–1996) began when a former government minister-turned-rebel, Charles Taylor, tried to topple the sitting government. This violence temporarily ended with a peace agreement in 1996 calling for elections the following year.

The 1997 presidential election was essentially a referendum on the peace agreement, and in a landslide, the warlord Charles Taylor won 75 percent of the vote. The election was held under the implicit threat of war should Taylor lose because his opponent, Ellen Johnson-Sirleaf, was too weak to prevent a post-election standoff if she were to win. Strength on the battlefield and at the ballot box were closely linked. In the 1997 election, Taylor's military strength and the fear of immediate renewed conflict were plausible explanations for Taylor's landslide victory. It is less clear whether this also explains the peaceful campaigning period. International engagement through UN peacekeeping, UN election assistance, and several observer groups likely also contributed to the peaceful pre-election atmosphere. Two years after these elections, Taylor's leadership was challenged by rebels, and Liberia returned to civil war. This second civil war (1999–2003) culminated in a new peace agreement in 2003, which stipulated elections by 2005.

Following on the heels of the second civil war, Liberia's 2005 elections were also at risk of election violence but again proved to be surprisingly peaceful. Due to Taylor's resignation and indictment for war crimes in 2003, no incumbent was running. This helped level the playing field in terms of access to state resources and access to the media.[41] Compared to 1997, the 2005 election was more contested, featuring two equally strong candidates. Given that Liberia had just emerged from two civil wars, infrastructure and state capacity—including NEC capacity—was quite low. Yet the campaigning period proceeded peacefully.

The 2011 elections were more distant from the civil war but had perhaps the clearest potential for election violence. On the eve of the election, opposition party protesters clashed with police and United Nations peacekeepers, resulting in one fatality. Yet the opposition party and its supporters did not escalate the conflict. Even when the opposition claimed fraud after the first round of voting, it decided to boycott the second round rather than take to the streets.

The 2017 elections posed two types of additional management challenges: for the first time since the end of the civil war, Liberia's NEC was fully responsible for election management. This challenge loomed perhaps larger given the recent Ebola pandemic and the drawdown of both the UN Mission in Liberia (UNMIL, which had previously helped with election security and logistics) and UNDP election assistance. The second management challenge arose after the first-round election, when one of the losing parties, the Liberty Party, challenged the announced result in court, which made the NEC review its own procedures, and nearly overwhelmed the capacity of the in-house hearing officer. Ultimately, the court dismissed the challenge. The two main contestants (Weah from the CDC and Boakai from the incumbent Unity Party) called on their supporters to stay calm. Although the 2017 elections were tense and accompanied by hate speech, some property damage, and isolated incidents of interparty conflict, where some election campaigns were again largely free of physical election violence.[42]

Why did Liberia—despite being a prime candidate for election violence—experience so little election violence? Why did campaign violence not erupt in the 1997 or 2005, was limited in 2017, and why did it not escalate after the single violent confrontation in 2011? Elections in other post-conflict settings are often accompanied by electoral violence, such as elections in Algeria, Sudan, and Colombia as well as Cote d'Ivoire. Why does Liberia's experience in post-conflict elections diverge from these and many other conflict and post-conflict countries? In other words, why is Liberia defying the odds?

An important part of the answer is that international election support played a critical role in keeping Liberia's elections relatively peaceful. International assistance made the elections more credible by substituting UN expertise for the lack of domestic election management in the 1997 and 2005 elections. In fact, UN assistance helped make these elections happen at all. Given the lack of domestic capacity after both the first and the second civil wars, election management in 1997 and 2005 was mainly the responsibility of the UN, which administered the elections in collaboration with the regional organization (the African Union). The electoral arm of UNMIL effectively administered these elections and helped increase the capacity of the national election commission (NEC), while several observer groups (such as the Carter Center and NDI) helped with reporting on election quality and voter education. The UN helped with the election law, district delimitation, voter registration, and many other aspects of the 2005 election, bridging a significant gap in domestic capacity. As Liberia's NEC chairman said after the 2005 election about this capacity supplement:

> For countries emerging from conflicts, the value added of international technical assistance cannot be over-emphasized. As in the case of Liberia, there exists a massive brain drain as a result of the protracted civil conflict. Consequently, technical assistance became an indispensable asset for the conduct of the 2005 elections. The virtual absence of local legal, delimitation, and IT specialists crucial to the conduct of elections was filled by international technical assistance.[43]

Technical assistance can help supplement domestic capacity for election management and electoral security. The UN mission to Liberia also provided security with fifteen thousand peacekeepers deployed during the 2005 election, guarding property, providing law and order, and thus deterring and mitigating the escalation of conflict into violence. In 2011, the Liberian NEC took over responsibility for the elections from the UN, although the UN again provided significant technical election assistance and security with ten thousand peacekeepers. This heavy security presence ensured that incitements of electoral violence would be detected early and de-escalated. In 2017, the UN provided more limited technical support than it previously did. UNMIL assisted with some logistical help and extended good offices, while the UNDP chief technical adviser was also available, with the UNDP office located inside the NEC building.[44] Further, the UNDP provided critical technical assistance to strengthen NEC dispute resolution procedures by hosting a refresher training for magistrate-level staff just before the run-off.[45]

The importance of the election commission for election security throughout the process is further confirmed by election observers, as many observer reports note the NEC's contribution for helping to secure the peace in this election. In addition to the UN support for more credible and peaceful elections, international observer groups also contributed to peaceful processes by making elections more credible. Observer groups attended Liberia's 1997, 2005, 2011, and 2017 elections and raised the accountability of political contestants for misbehavior. Observer groups reported that campaigning, including election-day, had been free from violence, as well as transparent and fairly well administered (with some more mixed reports for the self-administered election in 2017). This does not mean that the opposition never alleged fraud after the election—it did so in 2005 and 2011—but fraud was not "internationally certified": observer groups deemed the elections free and fair.

Perhaps most importantly, Liberians themselves think that election observers can reduce election violence. In a 2017 pre-election survey of over a thousand respondents that I conducted in collaboration with the U.S. Institute of Peace, Liberians reported great confidence in the ability of election observers to help reduce electoral violence. The survey was administered by a Liberian survey team from the Monrovia-based Center for Democratic Governance (CDG) in 150 at-risk towns across four vote-rich counties. Most Liberian respondents—88 percent—agreed somewhat or strongly that "election monitors can help reduce violence." This is just shy of the 91 percent who agreed that "election monitors can help reduce fraud/cheating." Liberians' confidence in observer effects on fraud aligns with a strong body of research on the fraud-reducing effect of observers, and there is little reason to doubt Liberians' confidence of observer effects on violence.

Liberians' confidence in observers' ability to reduce election violence is not unique. Together with the USIP, I conducted a very similar pre-election survey in Kenya, which had elections in August 2017, and found fairly similar responses. In Kenya, 73 percent of respondents agreed somewhat or strongly that election monitors can help reduce violence, and 85 percent concurred that they can reduce cheating. These numbers, speak to the local confidence in election observers to make elections both more credible (reduce cheating) and more peaceful (reduce violence).

This chapter empirically examines the effect of election support on campaign violence. As detailed in chapter 1, election support can increase the credibility of the electoral process by shaping the environment in which elections are held and make this environment more conducive to peaceful electoral processes. In particular, observation can increase the accountability of potential perpetrators. Observation makes it more likely that misbehavior is detected and independently verified and that the political actors behind these actions are publicly denounced.

By raising accountability for misbehavior, manipulation becomes more costly. While political elites may have incentives to use campaign violence in order to influence vote choice or turnout, the increased costs for such actions makes this a less attractive strategy. Therefore observation can help deter potential perpetrators from using violence in the campaigning period.

Further, technical assistance can increase the capacity of the election commission to administer smooth elections and to manage conflict. Technical support can help the NEC in acquiring sufficient material and staff to run the election and conduct voter education. It can also support the NEC in setting up institutions to prevent conflict and manage conflict where it occurs.

The quantitative and qualitative analyses provide empirical evidence for this argument: election support can significantly reduce campaign violence. The quantitative analysis of over four hundred elections in Africa and Latin America demonstrates that both types of international election support are associated with less campaign violence. Further, there is some evidence of a joint effect: when both types of election support are provided, campaign violence is lower than when no form or only one form of support was provided. These findings are robust to controlling for a host of domestic conflict factors from the baseline model of violence, and changes in the control variables.

The quantitative analysis has also tackled selection concerns, as these might provide a powerful alternative explanation. Testing for selection shows that observation is no more or less likely to be deployed at violent elections in Africa and Latin America. This means that the estimate of observation to reduce campaign violence is *not* biased by selection into more or less peaceful elections. The observer effect is not an artifact of selection. Testing for selection also shows that UN technical assistance tends to select into more violent elections. Technical assistance is somewhat more likely to be provided to elections that are expected to turn violent. It is significantly more likely to be provided to elections where UN peacekeeping troops are already on the ground and where economic development is low—all indicators of a conflict-prone environment. When accounting for this selection into more conflict-prone environments, the analysis reveals that technical support indeed has a violence-reducing effect. Taking into account that the UN goes to more violent places, it is still effective at reducing campaign violence in these circumstances.

Shifting gears from the quantitative analysis, a qualitative review of cases also supports the argument. Elections in Ghana, Benin, Malawi, and Guinea illustrate that the observer effect is not just an artifact of broad cross-country analyses but also holds within individual countries over time. Further, reviewing the activities undertaken by technical assistance in Sierra Leone's 2007 election highlights its link to conflict management and electoral security. Finally, a review of Liberia's post-conflict elections documents the joint effect of technical support and observation, as both were present at all elections and none of them experienced substantial campaign violence. The qualitative analysis sheds light on the proposed mechanisms that are often difficult to trace in statistical studies: how observation raises accountability and how technical assistance increases capacity for conflict management.

Given the apparent success of technical assistance for mitigating election violence, efforts to explore its dynamics and effects are an important contribution to scholarship and the policy community. I return to the effect of technical assistance on post-election violence in chapter 4, showing that this type of support is also associated with less post-vote violence. It thus is a force for good in terms of less electoral violence and perhaps for other domestic aspects that have yet to be systematically explored.

For election observation, chapters 2 and 3 demonstrate important and differential dynamics. On the one hand, observation can calm the campaign process by increasing accountability. On the other hand, this externally generated accountability can backfire after the election if election observers declare that the official result is not credible, increasing the loser's incentives to challenge the result. This suggests that observation can be a double-edged sword: fueling or calming violence depending on the electoral stage and actions taken. This argument is explored in more detail in the next chapter.

THE DARK SIDE
International Condemnation and Post-Election Violence

Chapter 1 presented a theory linking international election support to election violence. While chapter 2 provided empirical support for the pre-election argument, this chapter turns to the post-election period and specifically the effect of observer criticism on post-election violence. When international election observers issue negative verdicts—alleging that significant vote fraud has occurred—they cast doubt on the credibility of the election. Such a condemnation legitimizes the loser's dissatisfaction and facilitates mobilization among the loser's supporters. This influences the cost-benefit calculation of the electoral loser as he or she considers challenging or consenting to the result. Observer verdicts shape the incentives of domestic actors—losing candidates, parties, and their supporters—to challenge election outcomes, which can increase post-election violence.

In this chapter, I test the argument about condemnations and post-election violence empirically. I use quantitative methods to test the main effect: whether observer condemnations are associated with more post-election violence. In addition, I evaluate the proposed causal chain and the role of the key actor. I show that electoral losers are more likely to challenge a result when it is condemned and that loser challenges are associated with increased violence. This provides statistical support for the hypothesized causal chain, which is condemnation → loser challenge → violence. Further, I show that the results are robust to different model specifications and not driven by endogeneity. In the second half of this chapter, I provide more detailed, qualitative support for this relationship. I discuss several elections to illustrate the relationship between condemnations and post-vote violence. I draw on a comparative case study of two similar elections with divergent outcomes (Sierra Leone and Kenya 2007), another case to detail the loser challenge mechanism (Cote d'Ivoire 2010), and several additional cases to exemplify variation in which domestic actor initiates violence.

Quantitative Tests

If the theoretical argument in chapter 1 is correct, there should be a positive statistical association between negative observer verdicts and post-election violence. To test this, I use data on almost 250 observed national elections in sixty-eight countries in Africa and Latin America since 1990. I limit the sample to observed elections to get a cleaner counterfactual, as this allows us to compare elections that were at risk of receiving an observer condemnation. Examining the set of observed elections offers a more stringent test of the argument because only those elections are included in the analysis that "qualify" for condemnation by having observers in the first place. Monitors can only reveal election manipulation when they observe the election: they must be present in order to observe, evaluate, and assess the election in their press statements and reports. If we did not restrict the sample to observed elections, the counterfactual to condemnation would include both non-condemned and un-observed elections, which makes inference and interpretation challenging. The focus on observed elections also sidesteps the selection issue addressed in the previous chapter, as all the elections examined in this chapter had observers present. A remaining concern for inference is that the act of criticizing an observed election is not exogenous, and I address this issue in the robustness checks.

The dependent variable, *Post-election casualties*, is the count of election-related casualties in the three months after a national election. On average, fifteen people were killed or injured at observed elections; after some elections over a thousand people were harmed. These extreme cases include Kenya in 2007 and Angola in 1992. It is noteworthy that Africa has been more prone to post-vote violence than Latin America. Post-election violence affects about 17 percent of observed elections in Africa but only 9 percent of observed elections in Latin America. In terms of violence intensity, the average post-vote casualty count at observed elections is twenty-two in Africa but only two in Latin America. This means that violence risks and levels are substantially higher in Africa. It also means that there is more violence variation to explain in Africa than in the Americas, so that results are likely stronger for the African continent. To address this variation in violence, I run analyses on the pooled data (both regions) as well as on Africa separately;

this approach mirrors the main analyses in the previous chapter for campaign violence (table 2.1).

Since the outcome of interest is a count, I again use count models and cluster standard errors by country to account for lack of independence between elections within countries. Also in parallel with chapter 2, one stage of the model predicts zero violence as a function of development and conflict history, while the intensity of violence is predicted by the base model. Model diagnostics again confirm that zero-inflated binomial models are most appropriate for these data; I return to these diagnostics later.

The key independent variable is *Condemnation* in the form of a negative statement (press release or public report) by international election observers. This variable is a binary indicator coded 1 when any reputable observer group seriously questions the process or outcome of the election, that is, who the legitimate winner of the election is. This approach follows a body of research on international election observation, and the data is sourced from the Nelda dataset.[1] As detailed in chapter 1, reputable groups are more professional, independent, and willing to criticize elections than other groups. About 15 percent of observed elections were condemned in Africa and Latin America between 1990 and 2012.

My argument suggests that observer criticism by at least one reputable group should increase post-vote violence, so the coefficient estimate on *Condemnation* should be positive and statistically significant. The analyses also include a range of control variables from the baseline model of electoral violence introduced in chapter 1. These control variables are *Executive constraints, Post-conflict, Economic development, Natural resources, Population size, Ethnic fractionalization, Competition, Poll type, Past election violence,* and *Fraud.* Again following previous research on post-election contestation, *Fraud* is a binary variable that indicates whether there were "significant concerns that the elections will not be free and fair"; this measure relates to domestic or international concern about the quality of the election, including whether "elections were widely perceived to lack basic criteria for competitive elections."[2] I expect that fraud is positively associated with post-vote violence but also that condemnation has an additional, violence-increasing effect.

The statistical analyses also control for competition and previous election violence. As explained in chapter 1, the empirical measures for these two concepts differ between pre- and post-election analysis because we can use more accurate and relevant information about these issues once election-day has passed. For example, we know the vote share from the announced result, from which we can infer approximate support for the winner and the loser or runner-up—with some measurement error due to fraud. Thus competition is measured as the *Loser's vote share,* that is, the percentage of the vote received by the runner-up according to official election results. This controls for the fact that the loser's popular support may influence his or her incentive to challenge results and risk violence. As detailed in chapter 1, strength at the ballot box and in the street are linked: the more people vote for the loser, the more people are likely to come out and mobilize for the loser as well. Greater popular support for the loser should increase his or her incentives to challenge results and thus increase violence. In addition, more popular losers might also face more government crackdown in reaction to the challenge or as an attempt to prevent it. Hence, loser vote share should be positively associated with post-vote violence.

Further, I also include *Pre-election casualties*, that is, the count of casualties from the six months before and including election-day. This was the dependent variable in chapter 2 and now becomes a control variable, as pre-vote violence might influence post-vote violence. This is more proximate and more relevant for post-vote violence than taking election violence at the previous election, which tends to be several years in the past. However, I have no strong expectations for the direction of influence, as this issue is debated. While some have found a relationship between pre- and post-election violence or protest,[3] others have found no relationship or mixed results,[4] highlighting that electoral violence before and after voting follows distinct logics. The descriptive statistics of all variables and their data sources are in appendix 1C. Again, all controls—except the four election-specific variables—are lagged by one year to mitigate endogeneity.[5]

Table 3.1 presents the estimated impact of condemnation on post-election violence. Columns 1 and 2 include all observed elections, while columns 3 and 4 focus on Africa separately. The results in table 3.1 are consistent: the coefficient on *Condemnation* is positive and statistically significant in most models.[6] The results are particularly strong for Africa: condemned elections have significantly more post-vote casualties, while controlling for fraud and several other potential drivers of violence. Conditional on elections being observed, condemnation is associated with more post-election violence.

The effect of condemnations is also substantively important. To understand the magnitude of the impact, I estimate the predicted number of post-election casualties when *Condemnation* is varied from 0 to 1 while all other variables are set to their mean values. Condemned elections result in approximately nine additional casualties compared to elections that have also been observed but not condemned. That effect magnitude is about 50 percent of the average post-vote casualties in Africa (which is twenty casualties). This effect is substantively important. These findings support Hypothesis 2a, demonstrating that condemned elections have substantially more post-election violence than not-condemned elections, conditional on observer presence and controlling for a range of other variables.

TABLE 3.1 Effect of observer condemnation on post-election violence

	LATIN AMERICA AND AFRICA		AFRICA	
	(1)	(2)	(3)	(4)
Predicting violence intensity (count)				
Condemnation	1.415**	0.869	2.695***	2.593***
	(0.564)	(0.972)	(0.726)	(0.788)
Fraud		2.792*		1.490
		1.554)		(2.007)
Executive constraints	−0.209	0.232	−0.581***	−0.403
	(0.212)	(0.539)	(0.166)	(0.315)
Post-conflict	−1.611	1.199	−1.492	−0.174
	(1.463)	(1.227)	(1.073)	(2.073)
Economic development	0.659	0.773	2.298***	2.732***
	(0.639)	(0.597)	(0.794)	(0.862)
Natural resources	−0.014	−0.002	−0.065	−0.059
	(0.102)	(0.064)	(0.066)	(0.089)
Ethnic fractionalization	3.020	5.007	12.301***	13.563***
	(2.239)	(3.663)	(2.194)	(2.606)
Population size	1.033***	0.480*	1.041***	0.915***
	(0.293)	(0.257)	(0.270)	(0.337)
Poll type	−0.057	−0.531	−0.358	−0.652
	(0.423)	(0.469)	(0.336)	(0.444)
Pre-election casualties	0.002	0.032	−0.011**	−0.009
	(0.016)	(0.038)	(0.004)	(0.008)
Loser vote share	−0.066***	0.031	−0.038	0.010
	(0.024)	(0.051)	(0.033)	(0.080)
Predicting zero violence				
Post-conflict	−0.660	1.577	−0.703	−0.452
	(0.521)	(4.420)	(0.548)	(0.907)
Economic development	0.413**	3.460	0.288	0.429
	(0.189)	(6.095)	(0.227)	(0.297)
Log α	1.066**	3.089***	1.181**	1.461*
	(0.423)	(0.351)	(0.474)	(0.760)
Observations	246	242	155	152
Clusters	68	68	46	46
LL	−236.51	−235.46	−184.04	−183.07

Notes: The table reports estimates from count models (zero-inflated negative binomial models). The dependent variable is the count of election-related casualties in the three months after election-day. The unit of observation is the national election. The sample is restricted to observed elections. Robust standard errors are clustered on country. ***, **, and * indicate significance at the 1%, 5%, and 10% levels.

The results also indicate that the statistical model chosen is appropriate: the overdispersion parameter is significant in all models, suggesting that a negative binomial model is more appropriate than a Poisson model. As in chapter 2, I use model fit (AIC) statistics to assess model choice between the standard and zero-inflated negative binomial. These show that the zero-inflated model is preferred in all cases except column 4, where a negative binomial model provides a better fit. The substantive estimate of nine casualties is based on the negative binomial model. The effect estimate for zero-inflated models (as shown in table 3.1) is larger.[7]

The results are robust to using different measures for control variables, in particular replacing ethnic fractionalization with the percentage of excluded population from the Ethnic Power Relations dataset[8] and replacing fraud concerns with a fraud measure that takes into account election-day events.[9] The results are substantively similar with the different fraud measure or the exclusion measure.

While these analyses document the importance of condemnations by credible observers, I do not claim that condemnations determine violence or that they are the primary drivers of violence in every case. Domestic variables are also important. More populous countries tend to have more post-election casualties. In Africa, ethnic fractionalization is associated with more post-vote violence. These positive relationships are consistent with previous research, as outlined in chapter 1. The coefficient on fraud is weakly significant in column 2 and not significant in column 4. For Africa, this suggests that fraud alone is less likely to lead to violence than internationally certified fraud. Moreover, the effect of condemnations in Africa is robust to controlling for fraud.

Also, more constraints on the executive are associated with less violence in Africa. This points to political elites and specifically incumbents as the main perpetrators of violence as well as to the importance of accountability for political violence, as stressed in the introduction and chapter 1. Finally, it might surprise some that campaign violence is *not* consistently associated with post-election violence. It is only significant in one model, and the coefficient is negative, suggesting that more campaign casualties are associated with fewer post-vote casualties. This again emphasizes that pre- and post-election violence are two different phenomena that operate under distinct logics.

The quantitative results in table 3.1 support the argument that negative observer reports can increase post-election violence. If that is true, then do positive reports lower violence, essentially acting as a deterrent and mitigating conflict? I have tested this separately and found some evidence in favor of this, but the results should be treated with caution as they rely on a smaller set of elections and thus push the limit on what can be estimated. Recall that we cannot make any inference about the effect of positive reports from table 3.1 because

Condemnation = 1 indicates a negative report but *Condemnation* = 0 includes both positive and ambiguous (mixed) observer reports. To examine the effect of positive reports on violence, I use supplemental data from another source that has information on whether observer organizations deemed the election quality overall as positive, ambiguous, or negative. I coded *Endorsement* when all observer groups attending the election issued a positive report.[10] This ensures that condemnation and endorsement are distinct, because condemnation by any one group could provide leverage for the loser to challenge an election. These data are useful to distinguish clearly positive reports but have limited temporal scope (until 2004) and only cover about half of the elections marked as "observed" by reputable groups in the Nelda data. Consequently, the dataset drops to 116 observed elections in both regions and 73 observed elections in Africa alone. Running multivariate models—and especially more demanding count models—on such a small sample is not generally advisable, so inference, if made at all, should be taken as suggestive only.

Replicating table 3.1 with the alternative independent variable, the estimated coefficient on *Endorsement* is negative and significant in several models. This is in line with the argument that observer reports can significantly influence post-election violence; condemnations can increase such violence, while endorsement may mitigate conflict. However, as stated, results for the endorsement effect are based on a much smaller sample and should thus be treated with caution. Some elections support the notion that positive observer verdicts can at times play a conflict-mitigating role. For example, in the election held in Honduras in 2013, positive verdicts by the Carter Center, the European Union, and the Organization of American States—together with intense diplomatic pressure—helped undermine fraud claims made by the opposition.[11] The positive observer verdict on this election strengthened the position of the election commission and debunked efforts of the losing party to mobilize against the victor; no election-related casualties occurred after the election. This case also speaks to the importance of observer *verdicts* as opposed to their mere *presence* or opposition fraud claims when it comes to post-election violence.

THE CAUSAL CHAIN

While my main interest is in the effect of condemnation on post-vote violence, supplementary original data are sufficiently granular to also examine the plausibility of the causal mechanism and allow inference about the behavior of the key actor, that is, whether electoral losers are more likely to challenge a result when it was condemned, which then facilitates violence. For that purpose, I collected data on *Post-election loser challenge*, which is a binary indicator coded 1 if the losing party/candidate challenged the announced election result, and 0 otherwise. Loser challenges can take the form of statements, court proceedings, or demonstrations and must occur within three months of election-day in order to be included in the data. Since challenges are intentionally public events, information is sourced from comprehensive searches of newspapers and newswires using the OneSearch meta-search engine, which also searches within the popular LexisNexis database. More details on coding these original data are in appendix 1C.[12] Since this alternative outcome variable is binary, I use logit models. For the model specification I follow three prominent studies of post-election protests and rejections[13] and control for *Fraud concerns, Loser vote share, Executive constraints, Judicial independence, Economic development, Poll type,* and *Incumbent lost.* I do not include a control for observer presence since the sample is already restricted to observed elections.

Appendix table 3A.1 shows that observer condemnations are strongly and positively associated with a higher risk of loser challenges, while controlling for a range of other factors. The coefficient on *condemnation* is highly statistically significant across all models (p<0.01). Figure 3.1 illustrates the magnitude of this effect.[14] Condemnations are associated with a 36-percentage-point increase in the risk of loser challenges. This is a large shift in contestation. Another suggestive piece of evidence is that the coefficient on the *loser vote share* variable is positive (and borderline significant in the African sample), indicating that stronger losers are more likely to challenge the election outcome. This is in line with the argument. Since more people are likely to come out and fight for the loser, his or her chances of winning a potential post-election contest are heightened, which makes him or her more likely to challenge the election result. Such challenges turn violent when the initial challenge or the reaction to it involves physical force. Moreover, fraud is not a significant predictor of loser challenges in appendix table 3A.1. In other words, as in the main analysis, fraud alone is less likely to lead to challenges than "internationally certified fraud."

Further in the causal chain, loser challenges also significantly increase violence, as shown in appendix table 3A.2 (p<0.05). Violence after elections is lower when losers consent to results. In terms of substantive importance, loser challenges are associated with about a dozen more post-vote casualties than loser consent.[15]

These supplementary analyses of loser challenges support the causal mechanism outlined in the theory section, which states that condemnations increase the loser's incentives to challenge results and that loser challenges can exacerbate violence after elections. Taken together, these analyses provide evidence that condemnations can (unintentionally) contribute to violence after elections. This is strong support for the theory, particularly as the analyses control for other

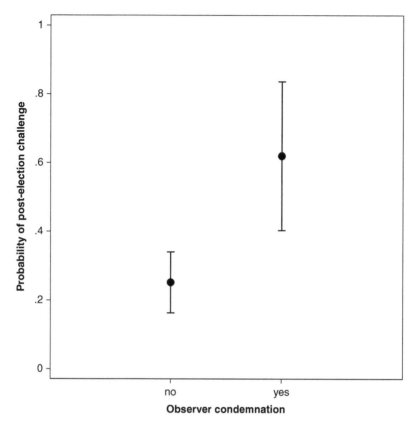

FIGURE 3.1.   Substantive effect of condemnation on post-election challenge

factors associated with violence. While some domestic factors also play a role, negative verdicts by international observers shape post-election violence.

ALTERNATIVE EXPLANATION: ENDOGENEITY?

However, it could be that the relationship between condemnation and post-vote violence is an artifact of reverse causality, which is a form of endogeneity. One can imagine a scenario in which observers hold off on their verdict, violence erupts after elections, and this already occurring violence leads observers to condemn the election.[16] I account for and examine this possibility in two ways: with original data on sequencing and with a statistical analysis of reverse causality. I replicate models 1 and 2 of table 3.1 but allow condemnations to be endogenous to a number of factors suggested in previous research. According to Judith Kelley, the determinants of observer verdicts include *Pre-election violence, Fraud, Official development assistance (ODA) per capita, First multiparty election, Turnover,* and *Capacity* (proxied with *Economic development* in the form of per capita GDP).[17] I use a two-stage model where the first stage predicts condemnations as a function of these variables, while the second/main stage is the same as in table 3.1. Following the discussion in chapter 1 and the robustness checks in chapter 2, I run treatment effects models, which are linear regressions with an endogenous binary treatment variable in the first stage.[18] As in the previous chapter, these models provide a test for whether the two stages are linked, that is, whether any unobservables influence both condemnations and violence. If the two equations are not linked, it is not necessary to use two-stage models, and the single-stage models (in table 3.1) are more appropriate.

The results in appendix table 3A.3 show that the two stages are not linked: the parameter ρ is near zero and its associated p-values are not significant in any of the models. In more technical language, we cannot reject the hypothesis that the two equations are not linked. This suggests that the two-stage setup is not needed, and single-stage models are more appropriate. That is, the single-stage models of table 3.1 are more appropriate for estimation and inference about the relationship between condemnations and violence. In table 3.1, the coefficient of interest is positive and significant. Even in the two-stage models, though, the coefficient estimates of *Condemnation* remain in the hypothesized direction (positive).

In the first stage, fraud concerns significantly influence condemnations; this is in line with other research, which has found that observer criticism is more likely at fraudulent elections. Pre-election violence is not strongly associated with condemnation. However, one previous analysis of the drivers of condemnation[19] had found the opposite empirical relationship—that campaign violence makes condemnation less likely and endorsement more likely—and interpreted this as evidence that observer groups withhold criticism at violence-prone elections in order to avoid fueling the fire. There are several reasons for why this difference in findings may arise. The analyses differ in dependent variable measures and models, in timeframe (1975–2004 vs. 1990–2012) and country sample. Further, the previous study's analysis did not measure post-vote violence in the second stage.

If it were the case that observer groups would regularly withhold criticism when they believe post-vote violence is likely, that would make it much more difficult to uncover the effect shown in table 3.1, as it would imply that elections with (more) post-vote violence do *not* get condemned. The results thus have two take-away points. First, test statistics indicate that the two equations are not linked, so the single-equation model in table 3.1 is more appropriate. Second, interpretation from table 3.1 suggests that condemnations are significantly and positively associated with more post-vote violence.

Original data on the chain of events also refutes reverse causality. I collected data on the timing of observer verdicts and the announcement of provisional results in relation to election-day.[20] In order for violence to influence observer reports—which would turn my argument on its head—reports would need to be issued several days, perhaps weeks after the election to allow time for announced results and responding violence. Yet figure 3.2 tells a different story: the vast majority of observer reports are issued within two days of the voting process, sometimes even before or on the day of polling itself. In this figure, the timing of observer reports from international organizations (IOs) are marked in light grey, and the timing of election results is marked in medium grey. Where they overlap, the color is dark grey. Observer reports almost always precede the announcement of election results. This finding is in line with earlier research noting that observer reports tend to be issued right after voting, usually before results are announced.[21] Since losers—if they challenge—generally wait for results to be announced in order to challenge them, this makes it difficult for post-election violence to influence observer verdicts. This supports the argument that the timeline at observed elections generally is: voting → observer verdict → results → potential challenge → potential violence.

There are four outliers in figure 3.2—two rather early and two late verdicts—but these are not cases of reverse causality. The two early outliers in terms of report timing are Guinea in 1993 with an IRI statement and Togo in 1993 with a Carter Center/NDI statement. These are cases where observer groups canceled or withdrew their missions before voting because the election would not be meaningful, effectively criticizing the election before election-day. In these cases, reverse causality (that is, post-election violence *before* condemnations) is a logical impossibility because post-vote casualties are only measured after election-day. The two late outliers in terms of report timing—Mozambique 1994 and Mali 2002—were both peaceful elections with *positive* verdicts. Consequently, the endogeneity concern—violence triggering a condemnation—does not arise in these cases. Thus the weight of the evidence casts doubt on concerns about reverse causality.[22]

Illustrative Cases

The statistical tests presented in this chapter provide empirical support for the hypothesis that international condemnations are associated with more post-election violence and that the mechanism involves loser challenges. This section provides qualitative case material to illustrate the hypothesized causal mechanism between condemnations and violence. I begin with a comparative case

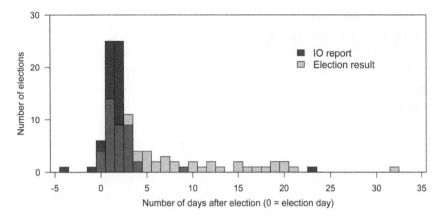

FIGURE 3.2. Timing of election, IO report, and result announcement

study about two similar elections—Sierra Leone and Kenya 2007—which had divergent observer verdicts and violence outcomes. While the election in Sierra Leone received an IO stamp of approval and was followed by a peaceful change in power, the election in Kenya was condemned, the loser challenged the result, and violence ensued for months. This case comparison, described more fully below, shows that elections that are similar across structural factors driving violence can follow substantially different violence trajectories and that observer verdicts play an important role in these dynamics. I then turn to the case of Cote d'Ivoire 2010 to zoom into the key actors and their actions, showing that the observer condemnation incentivized the loser to challenge the result, and that the winner responded to this challenge by attacking the loser's supporters. Finally, I return to the strategic interaction outlined in appendix figure 1B.1 and use case examples to illustrate how violence can break out at different points in the strategic interaction between loser and winner. Taken together, the case material provides qualitative support for the argument. It also highlights a few aspects that statistical analyses cannot reveal. For example, the cases show that domestic actors care about IO verdicts and at times use them to publicly justify their challenge.

CASE COMPARISON: SIERRA LEONE AND KENYA 2007

This section compares two elections to illustrate the mechanism linking condemnations and violence, that is, increasing the loser's incentives to challenge the result by indicating that the loser has more popular support than the official result suggests and providing a focal point for mobilization. Kenya 2007 and Sierra Leone 2007 were effectively similar along most control variables, as shown in table 3.2, so alternative explanations offer limited leverage for explaining why Sierra Leone remained peaceful while Kenya erupted in intense violence with more than a thousand casualties. Both presidential elections were held in ethnically diverse and fairly democratic countries and were highly competitive. Both elections were observed by credible international observers; the EU mission was the largest Western monitor at both elections. Further, both countries received technical election assistance in the run-up to their 2007 elections, focusing in both countries on election commission capacity building, staff and infrastructure, improved voter registration, and voter education.[23]

From a strictly domestic perspective, the difference in violence is surprising because of the similarity between cases and also because we might expect Sierra Leone to be more violent. To the extent that these two elections differ on domestic factors, the weight of factors points to Sierra Leone as the country expected to experience more post-vote violence. Sierra Leone was a post-conflict country, was poorer than Kenya, and had significant fraud concerns even before the election. Serious fraud[24] surfaced in both countries on election-day and during the counting of votes. Irregularities surfaced in the tabulation stage, and the announcement of the results took several days. In both elections, fraud occurred in the form of over-balloting, that is, turnout exceeding 100 percent of registered voters.[25]

A crucial difference between the cases was the observer verdict. In Sierra Leone, EU observers endorsed the election result. EU observers declared that the process was "generally well administered," with the conduct of polling and counting "either good or very good" in the vast majority of polling stations.[26] The national election commission (NEC) announced preliminary results on 10 September and released final results a week later, declaring challenger Koroma the winner with 54.6 percent vs. the incumbent party's Berewa's 45.4 percent of the vote. The EU's stamp of approval meant that the result was credible and that "the public's demand for political change"[27] was real: the incumbent party (Berewa's SLPP) had less popular support than the opposition. Deprived of a condemnation to use as a rallying cry, the loser conceded defeat the same day that results were announced. The winner Koroma visited Berewa at his residence to formally accept his congratulations. Consequently, the loser did not challenge the result and post-vote violence did not occur.

This stands in sharp contrast to Kenya's election a few months later. EU observers condemned the 2007 Kenyan election, which unintentionally helped embolden the loser to challenge the result violently. The EU chief observer first criticized the tabulation as "clearly disturbing"[28] on December 30, 2007, when the counting irregularities surfaced, and some election officials initially kept local results secret and excluded observers from some local polling stations.

TABLE 3.2   Similarity of Kenya and Sierra Leone's 2007 elections

	KENYA	SIERRA LEONE
Observers present	yes	yes
* Fraud concerns	no	yes
* Executive constraints	6	5
Post-conflict	no	yes
* Per capita GDP	442	243
Natural resources	no	no
* Ethnic fractionalization	0.86	0.78
* Population size	36.5	5.3
Poll type	general	general
* Pre-election casualties	70	0
Loser's vote share	44	45

Notes: Significant drivers of post-election violence in this sample are marked with *. All country-year variables are lagged by one year.

Later that day when results were announced, supporters of the electoral loser (Odinga) immediately challenged them by attacking some homes and businesses of the winner's (Kibaki's) supporters in Nairobi. The winner himself "tried to pre-empt any [further] challenge by having himself hurriedly sworn in."[29] This again prompted the EU chief observer to criticize the election, as he noted inconsistencies between local and national results and stated that the tallying process was not credible[30] so that "doubt remains as to the accuracy of the result of the presidential election as announced today."[31] In its preliminary statement, the EU reiterated that the elections had "fallen short of key international and regional standards" and called for an "independent investigation" of the vote count,[32] which received immediate support from the loser Odinga.[33]

The domestic press, the EU, and the loser's supporters linked the condemnation directly to the loser challenge: Odinga's "charges of fraud were lent extra weight by the EU election monitoring team."[34] Odinga "vowed not to back down" and called for a "million-man march [in Nairobi] . . . to protest what [he] called a civilian coup."[35] The loser's supporters were ready to join his cause. After international observers criticized the announced result, one Odinga supporter declared: "How can one man [Kibaki] cheat a whole nation? . . . If a guerrilla war starts, I am ready to join in."[36] Odinga supporters, even abroad, felt that that his decision not to accept the election result was justified by the observer criticism. One Odinga supporter linked the protest directly to the condemnation: "[Our elections] were marred by a lot of irregularities, and these have been documented by the European Union observer team. . . . So we are . . . expressing our dissatisfaction with the electoral process."[37] Furthermore, the EU later acknowledged the role that its negative report played: it "may have reinforced the narrative (of a vote stolen by the election commission on behalf of President Kibaki) which was driving violence."[38]

Taken together, this evidence supports both parts of the mechanism. First, the EU's criticism of the election result suggested that Odinga's popular support was larger than his official vote share. And second, this condemnation was an important factor contributing to the narrative of a stolen election and thereby facilitating mobilization among Odinga's supporters. A secondary but related question is why Kenya was condemned but Sierra Leone was not. One potential explanation for the divergent verdicts is "stability bias,"[39] meaning that observers did not condemn Sierra Leone's election because its history of recent conflict made it particularly volatile; election observers might not want to strike the match that ignites an explosion of violence. However, Kenya was no stranger to conflict either. In fact, Kenya had more pre-election violence in 2007 than Sierra Leone. Further, all three of Kenya's elections since the advent of a multiparty system were marred by high electoral violence.[40] Moreover, reputable observers have been willing to condemn elections in other post-conflict (Ivory Coast 2010, Rwanda 2003) and conflict (Uganda 2001, 2006) contexts. Hence such a stability bias, if it existed, may well have applied to both elections.

THE MECHANISM OF LOSER CHALLENGE: COTE D'IVOIRE 2010

The election in Cote d'Ivoire 2010 shows how observer condemnation can increase post-election violence and elucidates the role of loser challenge. The violent aftermath of the 2010 Cote d'Ivoire election led to widespread concern about the progress of African democracy. Although it was a multiparty presidential democracy, Cote d'Ivoire had not held elections in ten years due to the civil war (2002–2007) between the government-held Christian South and the rebel-held Muslim North. The incumbent, Laurent Gbagbo, represented the South and the party of the Ivorian Popular Front (FPI). His main rival, Alassane Ouattara, represented the North and the Rally of the Republicans (RDR), one of the two major opposition parties in the country. The first-round election on 31 October 2010 went well: voter turnout was high and reputable IO monitors—the United Nations (UN), the European Union (EU), the Carter Center as well as African organizations—approved the credibility of the election. However, neither Gbagbo nor Ouattara received a majority of votes. This led to a run-off election on 28 November.

After the run-off Cote d'Ivoire was left with two candidates claiming the presidency. The national election commission declared Ouattara the winner with 54 percent of the vote, which was verified by international observers. The UN observer team validated this result,[41] as the opposition candidate Ouattara noted.[42] Observer groups confirmed that voting had gone fairly well in most locations.[43] Further, observers from the EU and the Carter Center even congratulated Ouattara on his victory.[44] However, the constitutional court, which was packed with Gbagbo loyalists, invalidated voting from seven districts favoring Ouattara and declared incumbent Gbagbo the winner with 51 percent. Outraged by this turn of events, the EU observer group immediately condemned the court's decision and the announced election results.[45] The EU observer mission stated that it "condemns . . . [and] refuses to recognize the results announced by the Constitutional Council which it considers contrary to the will expressed by the Ivorian people in the polls."[46]

Ouattara, emboldened by the EU's condemnation of the judicial results and the UN's validation of the NEC result, refused to concede the election. The press linked the international condemnation of the court's result to Ouattara's decision to contest the election results: "Backed by the United Nations and the European Union, Cote d'Ivoire opposition leader Alassane Ouattara . . . declared himself president-elect."[47] Both men took an oath of office as president of the republic on 4 December. Ouattara's supporters took "to the streets to rally" and were lethally repressed when "security forces launched grenades at Ouattara supporters" and civilians, leading to fourteen fatalities.[48] Street fighting quickly escalated into broader civil conflict over the following four months. Overall, post-election violence led to over a thousand fatalities and more than one million civilians fleeing the violence.

Besides strengthening Ouattara domestically, the observer condemnation also had indirect effects by triggering further international reactions. The two main regional organizations, ECOWAS and the African Union, suspended the country over the disputed election until Ouattara would take office. The African regional reactions paved the way for a UN Security Council authorization for military action against Gbagbo in late March 2011, actively intervening in the ongoing civil conflict. The post-election violence came to an end in late April when French and UN troops bombarded the presidential palace in Abidjan. After months of fighting, Ouattara was sworn in as president in May 2011. Due to the military intervention, Ouattara won the military standoff and became the president of Cote d'Ivoire. Without external military support, the civil war may well have lasted longer. But without the initial international support from observer groups, which criticized the court's election result, Ouattara may not have challenged the announced result in the first place.

FORMS OF LOSER CHALLENGES

Loser challenges can take several forms, including verbal statements, court proceedings, peaceful street protests, and outright violence. Post-election challenges in the form of losers' verbal statements are relatively common, especially after internationally condemned elections. For example, after internationally criti-cized elections in Haiti in 1997, opposition parties denounced the results and called for their annulment. And again after the condemned election in 2000, the Haitian losing opposition leader called the election illegitimate and declared that the winner had no mandate to govern.[49] Similarly, Equatorial Guinea's 2009 elec-tion was condemned as it was "difficult to see how we can say that those elections are free and fair," and the main opposition candidate then refused to accept the results because polls were not free and fair.[50]

In addition to verbal statements, loser challenges of the election result can also take the form of court proceedings. For instance, after Uganda's condemned elections in 2001 and 2006, main opposition leader Kizza Besigye of the Forum of Democratic Change formally rejected the results in a statement given to the national election commission and then filed a petition to the courts to nullify the results.[51] Similarly, after observers cast doubt on the credibility of Nigeria's elections in 2003, most opposition groups challenged the outcome in public statements and in court. Specifically, the main opposition All Nigeria People's Party along with twenty-eight other opposition groups rejected the legislative results in a public statement. In addition, three key actors challenged the results in court: Muhammadu Buhari of the All Nigeria People's Party filed a court peti-tion to nullify the presidential election on behalf of twenty opposition parties, the Movement for Democracy and Justice filed a court injunction to the Federal Court of Appeal challenging the results of the presidential and legislative results, and Odumegwu Ojukwu of the All Progressive Grand Alliance also filed a court petition challenging the results.[52]

Beyond verbal challenges and court proceedings, loser challenges can also be outside of institutional channels, in the form of street protests. At times, these are prompted when international observers cast doubt on the credibility of the election result, as in Haiti and the DRC. After international observers con-demned Haiti's elections in 2006 and 2010, losing camps and their supporters poured into the streets.[53] At other times, protests by the electoral loser are already ongoing but further intensify after international condemnation, as in the Democratic Republic of the Congo (DRC) in 2011. Immediately following these elections, opposition leader Etienne Tshisekedi rejected the results and declared himself president; protests rose against the election results in DRC's capital, as well as in expatriate locations in Ottawa and Toronto. These loser protests further "intensified after a team of international observers reported that incumbent Joseph Kabila's win was so flawed it lacked credibility. . . . Elec-tion monitors from the Carter Center . . . added momentum to Mr. Tshiseke-di's refusal to accept the results, saying they 'lack credibility.'"[54] Similarly, after Nigeria's internationally condemned 2007 election, the opposition bloc led by

Muhammadu Buhari and former vice president Atiku Abubakar rejected the results and demanded their cancellation, filed a case to overturn the results, and staged peaceful protests.[55]

Violence—physical force and harm—then occurs when either the initial challenge by the loser is violent or when the winner violently represses a peaceful loser challenge. Loser challenges were violent in Nigeria in 1999. The election was criticized by the Carter Center, and this criticism was used by the losing camp for mobilization. A local reporter for *The Washington Post* noted that the Carter Center "said irregularities had clouded the outcome of the voting, and [losing opposition candidate] Falae's supporters seized on the statement as evidence for their case."[56] Specifically, Olu Falae staged protests and filed an appeal in the Abuja Appeal Court.[57] Supporters of the loser and radical anti-government (militant) groups poured into the streets and rioted, and government security forces responded by firing live ammunition at protesters and bystanders. Overall, at least six police and six rioters were killed in this post-election violence.[58]

The winner has violently repressed loser challenges in a number of countries, including Cameroon and Niger. Four days after the 1992 Cameroon presidential election, the chief observer of the National Democratic Institute issued a preliminary statement that this election had failed to meet international standards of fairness. When the incumbent president, Paul Biya, was declared the winner a week later, the results were rejected by the losing opposition camp around opposition leader John Fru Ndi. The winner reacted to those loser protests by sending police to break up marches and by placing the losing candidate, Fru Ndi, and other opposition leaders under house arrest.[59] At least three people died, ninety-two people were injured, and more than five hundred people were arrested.[60] Following this same pattern, Niger's 1996 election was condemned by international observers, which was followed by widespread street protests. The incumbent, who was also the winning candidate, arrested opposition leaders and hundreds of protesters, and riot police used tear gas against protesters.[61]

VARIATION IN THE VIOLENCE INITIATOR AND OUTCOME

As explained in chapter 1, I assume that it is the loser who challenges the result but I make no assumptions about who initiates the violence, which is difficult to establish empirically across countries and years. If and when the loser challenges the result, violence can be initiated by either actor and erupt at any of three stages of the post-election dispute: loser challenge, winner resist, or loser fight. To illustrate this, consider the following steps in the strategic game earlier introduced in figure 1B.1 with empirical examples of internationally condemned elections shown in figure 3.3. Once the loser challenges the result, violence can erupt:

1. if the loser challenges violently (as in Kenya 2007) rather than through a verbal announcement (as in Nigeria 2003), legal proceedings (as in Uganda 2011, Zimbabwe 2002, Cameroon 1992), or peaceful protest (as in Niger 1996, Equatorial Guinea 1999, Cameroon 1997),
2. if the winner violently represses the loser's peaceful protests (as in Ethiopia 2005, Togo 1998, Mauritania 1992, Panama 1989) rather than countering or acknowledging the challenge peacefully (as in Rwanda 2003), or
3. if the loser resorts to violence after the winner's resistance (as in Niger 1993)[62] rather than backing down (as in Uganda 2001, Kenya 2013).

How far political actors are willing to go also drives the outcome of this interaction, that is, where elections "fall" on the strategic game tree. The four terminal nodes of the game are perhaps best illustrated with several presidential and legislative elections, as shown in figure 3.3. For example, if the loser consents to the election result, as in Sierra Leone's 2007 election discussed above, then the interaction ends here, and the winner can assume political power. A similar case is Senegal 2012; here, too, the loser consented to the election result in the presence of a positive observer report (from the EU). The Senegalese incumbent Abdoulaye Wade secured a plurality in the first round against thirteen challengers, but then lost in the run-off against Macky Sall by a landslide (66% vs. 34%). Wade conceded without delay following certification of the results, and the power transition proceeded peacefully.

Cases where the loser challenges and the winner concedes are rather rare. One possible African example is Zimbabwe 2008. The presidential run-off was

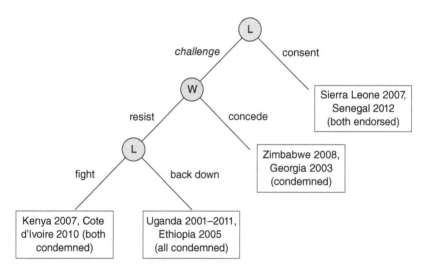

FIGURE 3.3.   The post-election game and cases examples

won by long-term incumbent Robert Mugabe after the opposition candidate Morgan Tsvangirai withdrew just before the run-off due to massive intimidation and violence against his supporters after the first round and also against the general background of continuing human rights violations. While the government did not allow election observers from Western countries, both rounds were criticized by African groups. The first round was criticized by observers from EISA, which raised "serious concerns regarding the credibility of the tabulation process, the integrity of the election materials, and the reliability of the results themselves."[63] The second round was criticized by observers from SADC and the African Union, which noted that the "elections did not represent the will of the people of Zimbabwe" and "fell short of accepted AU standards."[64] Tsvangirai's boycott of the run-off and the election dispute led to negotiations and an eventual power-sharing deal in which Mugabe (the winner) conceded some power to Tsvangirai in the form of a newly created post of prime minister.

There are also examples from other parts of the world. As an out-of-region example, some of the color revolutions fit this category. In the case of Georgia's 2003 legislative election, IO election observers criticized the process by stating that it "fell short of . . . international standards for democratic elections."[65] The military refused to support the government. The protesting crowds in Tbilisi further swelled, and the loser Mikheil Saakashvili challenged the official result by storming the parliament building. The following day, election winner, Eduard Shevardnadze, resigned. Similar dynamics unfolded in Serbia's Bulldozer Revolution in 2000, Ukraine's Orange Revolution in 2004, and Kyrgyzstan's Tulip Revolution in 2005.[66]

If the loser challenges the result following a condemnation and the winner resists, the loser decides whether to fight or back down from the challenge. Cases where the loser decides to fight include Kenya 2007 and Cote d'Ivoire 2010, as detailed above. Cases where the loser decides to back down despite an IO condemnation include Ethiopia 2005 and Uganda 2001, 2006, and 2011. Ethiopia's parliamentary election on 15 May 2005 was heavily criticized by international observers even before it was held. The EU chief observer noted that the murder of an opposition leader, the arrest of several hundred opposition supporters, intimidation, and the disruption of opposition rallies had a "negative impact on the entire electoral process."[67] On the afternoon of 16 May, early results for the capital, Addis Ababa, indicated a strong lead for the opposition. That same evening, the government declared a state of emergency, stationed military units throughout the capital, outlawed public gatherings, and closed state media to opposition parties.

On 25 May 2005, the EU chief observer again criticized the election board for its delay in releasing tallies, particularly since the results of many polling stations were available on election night. On 27 May, the elections board issued preliminary results showing that the government had won a majority. After the official results were released, the Carter Center also expressed concern over the vote counting and tabulation process.[68] Beginning 5 and 6 June, students and the opposition protested in Addis Ababa. Security forces responded violently and opened fire, resulting in over two hundred fatalities and twenty thousand arrests, most of them affiliated with the opposition.[69] The post-election violence after the condemned 2005 Ethiopian election also contrasts sharply with the relatively peaceful aftermath of the non-condemned election in Zimbabwe 2000. Like Sierra Leone and Kenya, the two legislative elections in Ethiopia 2005 and Zimbabwe 2000 were very similar along the structural conditions that influence violence (including fraud) and differed mainly in that the election in Ethiopia was condemned, challenged, and turned violent whereas the election in Zimbabwe was not condemned, was not challenged, and stayed largely peaceful.

While the link between condemnation, loser challenge, and violence is stronger in Africa than Latin America, cases show that this dynamic has also played out in the Americas. For example, Mexico's 1994 election was hailed as a step forward, but monitors criticized the uneven playing field in terms of media coverage and financing. The electoral loser (Cardenas) repeated this criticism almost verbatim as his motivation for challenging the outcome.[70] Similarly, Panama's 1989 election went sour when dictator Manuel Noriega's favorite candidate was trailing the vote count; Noriega replaced tally sheets and then annulled the election. As an international observer, former president Carter personally criticized this move, and the opposition followed with mass protests the next day, at which the main opposition leader (Guillermo Endara) was severely beaten by paramilitary forces.[71]

While much scholarship on election observation documents the positive effects of international involvement in strengthening developing democracies, it neglects the potential negative externalities associated with international condemnation. A negative observer report can increase the electoral loser's incentives to challenge results by indicating that popular support is larger than the official vote share and by providing a focal point for mobilization. Loser challenges can themselves be violent or provoke reactionary repression, resulting in casualties. These findings suggest that international observers may not have unequivocally positive effects but can also have significant side effects that contribute to domestic conflict.

I document the violent consequences of condemnations by analyzing observer verdicts and post-election violence for almost 250 observed elections in sixty-eight countries in Africa and Latin America since 1990. I also draw on original data on loser challenges, the timing of observer verdicts and results, and a comparative case study to trace the dynamics in more detail. Observed elections tend to be more violent when condemned (instead of being not condemned). The results show that condemnations can (unintentionally) contribute to post-election violence, even after controlling for a wide range of factors.

I also use case material to examine the link between condemnations and violence in more detail. We know that condemnations are widely disseminated through the domestic media, and cases show that both losers and winners reference condemnations. In the case of Kenya 2007, the loser and his supporters felt their protest was justified by the condemnation. There are similar references for Cote d'Ivoire 2010, which was also condemned and violent. Unsurprisingly, winners dislike observer condemnations and at times publicly criticize monitors for stoking violence, as in Ethiopia 2005 and Kyrgyzstan 2005.[72]

While the data used here focus on Africa and Latin America, the logic of the argument should apply to other developing democracies. The argument may not apply to the twenty-three or so advanced, liberal democracies. It does not apply here for three reasons: (1) observers rarely attend elections; (2) observers raise concerns about elections much less frequently; and (3) peaceful contestation has become a norm. Further research is needed to examine whether this dynamic also applies in the Middle East, the former Soviet states, or Asia, although a cursory scan of cases suggests that similar dynamics have also emerged elsewhere. Jordan 2010 was the first election to be criticized by international observers and also the first to erupt in peaceful mass protests, with the government using tear gas to disperse crowds. Similarly, Azerbaijan's 2003 election was condemned by observers and then challenged by the losing opposition, leading to mass arrests and at least one fatality from clashes with the police.[73] Subsequent elections in 2005, 2008, and 2013 followed the same script of condemnation, demonstrations, and police beatings and arrests.[74] Armenia's 1996 election was followed by peaceful protests, which turned violent after the OSCE condemned the elections; protesters stormed the parliament and physically attacked its speaker, resulting in two dozen casualties.[75] Such cases suggest that the argument applies beyond Africa, but more systematic analyses are needed.

Another interesting question is whether post-election violence leads to democratization. My finding is consistent with other research on the greater risk of protests and revolutions due to condemnations.[76] This research strand has largely been silent about actual violence costs and instead put the spotlight on such crises' *potential* for democratization. Whether and to what extent democratization actually ensues after election violence or even nonviolent protests is an open empirical question. The cross-regional cases highlighted above paint a mixed picture, but the question has not been examined in systematic, quantitative analyses.

Rich literatures have emerged on democratization and political violence—as well as the role of international actors in these domestic processes—but they have largely developed in parallel. Research on their intersection promises a deeper and more nuanced understanding of these often complex relationships.

From a policy perspective, the negative consequences of condemnations have important implications for democracy promotion and international election aid in particular. First, IOs should carefully consider not attending clearly undemocratic elections and explicitly state these reasons. While most reputable observer groups have agreed to avoid meaningless elections,[77] this strategy has not been fully implemented. For example, recent "elections" in the kingdom of Swaziland 2013 and Cambodia 2008 were observed by the EU, in Cameroon 2011 by the Commonwealth, in Azerbaijan 2010 by the European Parliament, and in Kazakhstan 2011 and Uzbekistan 2014 by the OSCE. Many of these elections are not meaningful, and the informational value gained from their observation is low. Worse, their attendance lends a veneer of legitimacy to electoral autocrats. Of course, not attending elections would also imply that fraud could not be detected and deterred, which needs to be taken into account. As the motivation and goals of observation can be myriad and complex, more nuanced consideration should be given to both fraud deterrence and violence risks.

Second, (more) observer groups could issue more frequent interim statements before election-day to lower the impact of a sudden condemnation. Instead of the first critical statement "hitting" immediately after voting, when tensions are high, observer groups could issue preliminary press statements regularly in the weeks leading up to polling. The Carter Center has begun doing that over the last few years, but more organizations could follow suit. By slowly adjusting expectations and reflecting political conditions as they evolve, the impact of a condemnation might be lessened.

Third, donor agencies and democracy promotion IOs may consider a budget shift from monitoring to technical assistance in some cases. If violence breaks out because election results are not seen as credible, then the clear policy implication is to strengthen electoral institutions to support fair, and thus more peaceful, elections. Instead of expending resources to establish that tainted elections were indeed not meaningful, donor organizations could support reforms in direct cooperation with the host country, such as strengthening election management bodies and conducting voter education. Since technical missions generally do not judge the election's credibility, their risk of stirring unrest is lower; if anything, these interventions should reduce post-vote violence by increasing domestic capacity and thus the credibility of the result and potential dispute resolution. Another alternative for IOs is supporting domestic election observation efforts—if domestic observer groups are widely regarded as unbiased by the local population and thus difficult to discredit by governments.

While we have a good understanding of international election observation, the research field is wide open to systematically explore the role of international technical assistance on domestic politics and conflict. The next chapter is a step in that direction, examining the effect of technical election assistance on post-election violence.

THE UPSIDE

Technical Assistance and Reduced
Post-Election Violence

Can technical election assistance reduce post-vote violence? In this chapter, I continue investigating the effect of international election support on violence *after* elections. While the previous chapter has examined the effect of observer verdicts (how reputable observer groups assess election quality after voting), I now turn to election assistance, which actively tries to improve election quality through financial, technical, and logistical help, hiring and training of election officials, voter registration, and voter education long before election-day. As outlined in chapter 1, election assistance should reduce violence in the aftermath of elections. Technical election assistance should increase the capacity and credibility of election management and thus make the election results more credible. Technical assistance also aims to change contestants' attitudes that losing is just part of the democratic game, which they may win in future competitions. Taken together, these efforts should increase trust in an election commission and the results that it announces, which should reduce post-vote violence.

Recall from the theoretical argument detailed in chapter 1 that election assistance does not necessarily change the probability of post-election loser challenges. This is because election assistance can have two countervailing effects on challenges. In principle, better election quality should mean fewer challenges. However, election assistance also informs contestants about their legal recourse options in case they want to challenge results, and it helps improve electoral dispute resolution. Strengthening the relevant institutions (usually election commissions or electoral courts) to investigate and adjudicate election disputes should make these institutions more capable and trustworthy arbiters of disagreements. This should make contestants more willing to challenge through legal institutional means instead of taking their dispute to the streets and the "court" of public opinion. Consequently, the effect of election assistance on *challenges* is unclear: assistance may increase challenges because reformed institutions provide greater prospects of fair arbitration; it may decrease challenges because higher election quality lowers the need for challenges; or it may leave challenges on average unaffected because both dynamics are present.

In contrast, the effect of election assistance on post-election *violence* should be negative. Assistance should lower violence because the election commission is more capable and the election result is more credible than otherwise, and *if* challenges occur, losers should be more likely to challenge peacefully (through institutions) instead of taking their contestation to the streets, which should lower violence intensity.[1]

In this chapter, I test this argument about election assistance and post-election violence and illustrate the causal mechanism with the cases of Guyana and Bangladesh. First, I present statistical evidence that technical election assistance significantly reduces violence intensity and that this seems to work through greater election commission capacity and higher election quality. Then I illustrate the mechanism of institution-building in the cases of Guyana and Bangladesh, documenting the capacity and credibility deficits surrounding their election commissions, the role of external technical support, and the connection to reduced violence after assisted elections.

Quantitative Tests

If the argument is correct, the provision of technical election assistance should be associated with less post-election violence. I test this prediction in a statistical analysis of more than four hundred national elections in Latin America and Africa from 1990 to 2012. The key independent variable is *Technical election assistance*, which is coded 1 if the United Nations provided such support in the run-up to an election, and zero otherwise. Since the outcome—violence after elections—is identical with chapter 3, I employ the identical estimation strategy and control variables. That is, the statistical model includes control variables for *Executive constraints, Post-conflict, Economic development, Natural resources, Population size, Ethnic fractionalization, Competition, Poll type, Past election violence,* and *Fraud*. As in the previous chapter and following prior research,[2] fraud indicates whether there was significant domestic or international concern that the elections would not be free and fair; competition is measured as loser vote share. The dependent variable is *Post-election casualties*, which is the count of election-related casualties in the three months after a national election. As before, I use count models (zero-inflated negative binomial models) and cluster standard errors by country to account for the lack of independence between elections within the same country.

Table 4.1 reports the estimates. Columns 1 and 2 are on the full sample, and columns 3 and 4 are on Africa separately. Odd-numbered columns include all control variables described above, and even-numbered columns (2 and 4) add a control for the presence of reputable election observer groups.

Table 4.1 indicates that technical election assistance is associated with less post-election violence. The coefficient on *Technical election assistance* is negative in all models, and it is statistically significant in the sample of 250 African elections (columns 3 and 4). The coefficient on *Technical assistance* is only weakly significant when we add Latin America (columns 1 and 2). There are several potential explanations for this. One possible explanation, as noted in chapter 3 and documented in figure I.5 in the introduction, is that post-vote violence in Africa is more common and more lethal than in Latin America. That means there is more variation to explain in Africa than Latin America, and results might be more pronounced on the African continent. If we were to run the same models on European countries, we would also find no significance because violence is rare and involves few casualties. Another potential explanation is that there is no strong relationship between technical assistance and post-vote violence in the Americas because election commissions are already relatively capable. There is some evidence for this, as figure I.6 in the introduction documented that election commission capacity is significantly higher in Latin America than Africa. On a range from 0 to 4, where higher values indicate greater election commission capacity, the mean value is 3.1 in Latin America but only 2.0 in Africa.[3] Taken together, that means technical assistance has a greater potential to improve election administration and reduce violence in Africa than in Latin America because improvements to already strong institutions and more peaceful elections can only be marginal, while improvements to weak institutions and conflict-prone elections can be substantial. This logic is supported by the prevalence of technical assistance across regions since 1990: technical support is more common in Africa (39 percent of elections) than in Latin America (24 percent of elections), as shown in figure I.4 in the introduction.

In Africa, technical election assistance is significantly associated with less post-election violence. The results are substantively similar when using negative binomial or hurdle models and when replacing the ethnic fractionalization measure with the percentage of excluded population from the EPR data. The

TABLE 4.1 Effect of technical election assistance on post-election violence

	LATIN AMERICA AND AFRICA		AFRICA	
	(1)	**(2)**	**(3)**	**(4)**
Predicting violence intensity (count)				
Technical election assistance	−1.049*	−1.355*	−1.233***	−1.435**
	(0.594)	(0.718)	(0.468)	(0.632)
Fraud	0.588	0.935	1.757**	1.847**
	(0.962)	(0.814)	(0.886)	(0.890)
Observation		0.831		0.990
		(0.531)		(0.907)
Executive constraints	−0.044	0.020	0.321*	0.402**
	(0.190)	(0.159)	(0.180)	(0.172)
Post-conflict	−1.202	−1.964	−0.095	0.913
	(1.629)	(1.862)	(1.225)	(1.260)
Economic development	−0.317	−0.572	−1.233	−0.991
	(0.466)	(0.430)	(0.892)	(0.955)
Natural resources	0.084	0.114*	0.193*	0.174
	(0.067)	(0.068)	(0.106)	(0.121)
Ethnic fractionalization	0.332	−0.030	−0.085	−1.970
	(0.931)	(0.904)	(1.420)	(2.350)
Population size	(0.593)	0.722	0.276	−0.004
	(0.530)	(0.606)	(0.211)	(0.286)
Poll type	1.314**	1.272**	1.801***	1.942***
	(0.587)	(0.609)	(0.415)	(0.484)
Pre-election casualties	0.005	0.006	0.011***	0.013***
	(0.005)	(0.006)	(0.003)	(0.003)
Loser vote share	0.024	0.020	0.064**	0.093***
	(0.039)	(0.045)	(0.028)	(0.033)
Predicting zero violence				
Post-conflict	−0.402	−0.675	0.139	0.207
	(0.551)	(0.627)	(0.530)	(0.573)
Economic development	0.537**	0.545**	0.110	0.158
	(0.218)	(0.236)	(0.293)	(0.329)
Log α	1.312***	1.488**	1.445**	1.538*
	(0.441)	(0.597)	(0.600)	(0.795)
Observations	392	368	246	232
Clusters	70	70	47	47
AIC	691.43	664.72	552.57	535.25
BIC	754.97	731.15	608.66	593.84
LL	−329.71	−315.36	−260.29	−250.62

Notes: The table reports estimates from count models (zero-inflated negative binomial models). The dependent variable is the count of election-related casualties in the three months after election-day. The unit of observation is the national election. Robust standard errors are clustered on country. ***, **, and * indicate significance at the 1%, 5%, and 10% levels.

coefficient loses significance when replacing the fraud variable with a different measure here, technical assistance and fraud are jointly significant.

Technical support is associated with three fewer casualties per post-election period (the mean casualty count in africa is 20).[4] While the magnitude of this effect might seem small, two things are worth keeping in mind. One is that technical assistance tends to be deployed in difficult or conflict-prone elections: elections held in poorer, less developed countries with weak institutions and previous peacekeeping. These country characteristics strongly predict technical election assistance, as shown in tables 2.2 and 2.3 in chapter 2. As discussed before, this means that technical assistance is deployed in violence-prone contexts and still contributes to violence reduction. The second thing to bear in mind is that violence reduction is often not the primary focus of technical support but one of several objectives. United Nations election assistance has three goals: helping member states hold democratic elections, building capable institutions for election administration that have the full confidence of contesting parties, and reducing the potential for election-related violence.[5] Thus, election quality and capable election management are as important foci as election violence. Election assistance can directly improve election commission capacity with financial support, staff hiring, hard and software purchase, training, and so on, but its effects on post-election violence are presumably more indirect, working *through* better institutions and election quality. Considering these two aspects, the effect on violence reduction is notable.

In addition to the violence-reducing effect of technical assistance, the analysis also reveals a couple of other noteworthy findings. Higher popular support for the loser is significantly associated with more post-vote violence in Africa. This supports the argument that post-election violence is often driven by whether the loser accepts the result and that a stronger loser is more likely to challenge it. Further, estimates also confirm the role of observer presence: the mere *presence* of observers is not statistically significant. That means that for post-election violence and observation, what matters is not observer presence—mere physical attendance—but their reports, as shown in chapter 3.

MECHANISM: CAPACITY AND CREDIBILITY OF ELECTION MANAGEMENT

In addition to the main result that technical assistance can reduce post-vote violence in Africa, there is also some empirical evidence for the hypothesized causal mechanism: that assistance lowers violence by improving the capacity and credibility of the election commission. To examine the influence of technical assistance on election commission capacity and election credibility, I run additional analyses. For the model specification I follow prior research on the effect of UN technical election assistance on election commission capacity. In particular, Anna Lührmann estimates the effect of UN assistance on commission capacity while accounting for the fact that such assistance is non-random.[6] In these two-stage treatment effects models, the first stage predicts technical election assistance and the second stage estimates the effect of election assistance on commission capacity. They are linear regressions with an endogenous binary treatment variable in the first stage. The first stage—or selection stage—modeling technical assistance is the identical specification as in table 2.3. That is, technical assistance is modeled as a function of the basic predictors: *Regime type, Economic development, Post-conflict, Peacekeeping, Poll type, Uncertain election, Opposition competition.* I replicate those models with the full predictors, which include the basic set plus *Economic wealth,* whether elections in the country where *Previously observed,* and a time trend. Following Lührmann, I specify the second stage estimating the impact of technical assistance on NEC capacity while controlling for *Autocracy, Post-conflict, Economic development,* and *lagged NEC capacity.* Controlling for the lagged level of commission capacity is similar to first-differencing, meaning that coefficient estimates relate to the change in commission capacity from the previous election to this election within the same country. The dependent variable in the second stage, *NEC capacity,* is an ordinal scale ranging from 0 to 4, with the highest value indicating "sufficient staff and resources to administer a well-run national election."[7]

In addition to election commission capacity, I also examine four other plausible intermediary outcomes: election commission independence, the degree to which voting was free of irregularities, a clean election index, and loser challenge. These variables are also measured on five-point scales and come from the Varieties of Democracy (V-Dem) Project.[8] As discussed previously, I have no strong expectations about the influence of technical election assistance on loser challenge. With regard to NEC autonomy, it is plausible that UN assistance increases election commission independence, as non-government funding (for instance, the UN covering parts of the election budget), external expertise, and external staff may make institutions less dependent on and less easily captured by the government. Also, as noted in chapter 1, some scholars have argued that commission independence (rather than underlying capacity) might be important for election quality. The measure used here captures de facto independence/autonomy: whether election commissions have "autonomy from government to apply election laws and administrative rules impartially in national elections." This is a five-point scale varying from not autonomous (0) to fully autonomous (4), with higher scores indicating more independent/less partial commissions.

The variable *Clean voting* indicates to which extent the election was free from intentional voting irregularities, such as ballot stuffing, intentional misreporting of votes, and false collation of votes. This scale varies from systematic irregularities (0) to no irregularities/clean voting (4). The variable *Clean elections index* is a five-point index of several election characteristics, constructed by taking the point estimates from a Bayesian factor analysis model of the indicators for election free and fair, election commission capacity and autonomy, clean voting, voter registry, vote buying, government intimidation or other electoral violence. The conflict measures here do not distinguish between pre- and post-election violence or the number of casualties. Note that this index includes three mechanism variables and some indication of election conflict and thus serves as an indicator of overall election characteristics, but the "cleanliness" index in the V-Dem terminology refers to a range of outcomes beyond the technical process of administering elections. Lastly, the variable *Loser challenge* indicates to what extent the election result was challenged, from no parties/candidates challenged (0) to all losing parties/candidates challenged (4), inverting the V-Dem acceptance measure. I use a scaled variable here to allow comparability to the other mechanism variables; results are substantively similar using the binary version as in the previous chapter.

All models have the same set of basic and full predictors in the first stage. In the second stage, the models predicting NEC capacity, independence, clean voting, and clean election index include controls for *Autocracy, Post-conflict,* and *Economic development.* The models for loser challenge are identical to the models in chapter 3, controlling for: *Fraud, Loser vote share, Executive constraints, Judicial independence, Economic development, Poll type, Incumbent lost,* and *Observer presence.* All second-stage models also include the lagged value of the relevant dependent variable; for example, in models of commission independence, the lagged values of commission independence from the previous election are included as a control. Results are substantively similar (and often stronger) without the lagged dependent variable. Robust standard errors are clustered on country.

The key coefficient estimates are shown in figure 4.1. Markers to the right of the dashed vertical line indicate positive coefficients and to the left indicate negative coefficients; horizontal lines around the markers indicate 95 percent confidence intervals. For the models predicting commission capacity, independence, and clean elections (left panels of figure 4.1), the first and second stages of the estimation are strongly related in many models and thus marked in black. The small p-values indicate that we reject the null hypothesis that these two processes are independent.[9] In other words, we should account for the non-random deployment of technical assistance when estimating its effect on NEC capacity and clean elections. For the other two outcomes of clean voting and loser challenge (right panels of figure 4.1) the first and second stages are not significantly related (thus marked in grey), so that single-stage models are more appropriate.[10] Thus the coefficient estimates on UN assistance shown in figure 4.1 are from single-stage models (indicated by hollow markers) for the panels on

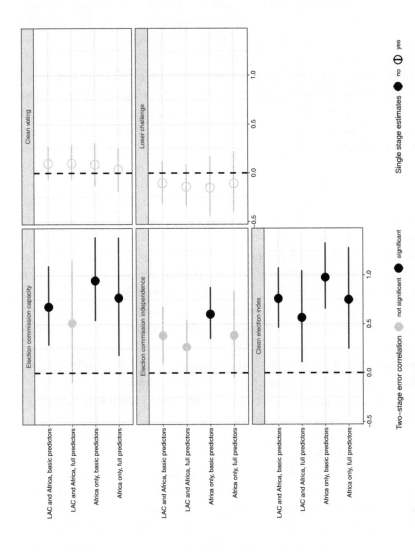

FIGURE 4.1. Effect of technical election assistance on election commission capacity, independence, clean voting, clean election index, and loser challenge

clean voting and loser consent while controlling for the drivers of selection; estimates are from two-stage models (indicated by solid markers) for the panels on commission capacity, independence, and clean election index.

Figure 4.1 indicates that when UN technical election assistance is provided before elections, election commissions become more capable, and elections become cleaner than the previous election in the same country. The coefficient estimates on these variables are consistently positive in all models, and they are statistically significant in most models. Even in the sample that includes Latin American countries, technical assistance is associated with more capable election management and cleaner elections. However, in line with expectations in this book, the coefficient estimates are larger and more consistent in Africa than Latin America. Recall that election commissions in LAC are already more capable and thus any improvements here, on average, are smaller than in Africa, similar to a ceiling effect. In terms of substantive importance, UN assistance is associated with a one-point increase on the five-point scale of commission capacity. This suggests UN assistance can raise capacity, for instance, from "serious deficiencies compromising the organization of the election" to "partial deficits in resources" or from partial deficits to no deficits. UN assistance is also associated with more independent commissions in Africa, which is approximately half a point on the five-point scale. Since more independent and less biased commissions should help level the playing field between contestants, this supports the argument that UN assistance may be able to level the playing field by making election commissions more capable and credible actors. Further, in terms of the clean elections index, elections with technical assistance are up to one point cleaner on the five-point scale than elections without such assistance. These are substantively important changes in election institutions and overall election quality associated with UN assistance.

In contrast to improvements in commission capacity, credibility, and overall election quality, UN assistance is not significantly associated with a cleaner voting process or loser challenge. None of the coefficient estimates on the right panels of figure 4.1 are significantly different from zero. With regard to loser challenge, the absence of an average effect is not surprising. The coefficients are consistently negative, indicating that assistance is weakly correlated with fewer challenges. However, as noted above and in chapter 1, this challenge-mitigating dynamic might be counteracted by the challenge-increasing dynamic of technical assistance because it also informs and trains parties on legal dispute resolution, that is, how to challenge election results through institutions (the election commission or independent court). After all, peaceful protests are a legitimate way of expressing dissent in a democratic system. Either way—reducing challenges or channeling them through institutions[11]—technical election assistance is associated with less violence and fewer casualties, as shown in table 4.1. This may be the case because all types of challenges (in the institutions or the streets) are reduced due to overall cleaner elections, because challenges take more peaceful forms (verbal announcements and court challenges instead of demonstrations, riots, and street clashes), or both of these reasons. There is no significant relationship between UN assistance and cleaner voting. This is perhaps surprising, as greater commission capacity should reduce voting irregularities. However, some actions may be outside of what election assistance can influence. Recall that the clean voting measure captures *intentional* irregularities and/or vote fraud by the incumbent and/or opposition parties, such as ballot stuffing, double IDs, or misreporting of votes. While technical assistance can bridge capacity gaps and presumably increase oversight to some degree, fraud may still occur.

As noted in the introduction, a technically clean election can still be fraudulent and subject to political interference. The empirical findings here suggest that assistance can improve election quality overall but is not effective in entirely preventing powerful local actors from interfering in the election process. This is an important caveat and a reminder to keep in mind the possibilities as well as the limitations of such external assistance programs. If parties/candidates want to cheat, they can likely find ways. While technical assistance can improve election quality in some ways (as indicated by improvements in the broader clean elections index), it is not a panacea. Even acknowledging this caveat, the empirics support the argument that technical assistance improves the capacity and credibility of the election commission and can boost election quality. When institutions are seen as more capable and credible, the result that they announce also tends to be seen as more credible.

There is also some empirical support for the argument that technical assistance and better election management improve trust in the national election commission. As discussed in the introduction, credibility is fundamentally about beliefs by the public and opposing political elites. What matters is often less an objective measure of accountability or capacity (as used for figure 4.1) and more public perceptions of these aspects. Probably the best measure of such perceptions or trust in election commissions comes from public opinion surveys.

I leverage two survey datasets here: publicly available data for Latin America, and two original datasets from fieldwork around the 2017 elections in Kenya and Liberia. Evidence based on the LAPOP measure is admittedly tentative, as the timing of these surveys is not perfectly interspersed with the timing of elections, so that it is difficult to measure changes in a consistent manner for a large group of elections, resulting in a smaller sample of elections. To measure NEC credibility, I use public opinion surveys on citizens' respect for the national election commission. I use data for Latin America because survey data from the Latin American Public Opinion Project (LAPOP) are evenly spaced in time and thus more compatible with election

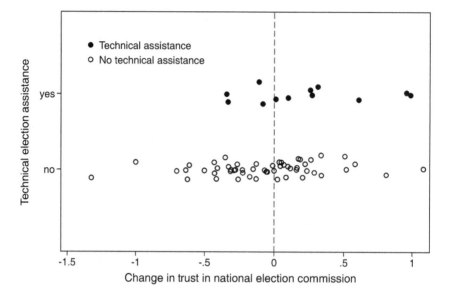

FIGURE 4.2. Change in NEC credibility conditional on technical election assistance

dates, which is not the case for the AfroBarometer. Data are available for twenty-six countries in two-year increments from 2004 to 2012. The question of interest is: "To what extent do you trust the supreme election commission?" Answers are recorded on a scale of 1 through 7, with higher values indicating higher trust.

To capture changes in credibility, I calculate the change in trust from the previous to the current election. Figure 4.2 illustrates changes in trust between elections. It shows that NEC credibility shows no clear trend toward either higher or lower values when technical assistance is absent. However, when election commissions receive technical support, their credibility tends to increase. Further, I create three comparison groups: (1) periods without elections, (2) periods with elections but no technical assistance, and (3) periods with elections that received technical assistance. Trust in the national election commission increases by 0.06 points without assistance and by 0.27 with technical assistance. This difference is only suggestive because it is a tri-variate comparison (elections, technical assistance, trust), and it is not statistically significant. It is noteworthy, however, that technical assistance is largely associated with an increase in trust (a positive change) even though these data cover Latin America, where capacity and credibility are already higher than in Africa.

A second and more fine-grained analysis of original survey data from Kenya and Liberia also shows that improved election management increases public trust in the election commission and mitigates election violence. These data are from extensive field research around the 2017 elections in Liberia and Kenya for a related project on what works in preventing election violence. In each country, we selected 150 towns as-if randomly from a larger pool of towns at risk of experiencing election violence and interviewed seven respondents in each town, resulting in 1,050 interviews in each survey.[12] We collected two waves of survey data: a baseline survey before the election and an endline survey after the repeat/run-off election. This allows us to examine *changes* in local attitudes over time, and link those changes to differences in election management. What we found is that higher NEC preparedness to manage elections locally is associated with increased trust in the election commission, an increased perception that elections are free and fair, and reduced election violence. These results are robust across the two countries and robust to including different sets of controls to account for individual, interview, and town characteristics. Further, in Kenya, delays in polling on election-day (deficient election management) were associated with reduced trust in the election commission and a lowered belief in elections being free and fair. These local experiences support the argument that election management and violence are strongly linked.

Illustrative Cases: Guyana and Bangladesh

The analyses above show that technical election assistance is significantly associated with less post-election violence. The quantitative analyses also provide support for the proposed causal mechanism, namely that technical assistance raises institutional capacity and election credibility. To explore this mechanism in more detail, this section draws on case material of elections in Guyana and Bangladesh. They are intended as a plausibility test illustrating the hypothesized mechanism—support increasing capacity and credibility and thereby reducing violence—rather than a definitive test of the argument. For each country, I provide some electoral background and then focus on the elections with significant assistance, documenting that these elections experienced reduced violence.

Elections in Guyana

Nestled between Venezuela and Suriname, Guyana gained independence from the UK in 1966. Before the British handed over governance, the electoral system was changed from first-past-the-post to proportional representation in order to reduce the effect of ethnic tensions. As one of the poorest countries in the Western Hemisphere and with a population of less than a million people,[13] Guyana's main fault lines run between the Afro-Guyanese and the Indo-Guyanese. Afro-Guyanese represent about 30 percent of the population and mainly support the People's National Congress (PNC), which dominated politics from independence to 1992. Indo-Guyanese comprise about 43 percent and mainly support the People's Progressive Party (PPP), which ruled from 1992 to 2015.[14]

Although four elections were held between 1968 and 1985, the 1992 election was hailed as the first free and fair election since independence. Observer verdicts on Guyana's elections were consistent after 1990: beginning with the 1992 election, none of Guyana's elections were condemned, and all of them were internationally endorsed as "free and fair." Yet violence erupted after the 1997 and 2001 elections, while 2006 and 2011 remained peaceful.[15] Since credible observers have endorsed all elections since 1992, their consistent verdict cannot explain variation in violence. Similarly, relatively little has changed on the (non-electoral) domestic scene since the 1990s, in terms of democracy levels, ethnic fractionalization, population size, resources, or civil war history. In contrast, technical assistance and the changes in electoral administration it helped generate are a plausible explanation for reduced violence in the 2006 and 2011 elections. Table 4.2 shows IO support and post-election violence for Guyana's national elections.[16]

A common theme for Guyana's post-vote violence is the refusal of some political parties to accept the election results, caused by parties' distrust of the Guyana Elections Commission (GECOM) and rumors spread by the local media: "In the decades following independence in 1966, voting . . . was a harbinger of instability and violence. With each poll came *accusations* of stuffed ballot boxes and election malpractice, stoked . . . by biased reports from the country's polarized media."[17] The skepticism of the election process and media reports to that effect regularly caused the opposition PNC party to challenge the announced results through violent street demonstrations. Guyanese came to expect violence around their elections. As the head of GECOM election commission put it, "Every single election in this country was associated with bloodshed, burning. . . . It was as if concomitant with an election there must be mayhem."[18]

TABLE 4.2 Technical election assistance and post-election violence in Guyana

ELECTION	TECHNICAL ELECTION ASSISTANCE	CONDEMNATION BY INTERNATIONAL OBSERVERS	POST-ELECTION CASUALTIES
1992	extensive	✗	0
1997	limited	✗	1
2001	limited	✗ (did not attend)	5
2006	extensive	✗	0
2011	limited	✗	0
2015	limited	✗	0

Forbes Burnham ruled Guyana as a competitive authoritarian regime from 1966 until his death in 1985. Under his tenure, the government used violence and intimidation against the opposition, elections were regularly rigged, and independent media was curtailed.[19] In 1974, Burnham declared the PNC paramount and the country a socialist state, tightened relations with Cuba and the Soviet Union, and nationalized most industries. After Burnham's death in 1985, economic and international pressure for reform mounted. President Desmond Hoyte took over, abolished the one-party state, rolled back socialist policies, and began electoral reforms. As part of these reforms, Hoyte transferred responsibility for the election process to a newly created, independent election commission (EC). The commission overhauled the voter registry, which made proxy and overseas vote fraud much more difficult. As a result, the PNC lost control over the election administration. Change did not occur overnight, though, as the extent of electoral reforms needed was overwhelming. Further, voter confidence in elections had been shattered by decades of manipulation.

Following Burnham's death in 1985, the first elections were held in 1992 after a two-year delay due to insufficient preparations.[20] President Hoyte's electoral reforms also included efforts for a new voters' list, rule changes, and a new chairman of the election commission. Beginning in 1991, the UNDP supported electoral reforms quite extensively: it "paid the monthly rent for the Elections Commission building; provided computer hardware, software, and technical personnel for voter registration, logistics, and vote tabulation efforts; and vehicles and staff for Election Day support."[21] IFES provided further technical assistance, while other international organizations provided logistical support (generators, ballot boxes, and signage).[22] The international observers—Carter Center and Commonwealth—endorsed the 1992 election, as did the domestic observer (called the Electoral Assistance Bureau, or EAB). Moreover, the 1992 election resulted in a power transition, with the PPP gaining a majority after PNC had ruled since the 1960s. The election result was implemented smoothly, with the PNC leaving power peacefully.[23] No post-election violence broke out.

In contrast to 1992, the 1997 elections received only limited technical support, and violence broke out when the opposition PNC challenged the result. In the run-up to the 1997 elections, technical assistance was limited: the UNDP did not provide election assistance at all, and IFES assistance consisted mainly of logistical support: special paper for the voters' list, UV lamps to verify ID cards, and a new computer system for the commission headquarters (hardware, software, training).[24] The PPP party received 55 percent and the PNC 40 percent of the vote. As before, domestic and international observers—IFES, CW, OAS—endorsed the election.[25]

However, administrative breakdowns delayed the announcement of results, triggering violent protests for weeks. After ballots were counted at polling stations, it took more than twelve hours for the results and ballot boxes to reach the commission's headquarters;[26] this was a significant delay given Guyana's small geographic dimensions. The transmission breakdown deepened distrust of the commission's work and led the opposition (and losing) PNC to protest the results violently with riots and massive demonstrations in Georgetown, the capital. A two-week delay in announcing the results[27] further aggravated tensions until mediators from the regional organization (Caribbean Community, or CARICOM) brokered an agreement, known as the Herdmanston Accord, for a full recount and electoral reforms. The international audit of the election confirmed the results, finding only marginal differences and thus no evidence of manipulation.[28]

The Herdmanston Accord of January 1998 ended weeks of post-election unrest and called for a re-drafting of the constitution, further electoral reforms, and new elections within three years. The election commission was established as a permanent body, the Guyana Elections Commission (GECOM), in 2000. Acknowledging the ethnic basis of election violence, new electoral laws made it a criminal offense for anyone to do or say something that can result in racial or ethnic violence or hatred—with deterrent costs. Any candidate or party found in violation of this law could be barred from running for five years, face a penalty of half a million U.S. dollars, and be subject to a special inquiry commission (which formed only after the 2001 election).[29]

While these were substantial reforms, they did not address the administrative shortfalls of 1997,[30] so that 2001 represented a déjà-vu of sorts: "The crisis of confidence surrounding the 1997 and 2001 electoral processes is . . . a direct result of electoral flaws—not fraud—compounded by a lack of political good will and trust. When added to misinformation, inflammatory statements and actions, the potential for civil commotion increases significantly."[31] Similar to 1997, the PPP won (with a slight majority), international and domestic monitors endorsed the election,[32] and administrative problems again led to the PNC challenge and violent demonstrations. The administrative problems included citizens missing from the voter roll and a four-day delay in the announcement of results by GECOM. Local media speculated about reasons for the delay, fueling rumors of malpractice. Again, the opposition PNC was convinced of rigging and rejected the results with weeks of violent riots, resulting in five casualties, including four deaths.[33]

GUYANA'S 2006 ELECTIONS

In the run-up to the 2006 elections, Guyana received extensive technical assistance from the UNDP and IFES, with international donors covering over half of the US$7 million budget. Reforms were implemented to support institutions (GECOM voter registry and tabulation, media monitoring) and to support civil society (voter education, communication, violence monitoring, and peacebuild-ing).[34] Guyana chose deliberately not only to request technical assistance but also to outsource important implementation positions to foreigners because domes-tic leaders would face greater distrust in the ethnically polarized climate.

Institutional reforms for GECOM focused on updating the voter registry and speeding vote tabulation. In previous electoral cycles, the voter registry was mainly updated in the few months prior to polling, which coincided with party campaigning. This politicized the registration process and undermined credibil-ity in the registry as well as voter ID cards. In response, GECOM changed the timing of this process by introducing a *continuous* registration system; this meant updating the voters' roll since October 2005 instead of summer 2006 for the elec-tion, which took place on 28 August 2006. It also established more permanent and temporary registration offices in each region, which were concentrated in the more populous coastal areas and Georgetown. In addition, GECOM intro-duced technological innovations, such as "check digits," parallel coding to reduce human error, and biometrics (photo and fingerprints) collected by door-to-door verification. To check fingerprints for multiple registrations, GECOM deliber-ately involved an external actor (a U.S. vendor) to allay parties' distrust of domes-tic institutions.[35] GECOM also chose a foreigner (a British citizen) to head the IT department "to quell public perceptions of political bias" after the two prior Guy-anese heads since 2001 resigned in frustration over the distrust against them.[36] The IT department at GECOM is responsible for entering and storing data on voter registration.

To speed the dissemination of results after polling—whose delay had previ-ously led to a rise in rumors and violence—it increased phone capacity and made each of the ten regions (instead of thousands of polling stations) report to the national headquarter. GECOM decentralized the process by having each poll-ing station tabulate and announce results locally and also added new staff and polling stations in overworked districts (the most populous regions).[37] These reforms were effective: the commission released results within three days of voting (instead of six days after 2001 and fifteen days after 1997), reducing the opportunity for rumors and frustration to build.

A third institutional reform, funded by the UNDP, focused on a media moni-toring unit (MMU), which was responsible for tracking and enforcing the media code of conduct. That code, drafted and signed by local media representatives, aimed to eliminate inaccurate, biased, or inflammatory statements, which had played a key role in instigating violence in earlier elections. Again, external help was enlisted for this purpose, with a veteran journalist from the BBC leading the effort.[38] The MMU kept a tab on inflammatory language and equality in the reporting (documenting inches in newspapers and minutes in broadcast media).

Violating media outlets were notified in writing and referred to an independent panel—also financed by the UNDP—composed of two veteran journalists from external Caribbean countries. As a result, the media was more responsible in its reporting.[39]

Apart from institutional reforms, technical assistance also worked with civil society. This included voter education about the process and implemented reforms, local monitoring of election violence, and a social cohesion program to mitigate ethnic tensions. IFES implemented its Election Violence Education and Resolution (EVER) program with a local NGO, the Electoral Assistance Bureau (EAB). The IFES-EAB collaboration trained citizens to monitor election violence in their communities by observing rallies and documenting cases of violence, intimidation, threats, and heightened tensions. The EVER project operated in seven of the most affected regions. This program was created to "monitor, report and analyze election-related violence,"[40] empowering civil society and creating greater accountability for (potential) perpetrators. EAB issued six reports between June and October 2006, detailing any tensions, accusations and incidents and naming perpetrators.[41] The program had some deterrent effect, as "politicians frequently cited the reports to warn supporters against using violence."[42]

Since Guyana's post-election violence had usually been triggered by citizens' distrust and *perceptions* of malpractice, institutional reforms were only of limited effect unless communicated broadly to citizens. Hence civil society work also focused on voter education generally and communicating GECOM reforms specifically. Three weeks before the election, GECOM released a statement about its "safeguards aimed at preventing (i) multiple voting, (ii) other forms of skullduggery, and (iii) any potential for dissatisfaction on election-day."[43] This six-page document outlined how difficult impersonation/multiple voting had become due to the photo ID verification and indelible ink. Ballot stuffing had also become more challenging due to transparent ballot boxes, the continuous presence of party representatives and the police in every polling station, the temporary presence of domestic and international monitors, and the local count of ballots in front of these stakeholders. GECOM pointed out that any violating elector or staff person "will be subjected to questioning, and possibly, be arrested immediately."[44] These were not empty threats. On election-day, a presiding officer from district 4 (which includes the capital) was immediately suspended "after allowing a number of people to vote, even though they were not on the list."[45]

Finally, another civil society initiative focused on nonviolence campaigning and ethnic inclusiveness. The EAB recruited local VIPs to convey the importance of peaceful elections on the radio and television. In addition, the UNDP financially supported the Inter-Religious Organization (IRO) to implement a "social cohesion program" to bridge the divide between the Afro- and Indo-Guyanese communities. This program organized marches for peace and thousands of conversations between ethnic groups and gave them an opportunity to interact with each other and build trust on the local level.[46] Again, the UNDP took the lead in implementing the program and enlisted the help of a foreigner, this time a European development adviser, because of mistrust against Guyanese government officials.

The extensive technical assistance contributed to the first peaceful election since 1992. Not only did the losing PNC accept the results in 2006, it even conceded defeat a day before the official results were announced, thereby allowing a peaceful implementation of the election result. The EAB directly attributed post-election peace "to the acceptance of the election results by all contesting parties" and noted that in prior elections "the main opposition party had not been satisfied with the elections or their results, and in marching to air grievances, violence and looting broke out."[47] The front page of *The Guyana Chronicle* summarized this as a "peaceful poll surprise."[48] IO technical assistance was key in creating the conditions for more peaceful elections. The UNDP concluded that facilitation by the international community converted what was almost universally expected to be an elections process fraught with violence into the most peaceful and universally endorsed electoral process in Guyana's four decades of post-independence history.[49]

Guyana demonstrates the importance of running "administratively credible elections that limit the space for rumor and suspicion to take hold."[50] In the run-up to the 2011 and 2015 elections, the UNDP offered limited assistance,[51] mostly focusing on media monitoring and social cohesion, and these elections again remained peaceful in their aftermath. Guyana also illustrates how IOs can substitute for local processes when domestic capacity is insufficient or trust has eroded. Guyanese officials consistently "out-sourced" programs to the UNDP and deliberately chose foreigners for key positions because local officials faced higher skepticism in the charged political environment.

ALTERNATIVE EXPLANATIONS

Several competing explanations of the switch to peaceful elections in 2006 can be ruled out. First, international election monitoring has low explanatory leverage because external observers were present at all elections since 1992 and consistently endorsed each election.[52] Their positive verdict did not keep Guyanese parties and voters from challenging election results in 1992, 1997, and 2001; the latter two resulted in street protests and violence.

Second, several domestic factors can be ruled out as causes. The electoral system (PR) and winning party (PPP) did not change between 1992 and 2015. The

PNC lost every election between 1992 and 2015, but the same outcome (defeat) was sometimes accepted (when seen as fair) and sometimes rejected (when seen as not fair). Economic development did not notably improve until 2011 when it cleared the US$1,000 per capita GDP hurdle. One potential competing explanation, decreased voter interest, is plausible but has quite different effects in other countries. While turnout decreased by 20 percent in 2006 compared to 2001, it remains unclear whether this reduction in voter interest causes less violence. A more promising competing explanation is that citizens became tired of election violence and were ready for a new approach. However, that citizen tiredness/weariness may itself be a result of the nonviolence programs implemented with UNDP and IFES support. Peacebuilding programs addressing the need for peaceful elections, the consequences of violence, and mediation initiatives were intended to make citizens more aware of the human cost. Therefore, if the technical assistance had any effects, it *should* make citizens weary of violence and stimulate discussion about alternative means. In that way, a change in voter and party attitude may well have contributed to peaceful elections, but it would represent an indirect effect of technical assistance on violence rather than a competing explanation.

Elections in Bangladesh

While the quantitative tests and many of the illustrative cases in this book have focused on Latin America and Africa, there are also elections outside these regions to which the argument can apply. The region-specific factors discussed in the introduction (democracy, development, capacity for election management) are important to keep in mind for the link between technical election assistance and election violence, but some countries in other regions have similar characteristics. For example, Bangladesh's election commission has had a similarly low capacity level as the average African country since 1990 (with reference to figure I.6, a score of 2). Thus Bangladesh is an "out of sample" example that can help us understand how the basic dynamics work in other regions but with similar structural context and where technical election assistance helped de-escalate conflicts inflamed by the electoral process.

In contrast to Guyana's small size, Bangladesh is the eighth most populous country in the world and has a single ethnic group (98% of the 150 million people are Bengali), so the fault lines of political conflicts are different. Many voters are not permanently allied with a single political party but rather evaluate individual local candidates in their constituencies. Bangladesh is quite poor, with a per capita GDP of less than US$1,000; only half of the population is literate, which poses additional challenges for election administration and voter education. After gaining independence from Pakistan in 1971, Bangladesh initially became a multiparty democracy but experienced two turbulent decades of coups and states of emergency. In 1991, President Hussain Muhammad Ershad—who had come to power through a coup—resigned amid large-scale opposition pressure and the loss of Western support.

Ershad arranged for a caretaker government to prepare democratic elections—a system that would later become institutionalized. In addition, Bangladesh was transformed from a presidential to a parliamentary democracy with a prime minister and only a ceremonial role for the president. The electoral system is first-past-the-post in single-member districts, which tends to be associated with more conflict and violence than elections in proportional representation systems. A strong anti-incumbent trend has emerged: the incumbent party—regardless of its identity—has effectively lost each parliamentary election between 1991 and 2008. For seventeen years, power has changed hands regularly between the two major parties: the Awami League (AL) led by Sheikh Hasina and the Bangladesh Nationalist Party (BNP) led by Khaleda Zia. The most recent 2014 and 2018 elections broke with this trend and were controversial.

After 1991, democracy regained its foothold, but the regularly held elections have been marked by "mutual suspicion and violent confrontation."[53] Table 4.3 gives a brief overview of the six elections held since 1991, including post-election violence levels and engagement by technical assistance and observer missions. Relating back to chapter 3, this table shows that the condemnation/withdrawal of observers may have helped explain violence after the February 1996 election, but the same factor cannot explain the absence of violence in 2014. Perhaps more importantly, table 4.3 also shows that the UN selected into a violent situation when it became active in the run-up to the 2008 elections: the previous contest in 2001 was intensely violent, resulting in several dozen casualties in the three months after voting.[54]

In 1991, the BNP won in a tight race over the AL, with the party of outgoing President Ershad trailing third with only 11 percent of the vote. The election was relatively peaceful and without external technical assistance. The election in February 1996 was boycotted by the AL and many voters; consequently, the BNP won in a landslide. Unsurprisingly, opposition parties rejected the legitimacy of the resulting legislature and staged riots and protests, so much so that the BNP soon dissolved parliament.

After the failed February 1996 elections, the BNP handed responsibility for holding elections to a nonpartisan caretaker government. This was intended to solve the political crisis, instill confidence, and remedy distrust between the par-

TABLE 4.3 Technical election assistance and post-election violence in Bangladesh

ELECTION	TECHNICAL ELECTION ASSISTANCE	CONDEMNATION BY INTER-NATIONAL OBSERVERS	POST-ELECTION CASUALTIES
1991	no	✗	0
1996 (Feb.)	no	✗ (withdrew)	1,115
1996 (June)	limited, post-election	✗	0
2001	no	✗	46
2008	extensive	✗	3
2014	limited	✗ (withdrew)	0

ties by making it harder for incumbent parties to rig elections in their favor. Under that system, the incumbent government hands over administrative powers to a non-party technocratic government three months before the next election to ensure that the playing field is relatively level. In the immediately following June 1996 election, the AL won an absolute majority. The June 1996 election was marked by a record turnout (75%), limited technical assistance by the UN, and relative peace.

The 2001 elections were also held under the caretaker system and were deemed credible by observers, but its results were still rejected by the loser. The UN did not provide any technical election assistance and only helped coordinating observers. The AL—which lost in a tight race—claimed "crude rigging" and challenged the result.[55] It boycotted the first session of the new parliament and threatened street protests. Four days after the election, it held a demonstration in Dhaka, the nation's capital, and demanded the cancellation of the election results. Post-election turmoil turned violent, leading to more than forty-six fatalities in the three months following the election.

The situation deteriorated further in the run-up to elections planned for 2007. Already a year before the scheduled elections, in the summer of 2006, political violence was widespread. This "muscle power" was usually organized by the two major parties and implemented through its youth groups, labor wings, and criminal connections.[56] Victims of such pre-election violence included candidates and political activists of the other party, as well as election officials, journalists, and civil society organizations. There were serious concerns about escalating violence on and beyond voting day.[57]

The lack of trust in the electoral process caused the breakdown of the planned 2007 election. Although the opposition party AL had voiced its concerns repeatedly, the incumbent party BNP did not offer substantial remedies. Given its lack of confidence in the possibility of fair elections, the AL boycotted the election, withdrawing all of its 2,400 candidates. The international community agreed: observer groups declared they would not send a mission, and the UN suspended the technical assistance program it had begun in 2006. Street violence escalated. During the political crisis in early January 2007 and under pressure from the military, the incumbent president and chief adviser to the caretaker government, Iajuddin Ahmed, postponed the elections indefinitely, imposed a state of emergency banning all political party activities, and resigned from his post.

BANGLADESH'S 2008 ELECTION

While the state of emergency became more controversial as it dragged on for almost two years until mid-December 2008, it gave the caretaker government an opportunity to push through key electoral reforms. In particular, it addressed the four major concerns that the opposition had voiced about the prospects of a level playing field:[58]

- It doubted the nonpartisanship of the caretaker government because the BNP had influenced the appointment of its chief adviser—this was addressed by the resignation of the chief adviser (the former president).
- It doubted the independence of the Bangladesh Election Commission (BEC) because the sitting president had appointed its members—all sitting commissioners resigned and were replaced through appointment by the caretaker government.
- It noted grave inaccuracies in the voter list, which reportedly featured more than twelve million ghost voters[59]—the BEC undertook a massive effort to create a new voter roll, registering more than eighty-one million voters with their photographs in all parts of the country. External audits found the new voter roll to be remarkably accurate.[60]
- It called for the introduction of transparent ballot boxes to minimize room for ballot box stuffing—these were purchased by the UN.

These electoral reforms were only possible with international technical and financial support. The UNDP was the lead organization in providing and channeling this support, accompanied by the Asia Foundation, USAID, and smaller donors. The centerpiece of UNDP technical assistance was voter registration. The "Preparation of Electoral Rolls with Photographs" (PERP) project began in the summer of 2007 with a budget of US$82 million. Its aim was to "establish technical requirements, develop infrastructure, and build capacity" for credible electoral rolls.[61] This included the purchase of technical equipment, including thousands of laptop computers, web cameras, and fingerprint scanners as well as the payment of staff salaries.[62] Workers needed to be trained to conduct voter registration, collect and integrate data, and manage it to ensure the sustainability of the process for future elections.

The other two key reforms were also supported through UN technical assistance. The electoral commission received substantial funding, advice, and material support through the "Support to the Electoral Process in Bangladesh" (SEPB) project, a five-year program designed to strengthen the capacity of the BEC. This was mainly aimed at constituency delimitation—which had not been reformed since 1984 and was marked by high discrepancies in constituency size. It also supported a nationwide system for candidate declaration and nomination and one for the reporting of results.[63] Regarding the final opposition request, the UN also purchased 240,000 translucent ballot boxes at a cost of US$6 million.

These fundamental reforms of the election management paid off in terms of voter confidence and electoral integrity as well as the relative lack of violence following the 2008 elections. The BEC was credited by voters for its reforms, especially the voter registration effort. The electoral commission enjoyed a high level of trust among the population, with 87 percent of voters expressing confidence in the BEC in the month before elections.[64] This was notable since the previous BEC was one of the key reasons the opposition had undermined the planned 2007 election. Election-day was "far calmer and more peaceful than previous national elections."[65] This was undoubtedly helped by the state of emergency and a strong security deployment. However, since both ended on election-day, they cannot explain the absence of violence *after* the election. More than a hundred people died in violence after the 2001 elections, but "only" three died after the 2008 elections.[66] This substantial reduction in violence was in large part the result of a credible election.

After 2008, UN technical election assistance continued to help further institutionalize domestic reforms, albeit on a much smaller scale than before.[67] The January 2014 elections were again marked by heated pre-election contestation but once again had remarkably little post-election violence. Months before the elections, the BNP and affiliated opposition parties called for the incumbent AL party to transfer power to a caretaker government three months before the election. While that was normal procedure in previous Bangladeshi elections, the AL had "abolished the caretaker system in 2010, arguing that it was no longer necessary," given the wealth of electoral reforms.[68] When this and related demands were not met, opposition parties staged three months of nationwide strikes and boycotted the election.

Adding fuel to the fire, the Islamist opposition party, Jamaat-e-Islami, engaged in protests and violence beginning in mid-December 2013, when one of its leaders, Abdul Quader Molla, was the first to be executed for war crimes committed in the Bangladesh Independence War of 1971. As in 2001, international observers (EU, Commonwealth) announced that they would not attend because they doubted that a meaningful election was possible.[69] And again as in 2001, the election was marked by low voter turnout (22 percent). Due to BNP not contesting the election, the AL won a landslide victory with 79 percent of the vote. This marked the first time in recent Bangladesh history that *no* power transition took place as the AL continued as the ruling party. Despite all these factors, protests and violence were limited to the period before elections and election day. The BNP conceded defeat, and the aftermath was largely peaceful.

In all, Bangladesh illustrates two trends in the selection and effectiveness of technical assistance. First, the UN tends to provide technical support to places that need it most—including countries where administrative shortcomings have led to instability and political violence in the past. In this sense, the UN selects into more difficult, volatile settings. Second, UN technical assistance can address specific, major challenges to electoral integrity and thus reduce incentives to challenge the electoral process or its outcome violently. By strengthening the capacity and credibility of the Bangladesh Election Commission and its voter register, the UN helped increase confidence in the BEC itself and the result that it would announce. In the case of Bangladesh, this reduced motivations for the losing party to challenge the outcome or decline to accept defeat, so that violence after elections was lower.

Technical election assistance can mitigate violence after elections. An important mechanism linking UN assistance and reduced post-vote violence is election credibility. When citizens deem the electoral commission more capable and credible, they are more likely to perceive the outcome as fair and acceptable, which should lower incentives for election challenges and violence after voting. This mechanism linking assistance and reduced post-election violence is documented for Africa in the quantitative analyses and also detailed with the cases of Bangladesh and Guyana. Beyond documenting the hypothesized mechanism of boosting capacity and credibility of the election commission, the case of Guyana also illustrates another important feature of international election support, that it can *substitute* for local processes when domestic capacity is insufficient or when trust is eroded. Guyanese officials consistently "out-sourced" programs to the UNDP and deliberately chose foreigners for key positions because local officials faced higher skepticism in the charged political environment.

International technical assistance is not a panacea; changes crucially depend on domestic political will, and they also take time. But it is a promising tool of conflict management and democracy promotion that has been underappreciated. As one form of peacebuilding, election assistance can be an effective tool of conflict management, preventing conflicts from escalating in the first place as well as reducing the risk of *re*-lapsing into intense violence.

This finding is important because it is based on a much broader set of countries than commonly considered in peacebuilding research. Peacebuilding research tends to focus on conflict or post-conflict countries but rarely widens the horizon to all developing countries. As such, this chapter contributes to the debate on the effectiveness of the UN in conflict management by expanding the universe of analyzed countries to developing countries broadly (instead of just conflict countries) and examining a prominent form of peacebuilding. Within the UN effectiveness debate, the weight of the evidence points to the UN being effective at keeping the peace once civil wars end[70] and even being able to reduce fatalities in active conflicts.[71] Apart from keeping the peace, a related literature has explored the UN's effectiveness in building peace in post-conflict settings,[72] which intersects with research on post-conflict elections.[73] Among the different types of UN peace operations, peacebuilding has a large effect on reducing violence and perhaps even improving democracy.[74] But again this finding is based solely on the subset of civil war countries. Moreover, peacebuilding itself encompasses a wide range of elements, making it important to be able to attribute success to one tool over another, in order to develop actionable policy implications. This chapter is a step in that direction.

IMPROVING DEMOCRACY AID FOR CREDIBLE AND PEACEFUL ELECTIONS

Virtually all states hold elections, even in conflict-prone places like Afghanistan or authoritarian countries like Uganda and, until recently, Zimbabwe. Yet the quality and meaning of elections vary widely. A substantial share of elections are accompanied by unrest, where competition is violent rather than peaceful. Elections often result in casualties when domestic agents use violence as a tool of political competition. About a quarter of national elections worldwide are accompanied by electoral violence.

Developing country elections usually take place in an international context. Sometimes, international actors act directly to reduce election violence. Yet even when international actors are focused on election credibility rather than violence reduction, they still have the potential to influence political violence in important ways. International organizations have invested substantial resources in election support in developing countries over the last three decades. This reflects a widespread consensus among policymakers, practitioners, and scholars that this support matters. This consensus, however, obscures how little we actually know about the effectiveness of election aid. That international election support—specifically observer *criticism*—can have the unintended negative consequence of increasing violence, for example, stands in stark contrast to the largely positive research on observation. This book provides an explanation of why and when election support can increase election violence and also when it can reduce such violence.

Policymakers and scholars have focused on improving electoral integrity and, for more than a decade, specifically on the problem of election violence, that is, political violence intended to influence the election process or outcome. Funders and implementers have issued guidelines on how to mitigate election violence, and researchers have provided (case) studies on domestic risk factors. However, theories and systematic, cross-national evidence have been in short supply, and our understanding of the relationship between external election support and election violence is quite limited. *When* does election support matter: under what circumstances can such support influence election violence, and at which points during the electoral cycle? *How* does election support matter: how can it shape the incentives of domestic actors to engage in violence? And does support help reduce violence, increase it, or leave it unchanged? Finally, since election support is comprised of both observation and technical election assistance, *which* type of support is better when?

The book addresses these questions by providing a theory and detailed cross-national evidence for explaining how international election support can influence election violence. Throughout this book, I focus on two forms of international election support: technical election assistance and election observation. I develop a theory about the importance of credible elections for election security, test it using original data on over four hundred elections in Africa and Latin America, and provide qualitative case material to document the proposed mechanisms. The following sections summarize the argument, findings, and implications for research and policymaking.

Argument

Credible Election Theory (CET) explains how international democracy aid can influence election violence. Credible elections are less likely to turn violent, and international election support can make elections more or less credible and thus alter the incentives of domestic actors to engage in election violence. Elections are credible when they are competently managed and held on a level playing field. For an election to be perceived as credible, election management (usually in the form of an election commission) should be capable and trustworthy, and parties and candidates should be held accountable for their behavior.

Yet external influence is a double-edged sword: Election support can reduce violence in some circumstances and increase it in others. The effect depends on the type of support (technical assistance or observation) and the election phase (before or after election-day). Both types of support increase international scrutiny of sensitive domestic political processes. But they operate through different mechanisms.

Observation provides information about the behavior of stakeholders while technical assistance builds institutional capacity for election management. In the run-up to elections, both types of external support can help calm tensions and lower the risk of election violence. However, in the wake of elections they can have divergent effects: technical assistance can reduce violence, whereas observers' negative verdict about the elections' credibility can contribute to violence.

Before elections, campaign violence tends to be used to influence vote choice or turnout. International observation can increase the accountability of potential perpetrators of fraud and violence because external scrutiny increases the likelihood that perpetrators are identified and publicly shamed. Reputable observer groups send pre-assessment missions and issue statements about the possibility of a meaningful election. These statements detail institutional shortcomings and malpractice by domestic stakeholders, including violent and nonviolent manipulation (e.g., misuse of state resources, failure to update the voter register, attacks on opponents). The anticipated public exposure of manipulation generates incentives for domestic actors to limit manipulation or at least adopt less overt strategies. External scrutiny increases the costs of engaging in violence, making it a less attractive strategy to use violence as a tool of political competition in the campaigning period. Given increased accountability costs, perpetrators have incentives to reduce manipulation or abstain from it entirely; they are more likely to play by the rules.

Technical election assistance can improve election management by increasing the capacity of the election management body (usually the national election commission) to run a smooth and clean election, removing potential conflict triggers, and keeping conflict from escalating. Technical assistance can help reform conflict-prone procedures. It can help mitigate violence by increasing the election commission's resources for electoral security and sponsoring local mediation bodies. These forms of election support can make the campaigning period more credible and remove potential triggers of violent contestation, thus reducing pre-election violence.

After election-day, violence often erupts when the election process or result is seen as not credible. During this time, the effect of external support depends on its type. Technical assistance can reduce violence in the aftermath of elections by raising the capacity and credibility of the election commission. When political elites trust and respect the election commission, they are also more likely to trust the announced result and channel any disputes through said institution. Both of these should result in less post-election violence. Besides increased institutional capacity and credibility, technical assistance also encourages contestants to stay calm and aims to socialize citizens and parties to acknowledge that losing is just part of the game, which they may win in future competitions.

In contrast, critical observer verdicts can strengthen the loser's incentives to challenge the election outcome, thus potentially leading to more violence. Independent validation of election quality is an important factor in post-vote violence. A negative observer report alleges that significant manipulation occurred and casts doubt on the accuracy of the announced result. Such a condemnation strengthens the loser by indicating that the loser might have more popular support than the official vote share suggests and by serving as a focal point for mobilization. Negative observer reports can shift the probability of winning a potential post-election contestation in favor of the loser by increasing the number of people who are willing to mobilize for the loser. If the loser is more likely to win a potential post-election contest, the loser is more likely to challenge the result. Challenges can result in violence when the loser challenge is violent or when the loser challenge provokes reactionary violence by the winner. Therefore, a negative observer report increases incentives to challenge the result, which can contribute to violence.

Findings

To test these arguments outlined in chapter 1, I use statistical analyses, illustrative case material, and the compilation of original datasets. The original data collected and analyzed for this project cover more than four hundred national elections in seventy countries in Africa and Latin between 1990 and 2012. The data include information on technical election assistance, election-related casualties before and after elections, and loser challenges after elections. Importantly, the data distinguish electoral violence before and after elections. Using original data on casualties—the number of people killed or injured in election-related violence—I show that pre- and post-vote violence are indeed distinct phenomena. In many countries, election violence is not a structural factor that pervades elections both before and after every election. Empirical patterns in the frequency and prevalence of violence before/after election-day document that these two are distinct processes and that they are strategic rather than simply structural.

In the absence of a good deductive theory of election violence in past research, chapter 1 introduced a baseline model of violence. In this baseline model, I outline which domestic factors are frequently associated with election violence. These factors include institutional constraints on the executive, conflict history, economic development, natural resources, population size, ethnic fractionalization, competition, poll type, past election violence, and fraud. Moreover, I explain which of these domestic factors can be influenced by international election support: constraints on political elites and (real and perceived) election fraud.

In chapter 2, I test the argument about election support and campaign violence. I estimate the effect of observation and technical assistance on the number of casualties while controlling for the domestic factors from the baseline model. The results indicate that the presence of reputable observer groups is significantly associated with less campaign violence. Moreover, the analyses find a joint effect: when both forms of election support are provided, campaign violence is lower than when only one or neither was provided. This suggests that they work through different mechanisms to calm tensions in the campaigning period.

The analyses also test for the selection of support into more or less violent elections. There is no evidence that expected violence drives where observers go; the observer effect does not seem to be an artifact of selection. However, there is some evidence that technical assistance selects into *more* violent elections. Accounting for this selection into more conflict-prone environments, the analyses document that elections with technical assistance have less campaign violence. Taking into account that the UN goes to more conflict-prone countries, it is still effective at reducing campaign violence in these circumstances. To illustrate the proposed mechanisms of accountability and capacity, I draw on case material from Liberia, Sierra Leone, Benin, Ghana, Malawi, and Guinea. For example, the case of technical assistance in Sierra Leone illustrates how party registration proceeded more peacefully than expected because regulations were changed to have parties register on separate days, avoiding run-ins between political contestants.

Chapter 3 turns to post-election violence and the effect of international condemnations. Again, the quantitative analyses control for a host of domestic characteristics from the baseline model. The results indicate that condemnations are associated with more post-election violence. Further, they suggest that it is often internationally "certified fraud," not fraud alone, that exacerbates loser challenges and violence. I also tested for endogeneity (observer verdicts being influenced by violence) but found no evidence of reverse causation. In addition, I use newly collected data to show that verdicts are issued within a couple of days after the election while violence is measured up to ninety days after the election, which makes it difficult to explain the effect with reverse causation. For post-election violence, what matters is not observer presence—their mere physical attendance—but their reports. Observer verdicts of election credibility matter for election violence.

To document that the mechanism linking condemnations and violence works through loser challenges, I show that condemnations significantly increase the probability of loser challenges, and that loser challenges significantly increase post-vote violence. Further, I use a case comparison of two similar elections that differed in condemnation and violence: the 2007 elections in Kenya and Sierra Leone.

This shows how similar domestic contexts can yield different outcomes because the condemnation (unintentionally) encouraged the electoral loser Odinga to challenge the result in Kenya whereas the endorsement in Sierra Leone did not give the same legitimacy to loser Berewa.

Chapter 4 tests the argument about technical election assistance and post-election violence. Again using a count model of casualties, technical assistance is significantly associated with reduced violence in Africa. I also document the proposed mechanism of building the institutional capacity and credibility of the national election commission. I show that technical election assistance significantly increases the commission's capacity in Africa and Latin America. This effect is substantial, raising institutional capacity by about one point on a five-point scale. Survey data from Kenya, Liberia, and countries in Latin America support the argument that election commissions that receive technical assistance tend to become more credible in the eyes of citizens than commissions that did not receive such support; and that better election management improves local trust in the commission and perceptions of free and fair elections. Elections in Guyana and Bangladesh illustrate the mechanism of technical assistance increasing trust in the credibility of elections, which limits incentives to engage in post-election violence. In sum, quantitative and qualitative material supports the argument that international organizations providing election support can influence election violence by altering election credibility and changing the incentives of domestic actors to engage in violence.

To revisit the questions posed in the introduction, this book provides answers to several important questions about international democracy aid and election violence. The study suggests *when* election support matters for violence and *which* type is "better" when. Campaign violence can be substantially reduced by observation and technical assistance. Post-vote violence can be reduced by technical assistance in Africa but does not seem to have the same effect in Latin America, where election commission capacity tends to be already higher and violence less frequent and less intense than in Africa. Critical observer reports can fuel violence in the wake of elections.

The book also provides an explanation for *how* election aid changes violence: by altering election credibility. Observation can raise the accountability of political elites which may otherwise engage (more) in violent and nonviolent manipulation. It increases the costs of using violence by making it more likely that misbehavior is detected and publicly denounced. It thereby raises the constraints on political actors, making violence a less attractive strategy in the campaigning period. However, accountability can also backfire. When observers certify significant manipulation, they cast doubt on the credibility of the election and thus strengthen the electoral loser's incentive to challenge the result, which can lead to violence. In contrast to observation, technical assistance works through institution building. It can increase the capacity of electoral commissions and thus make the electoral process more smooth and less prone to conflict. Before elections, this can help prevent violence by removing triggers and mitigate violence where it erupts, keeping it from escalating. After elections, the higher credibility of the election commission can also make the result that they announce more credible and provide a better forum for dispute resolution, thus lowering incentives for post-election unrest.

Implications

The relationship between international election support and election violence has important implications for scholars and policymakers. The findings here challenge a still-common assumption in comparative politics that domestic politics is mainly driven by domestic factors, advance research on democracy assistance, and suggest new avenues of research about the conditions under which IOs influence domestic politics. In addition, the empirical findings provide important insights for policymakers who wish to mitigate election violence or work with international organizations in the election field.

RESEARCH

This book advances research on international organizations by proposing and testing a theory about how international organizations can influence election violence. In an effort to explore *how* international institutions matter,[1] this study has revealed mechanisms, illustrated the role of domestic politics, and documented how international institutions are consequential as well as objects of state choice. More specifically, the book contributes to the literature on the domestic politics of international relations,[2] and adds another domestic political outcome (election violence) that can be influenced by international factors. Further, this study shows how international organizations can to some degree *substitute* for domestic practices. When domestic capacity is low, technical assistance can support and expand election management. As an investment in local institutions and agents, international assistance boosts domestic capacity through logistical help and advice. In rare cases, governments transfer domestic authority to international organizations for administering elections entirely. More often, governments transfer some authority to monitor elections to IOs.

Democracy aid by international organizations is consequential for domestic politics. By documenting effects on election violence, this study explores new ground in four ways. First, it shifts the focus from fraud[3] to violence as an important dimension of politics that election aid can influence. This contributes to institutionalist research on the "second image reversed"[4] as well as research on the effect of third-party actors in domestic conflict.[5] Second, this study shifts attention away from the limits of observation and the extent of its positive effects[6] to the potential negative effects of observation and observer verdicts in particular. In this way, it adds nuance to research on election monitoring and, more broadly, contributes to the literature on the negative unintended effects of international organizations.[7] Third, this book helps to open up a new research field: technical election assistance. External support of political infrastructure has received relatively little attention.[8] The scarce research that exists on technical election assistance and conflict often relies on case studies and offers mixed results, ranging from carefully optimistic to inconclusive and skeptical of any pacifying effects.[9] In contrast, this book provides systematic empirical evidence and shows that such assistance can reduce violence in some contexts.

Fourth, the book contributes to research on international democracy assistance. This line of work has moved on from the initial debate of whether democracy aid is effective[10] to when (or the conditions under which) it is effective. Recent work suggests that democracy aid is more likely to help democratization in countries with multi-party elections, with a greater need of external support, and without competing foreign policy priorities by donors.[11] In the statistical analyses, this line of research has also shifted from aggregate measures of "democracy aid" and broad outcomes of interest ("democratization" writ large) to types of aid and more specific outcome components, such as cleaner elections, more human rights, and stronger civil society.[12] This makes sense, as it is unlikely that election quality is influenced by unrelated democracy and governance programs, such as aid for parliamentary efficiency. The book contributes to this line of work by showing how the two major types of election aid can influence plausible outcomes (election quality and election violence).

Using *specific* measures is important for testing theoretical predictions and deriving policy implications. Much existing work measures election support as an aggregate variable and as one of many components. This is largely a function of available data: USAID data include a variable for "elections and political processes" that combines funding for political party support, technical assistance, and observation; OECD data feature a variable for "elections" that combines support for election observation, electoral management bodies and processes, and voter education; and AidData builds on this OECD "elections" variable and adds projects. Using aggregate data on "election aid" (or broader still, democracy aid) can mask important dynamics in how the effects differ by type of aid (observation and technical assistance), type of outcome (election quality, violence, or broad democratization) and timing (before or after elections). Using more specific empirical measures to test specific theoretical predictions is a promising way to advance this research, solve some of the debates, and derive actionable policy implications.

For both academic and policy researchers in democratization, election violence is a—perhaps *the*—missing link in understanding the transition to truly democratic regimes. In loose parlance, it is hard to conceive of a society that regularly experiences election violence as democratic. On the other hand, any system that regularly has nonviolent and fair elections is more likely a consolidated democracy. For political theorist Robert Dahl, peaceful, regular, and fair elections are an essential component of the democratic process: "A democratic government provides an orderly and *peaceful* process by means of which a majority of citizens can induce the government to do what they most want it to do and to avoid doing what they most want it not to do."[13]

Thus, by definition, election violence undermines democracy, and eliminating such violence is crucial to democratic consolidation. Despite this, election violence still remains relatively understudied, especially compared to the large bodies of research on democratization and other forms of political violence (such as civil wars, human rights violations, and coups).

Much comparative politics research on election violence focuses on domestic causes, skeptical that there are important influences outside the nation-state. In contrast, this study has shown that even when controlling for domestic drivers of violence, international organizations still exert a significant and substantial effect on violence. The argument does not minimize the role of domestic factors; to the contrary, it complements existing work as domestic factors build the baseline model of election violence and clarifies which entry points exist for international efforts to mitigate violence. The book points out that international influences should be taken into account to paint a more complete picture. While there are certainly cases in which external support is not consequential, in many cases it is worthwhile to consider international influences.

POLICYMAKING

What works in international democracy assistance? Prominent policy researchers have written little about aspects of international democracy support that I have found essential. Technical election assistance can and does play an important role in improving elections, institutions, and civil society. As chapters 2 and 4 have shown, technical assistance can support civil society through civic and voter education as well as programs on nonviolence and social cohesion. It can also reform state institutions—helping to transform national election commissions into more capable and credible bodies, and furthering interaction between election management and the security sector. Most centrally, technical assistance can help improve the administration of elections, making elections more legitimate fora for competition. That is not to say that technical assistance is a panacea—changes crucially depend on domestic political will[14]—but it is a promising tool of democracy promotion that has been under-appreciated compared to the wealth of work on party aid and election observation.

How can external actors help countries conduct more credible elections and more *peaceful* transitions of power? At the beginning of this book, I noted the gap between the widespread practice of international election support and the scarcity of research on how such support influences election violence. As one of the leading democracy promotion scholars and practitioners, Thomas Carothers, noted, how can we support elections to help reduce the chance of sectarian conflicts?[15] Let's reconsider that question in light of the empirical evidence presented here. My findings suggest that technical assistance has pacifying effects while election observation is conflict-mitigating before elections but can potentially contribute to violence after elections by issuing a negative verdict. Some scholars argue that when election observers condemn elections and contribute to post-election *protests*, this is constructive conflict because it can help shape incumbent incentives and potentially helps enforce democracy in the long run.[16] *Violence*, however, may be a different matter. Apart from the ethical issues involved, whether election violence is constructive violence and has democratizing effects remains an open empirical question. The scarce work on this question to date focuses on the attitudinal effects of election violence and indicates that fearing election violence lowers popular support for democracy and boosts support for a return to autocracy.[17] To the extent that election violence does not have democratizing effects, this book suggests that for some elections, donors and implementing organizations may wish to carefully reconsider whether funding or providing election observers is indeed the best way forward in a given context.

This book's findings offer several policy implications regarding the usefulness of international election support (observation and technical election assistance) for addressing election quality and, in particular, election violence. As mentioned at the beginning of this book, a caveat is in order: the focus of external election support is usually on improving election quality broadly rather than specifically on election violence. That said, for some providers mitigating electoral violence is indeed a core goal. United Nations election assistance has three goals: helping member states hold democratic elections, building capable institutions for election administration that have the full confidence of the contesting parties, and reducing the potential for election-related violence.[18] Further, core funders of election support such as USAID and the European Union have issued best practice documents on how to address electoral violence, which underscores that election support has increasingly been seen through a conflict lens.[19] And even

when international actors are not explicitly trying to affect election-related violence (but election quality more broadly), they still have the potential to alter
domestic outcomes—including violence—in important ways. So how can election support be designed to lower election violence?

Observer groups face a dilemma when they have hard evidence about manipulation. They can follow their mandate of providing accurate information, condemn the election, and risk exacerbating post-vote violence. Or, alternatively,
they can endorse a fraudulent election in the hope of delaying or deterring violence but thereby legitimize a potentially manipulating government and also
risk their own observer reputation in the long run. How can this dilemma be
solved? One way to avoid this dilemma is for observers to not place themselves
in this situation in the first place. Observer groups could avoid attending clearly
undemocratic elections and explicitly state these reasons. That is, after careful
analysis, observer groups could decide not to attend elections that are unlikely to
have meaningful competition. After all, it is unclear what added value in terms of
information about election quality can be gained from observing elections that
many expect to be deeply flawed long before they start.

At times, observer organizations have already done exactly that—choosing
not to attend clearly undemocratic elections—but if it were a standard, observer
absence would be even more common. Since 1990, observer groups seem to have
refused to attend a few dozen elections because they believed that it would not be
free, fair, or democratic. Those include Honduras 2009, Haiti and Cote d'Ivoire
2000, and several elections in Equatorial Guinea, Guinea, Togo, and Sudan and
in former Soviet Union states (Uzbekistan, Turkmenistan, and Tajikistan).[20] The
OAS, NDI, and Carter Center withdrew from Peru's 2001 election, which the
incumbent rigged in his favor, and more recently the EU chose not to attend
Sudan's government-controlled 2015 election (whereas the African Union did).[21]
Of course in some cases, withdrawing observers becomes imperative when the
security situation deteriorates, such as in Afghanistan 2014 or Sudan 2010. But
even if the physical safety of observer teams is not at risk, observation groups may
want to consider whether to withdraw or not attend when meaningful competition is unlikely. Many "bad" elections still get observed around the world. Some
organizations attend farce elections, such as those in Zimbabwe (until Mugabe's
resignation in 2017), Swaziland, and Ethiopia. Instead of investing in elections
with little potential for fair competition and the risk of fueling violence with an
observer condemnation (as in Ethiopia 2005), observer groups and funding organization may want to weigh more carefully the benefits and costs of attending.

The suggestion to carefully weigh the pros and cons of attending particular
elections is not new. The 2005 "Declaration of Principles for International Election Observation" and the "Code of Conduct for International Election Observers"

already included some preconditions.[22] This book suggests an additional factor that organizations may want to take into account when deciding whether to send an observer mission: whether the particular election may turn (more) violent if observers criticize election quality. In the 2005 Code of Conduct, observer organizations already agreed not to send missions if it is "likely that its presence will be interpreted as giving legitimacy to a clearly undemocratic electoral process."[23] This is often a risk because some domestic competitors have incentives to cite observer *presence* as proof of better election quality, regardless of observer actions or findings. Choosing not to attend clearly undemocratic elections would avoid the risk of observer presence being interpreted as a stamp of approval and would also avoid the dilemma of having to issue a negative observer verdict in a possibly fragile or conflict-prone environment. Alternatively, if observers are already deployed on the ground, they could consider withdrawing in order to avoid legitimizing sham elections with observer presence and potentially violent repercussions after voting.

Of course, not attending particular elections would have some drawbacks: observers would be unable to detect and deter fraud and violence before voting—so the violence-reducing effect documented in chapter 2 could not occur—and observers would not be able to issue informed, detailed recommendations for reforms for future elections.[24] One possible solution to limit these drawbacks is to support domestic election observation efforts. After all, in many countries today domestic observers have become quite professionalized and similarly assess electoral processes, outline deficiencies, and evaluate overall election quality. While domestic efforts are often seen as more partisan (with an interest in election outcomes as well as process) and thus potentially less reputable,[25] supporting domestic observer groups when internationals decide not to go could strengthen accountability.

Second, if observer groups attend non-credible elections, they should not hold back criticism and should consider issuing more frequent interim statements. The first part may seem counterintuitive given the empirical findings that negative observer statements can fuel domestic contestation. More importantly, by softening the statements, observer groups may falsely legitimize incoming governments and also undermine their own observer reputation which is their main currency. While my analyses suggest that reputable groups predominantly are truth tellers,[26] there have been cases in which observers were less than forthright with their findings. Earlier work by Judith Kelley noted three elections in which observers may have softened their statements because they were concerned that a critical statement would fuel violence: Zimbabwe 2000, Kenya 1992, and Nigeria 1999.[27] My systematic analyses and empirical findings provide compelling evidence that such concerns are justified. To those three elections we might add Afghanistan 2014, where local institutions cut corners, politicians engaged in vote buying, and election mismanagement was evident. Yet observer groups deemed these elections "good enough" and a step forward. Some may also add the 2017 Kenyan election, which was deemed fairly credible by international observers—possibly reluctant to criticize because of concerns over election violence as in 2007–08—but then was annulled by the country's Supreme Court. Kelley would denote this as a stability bias, but we could also usefully think of it as the observers' credibility-peace trade-off.

While endorsing a deeply flawed election may seem the right choice in the short term to avoid fueling violence, it risks eroding observer reputation in the medium and long term, risking the health of an industry and losing a key tool to hold governments and opposition forces accountability to democratic standards. Hence observer groups may sometimes be better off choosing not to go than to go and soften their findings. It is important not to antagonize domestic politics, but it is also important to give unbiased assessments. Of course, in practice, making decisions on observer presence and observer verdicts is often a sensitive and complex matter. Decisions need to be made on a case-by-case basis and with detailed discussion of context, opportunities and goals after careful assessment of the advantages and disadvantages of available options.

Apart from not holding back criticism, observers should also consider issuing more frequent interim statements before election-day to lower the impact of a sudden condemnation. Instead of the first critical statement "hitting" immediately after voting, when tensions are high, observer groups could issue preliminary press statements regularly in the weeks leading up to polling. By slowly adjusting expectations and reflecting political conditions as they evolve, the impact of the condemnation might be lessened. This is essentially applying the "electoral cycle approach" from UNDP, IDEA, and EU assistance to election observation. The electoral cycle approach has become a standard way of looking at the different activities in the electoral process, such as voter education, candidate registration, voter roll updates, and so forth. While observer statements often include a section on these activities, it would be worthwhile to standardize these efforts by issuing regular (say monthly or bi-weekly) statements on the quality of these processes by applying a common set of criteria. The Carter Center has already begun doing that over the last few years, but more organizations could follow suit.

Third, donors could consider increasing funding for technical election assistance or shifting some of the budget for international election support from observation to technical assistance. Independent of the findings for election observation, the findings on technical assistance for commission capacity and electoral security indicate that these programs are worthwhile and should be expanded where possible. Policy interest on the nexus between technical election assistance and electoral violence has increased, with several leading organizations issuing guidance on best practices for technical assistance. The UNDP issued its programming guide for elections and conflict prevention in 2009, followed by USAID's electoral security framework in 2010 and best practices guide in 2013.[28] IFES has made efforts to streamline violence resolution into regular elections programming, and the U.S. Institute of Peace has regularly held workshops for policymakers to transfer practical tools for election violence prevention.[29] Organizations usually evaluate the success of such programming based on case studies of individual elections. Using large-N statistical analyses of technical election assistance, I have shown that technical assistance can act as a pacifier around elections. This implies that investment in technical support is worthwhile and should be expanded when possible.

Technical assistance needs a permissive political environment, so it is not always an available option. Further, technical assistance is unlikely to provide much added value when election management is already quite capable (including a high-quality voter roll, high voter education, high commission capacity and credibility). But many elections in the developing world stand to benefit from technical assistance in the foreseeable future. This calls for needs and risk assessments to be made at an early stage, to enable experts to identify particular sources of conflict in upcoming elections (just like voter registration was identified as a source of conflict in Bangladesh) and to allow funding to come through early to then de-escalate the conflict around elections.

Moreover, to enable a more detailed evaluation of assistance programs, it would also be beneficial to collect more in-house data on the timing, scope, and shape of such programs and to publish that information. The UNDP has made efforts to put project documents of its activities in the public domain. That is laudable. It is worth noting that without these data, some of the analyses in this book would not have been possible. But to enable more detailed quantitative research (which components of technical assistance are most important? which timeframe is best? what is the ideal budget?), such information would need to be more consistent in terms of project duration, size, budget, and components—and be provided by other organizations as well.

Finally, it is important to issue two disclaimers. Recall that international election support—as argued in this book—seems to be most useful when election credibility is at stake. Actors with primarily criminal motives—insurgents such as the Taliban in Afghanistan or drug cartels in Mexico—are likely unresponsive to this kind of programming. Here, electoral violence is not so much a political issue as a straight-up security issue. Also, much recent discussion surrounds the use of technology in elections. Technology and social media, in particular, are tools that many actors can seize upon. They can be used to track violent incidents, enable rapid response, and thus keep conflicts from spiraling out of control. But they can also be used to organize violence, spread rumors, issue threats, and digitally manipulate and disrupt elections. In this regard, it is important to support and learn more about ongoing efforts to track, forecast, and address electoral violence through social media platforms, such as Ushahidi, Aggie, and others.[30]

Future Research Avenues

This book has just scratched the surface of this relatively new research field, and several new puzzles have surfaced during the course of this research. I outline a few directions of future research that could add to this body of knowledge. First, technical assistance provides fertile ground for future research. Almost two decades ago, Robert Pastor drew attention to the fact that the administrative side of elections is critical but overlooked.[31] With few exceptions, that situation has not changed. Credible election commissions are an important foundation of democracy and democratization. If commissions are more credible, elections are more likely to be peaceful regardless of the presence or actions of international organizations. However, to help commissions reach that level of institutional quality, external support can be crucial. Democracy has to be learned; no country was born with advanced institutions. In established democracies, citizens solve their disputes through ballots rather than bullets. What does it take to achieve a political system in which competing interests are resolved nonviolently, citizens feel they can meaningfully participate, and democratic institutions are seen as legitimate? What are the different types of democratic technical assistance that countries can draw on to achieve a more democratic state? Perhaps most importantly, once technical support has been provided, how durable is its effect? This calls for more research on the causal processes and effects of technical assistance on related outcomes.

Second, can combining or sequencing different types of international election support generate greater changes in domestic politics? The analyses in chapter 2 suggest that the presence of *both* technical and observer groups has a greater effect on campaign violence than either type by itself. They operate under different mechanisms and thus generate a greater joint effect. Future research could explore how to best sequence or coordinate these two types of support. For example, the effect of observation on post-election unrest may depend on institutional trust: very low or very high trust in domestic electoral institutions may render international observation ineffective in terms of changing election credibility and violence levels.[32] As institutional trust improves to middling levels, a combination of technical assistance and observation could improve election credibility. But these are ultimately empirical questions warranting further research.

More than thirty years of experience have shown that the seeds of democracy assistance may fall on sandy soil, rocky soil, and, sometimes, fertile soil. Even on fertile soil, democracy assistance does not always achieve its goals and sometimes has unintended effects. Domestic political, economic, and social characteristics are important drivers of local politics. International aid, however, can help shape institutions and incentives that support the transition to peaceful elections and, over time, can help consolidate democracy. The challenge for academics and practitioners alike is to continue to identify which policies strengthen these institutions (and which do not). This book suggests that reducing election violence through credible elections is an important step in this process. Further, rigorous election observation can help detect and deter manipulation in the run-up to elections, but may exacerbate violence where an election is tainted by fraud and thus condemned. Finally, technical assistance aimed at building credible election management bodies can be an important pillar of peaceful elections and democracy.

Appendix to Chapter 1

Appendix 1A: Election Administrative Challenges

This list is adapted from Pastor 1999b, 8–9.

Pre-Election Stage

1. Designing a system to appoint registration and election officials and then training them;
2. Delineation of the boundaries of voting areas;
3. Designing a voter registration system, establishing voting sites, and notifying the voters;
4. Registering voters on-site or at home and aggregating a voters' list at the national and local levels;
5. Publishing and distributing a preliminary list to allow voters and parties an opportunity to review and correct the list, adding, deleting, or modifying data or the voting sites;
6. Collecting information on voters and processing the data into voter identification cards;
7. Finalizing the registration list and sending copies to the regions and to the voting sites;
8. Distributing voter identification cards (sometimes at the same place as registration and voting) and assuring that they are received by the right people;

9. Registering and qualifying political parties and candidates;
10. Establishing and enforcing rules on campaigning, access to the media, and financing;
11. Ensuring security of the voters, the candidates, and the polling stations;
12. Developing rules for the proper observation of elections by domestic and international monitors and giving credentials to them;
13. Production of election materials; printing and securing the ballot; delivery of the election materials to designated sites.

Election-Day

1. Polling officials should set up their booth and verify receipt of the materials in the presence of monitors before the polling officially begins;
2. Polling officials should open the ballot boxes in the presence of voters, then close and seal them, and begin the voting;
3. Polling officials should certify that voters are on the registration list and that they vote privately and in accordance with the procedures (often including dipping one's finger in ink to preclude multiple voting);
4. Election officials should monitor the voting of all sites during the day and have quick-reaction teams ready to distribute election materials and resolve problems during the day;
5. Ballots should be counted in the open, preferably at each site and in the presence of monitors from all major political parties or the public; other procedures for identifying, counting, and organizing blank or invalid ballots should be followed;
6. Tally sheet should be jointly signed by all the poll-watchers, and results should be delivered to sub-regional offices and the national election commission as expeditiously as possible;
7. At the national election commission, results should be announced as they arrive, but precautions are needed to avoid double-counting.

Post-Election Verification and Dispute Settlement

1. Electoral Tribunal or appropriate body should investigate and adjudicate complaints;
2. Electoral Commission, or designated body, should verify the final count and certify the final results.

Appendix 1B. Formal Model of Post-Election Violence

This section complements the "Support and Post-Election Violence" section of chapter 1 by formally presenting a deterrence-type game to generate hypotheses about the effect of IO election support on post-election violence. The post-election model is illustrated in appendix figure 1B.1 and captures the interaction between the two key players, the election loser and the election winner (L and W).[1] The model is sufficiently general: it can capture the incentives of candidates and parties and thus applies to both presidential and legislative elections; the loser may be either the incumbent or the opposition.

For the game shown in appendix figure 1B.1, I assume that players are rational actors who seek to maximize their payoffs. Winning the post-election contest, thus presiding over the government and its resources, gives a payoff of 1. Note that the probabilities of winning, P_W and P_L, must always sum to 1, or more formally: $P_W = 1 - P_L$. Losing the post-election contest gives a payoff of 0. The payoff for fighting is the probability of winning a post-election dispute (P_i) times the material benefit of presiding over the country (1) minus the cost of fighting (c_i). Since fighting is costly, c_i is never zero and is always positive; this fighting cost can include anything from people, weapons, logistics to intangible reputational costs.

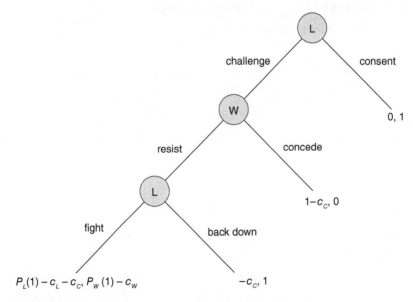

APPENDIX FIGURE 1B.1. The post-election game

I assume that both sides have sufficient resources to start a street fight. If the loser challenges, the loser incurs an additional, marginal cost c_c.[2] Payoff components are summarized in table 1B.1 and discussed in more detail below.

Equilibria

Solving the game in appendix figure 1B.1 through backward induction, three equilibria arise. Appendix figures 1B.2 and 1B.3 display the solutions of backward induction. The sufficient condition in equation 1 gives rise to the Subgame Perfect Nash Equilibrium in which the loser consents to the election outcome. Equation 2 shows the conditions for the equilibrium in which both players fight. Finally, equation 3 gives the conditions for the third equilibrium in which the winner concedes after a challenge.

In appendix figure 1B.3 the white area shows the sufficient condition for the loser to consent, equation 1. The light-gray area shows the conditions for the winner to concede after a challenge, which is equation 3. The dark-gray area shows the conditions for both players to fight, equation 2.

APPENDIX TABLE 1B.1   Formal notation in the game

P_i	Probability of winning the post-election contest
c_i	Cost of fighting
c_c	Cost of challenging incurred by the Loser

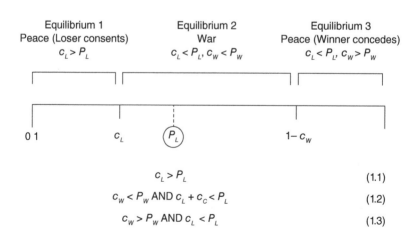

$$c_L > P_L \tag{1.1}$$

$$c_W < P_W \text{ AND } c_L + c_c < P_L \tag{1.2}$$

$$c_W > P_W \text{ AND } c_L < P_L \tag{1.3}$$

APPENDIX FIGURE 1B.2.   Equilibria and the loser's strength

Proof of Equilibria

To solve this game through backward induction, consider the decision of the last player, the loser. The loser chooses between backing down and fighting. The loser backs down if and only if the loser's payoff for fighting ($P_L - c_L - c_c$) is smaller than the loser's payoff for backing down ($-c_c$), and he or she will fight otherwise. In other words, the loser backs down if and only if the loser's cost of fighting is greater than the loser's probability of winning the post-election contest (iff $c_L > P_L$). Given that the loser backs down, the winner will resist because the winner's payoff for resist and back down (1) is always greater than the winner's payoff for concede (0). Given that the winner resists and the loser backs down (iff $c_L > P_L$), the loser prefers to consent because the loser's payoff for consenting (0) is always greater than the loser's payoff for challenging and backing down ($-c_c$). The following is a sufficient condition for the loser to consent. Thus equation 1 is the Subgame Perfect Nash Equilibrium:

$$c_L > P_L \qquad \text{(equation 1)}$$

If instead of backing down the loser decides to fight (iff $P_L > c_L$), then the winner will resist as long as his or her payoff for fighting ($P_W - c_W$) is greater than his or her payoff for conceding (0), meaning that $P_W > c_W$. Given that, the loser will

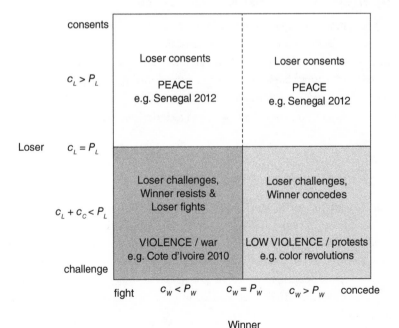

APPENDIX FIGURE 1B.3. Equilibria summary

challenge as long as the payoff for challenge, resist, fight $(P_L - c_L - c_c)$ is greater than that for consent (0): $P_L > c_L + c_c$. Thus there is a combination of two individually non-sufficient conditions that induces the loser to challenge: if and only if for each player the cost of fighting is smaller than the probability of winning. This is captured in equation 2.

$$c_W < P_W \text{ AND } c_L + c_c < P_L \qquad \text{(equation 2)}$$

If the loser decides to fight (iff $P_L > c_L$), the winner alternatively chooses to concede if and only if the winner's payoff for conceding (0) is greater than the winner's payoff for fighting $(P_W - c_W)$, meaning that $c_W > P_W$. Given that the winner prefers conceding, the loser challenges because by assumption the value of holding office exceeds the marginal cost of challenging the result: $1 > c_c$.[3] Thus there is a second combination of two conditions that induces the loser to challenge, but here the winner concedes. This is captured in equation 3.

$$c_W > P_W \text{ AND } c_L < P_L \qquad \text{(equation 3)}$$

Appendix 1C. Variables and Data

This book draws on original as well as publicly available data. The unit of analysis is the national election, and the scope of statistical analyses are countries in Africa and Latin America from 1990 to 2012. The variable sources and measurement are summarized in appendix table 1C.1; their descriptive statistics are in appendix table 1C.2. Subsequently, I provide information about the original data collection for election violence, post-election loser challenges, and technical election assistance.

Election Violence Data (GEVD)

I collected original data on election violence. The resulting dataset, the Global Election Violence Dataset (GEVD), covers over 1,400 national elections and referenda worldwide from 1990 to 2015. In this book, I draw on a subset of these data—variables about deaths and injuries—and concentrate on national elections. The introduction presents data globally while the remaining chapters focus on Africa and Latin America, as detailed in the empirical strategy section of the introduction.

I collected original data on election violence intensity for each stage of the electoral cycle—including the number of people killed and injured before, during,

APPENDIX TABLE 1C.1 Variable descriptions

TYPE	VARIABLE NAME	CODING	SOURCE
Dependent variables	Pre-election casualties	Number of people killed or injured in the six months before and on election-day	von Borzyskowski 2018 (see GEVD in appendix 1C)
	Post-election casualties	Number of people killed or injured in the three months after election-day	von Borzyskowski 2018 (see GEVD in appendix 1C)
Independent variables	Technical election assistance	Binary indicator for whether the United Nations provided technical election assistance	von Borzyskowski 2016, (see TEAD in e_v2el_frefair appendix 1C)
	Observation	Binary indicator for whether at least one reputable observation group attended the election	Hyde and Marinov 2012, variable nelda46
	Condemnation	Binary indicator for whether at least one reputable observation group alleged significant vote fraud	Hyde and Marinov 2012, variable nelda47
Mechanism variables	Post-election loser challenge	Binary indicator for whether the loser challenged the election result; for robustness, also used binary/scale from V-Dem	Original data (see appendix 1C); Coppedge et al. 2015 (V-Dem) inverted variable v2elaccept
	Election commission capacity	5-point scale of capacity of the national election commission	Coppedge et al. 2015 (V-Dem), variable v2elembcap
	Election commission independence	5-point scale of autonomy of the national election commission	Coppedge et al. 2015 (V-Dem), variable v2elembaut
	Clean voting	5-point scale of freedom from intentional irregularities	Coppedge et al. 2015 (V-Dem), variable v2elirreg
	Clean election index	5-point index of multiple election quality variables	Coppedge et al. 2015 (V-Dem), variable
Control Variables	Executive constraints	Number of institutional constraints on executive authority, lagged	Marshall and Jaggers 2011 (Polity IV), variable xconst
	Post-conflict	Binary indicator for whether the country experienced a civil war in the previous ten years	Gleditsch et al. 2002 (UCDP/PRIO)
	Economic development	GDP per capita, measured in constant USD, lagged and logged	World Bank WDI 2012

(continued)

APPENDIX TABLE 1C.1 (continued)

TYPE	VARIABLE NAME	CODING	SOURCE
	Natural resources	Per capita value of oil and gas production to a government once subsidies are accounted for, lagged and logged	Ross 2012
	Population size	Population size measured in millions, lagged and logged	World Bank WDI 2012
	Ethnic fractionalization	Index of ethnolinguistic fractionalization from 0 (perfect homogeneity) to 1 (extreme heterogeneity)	Finkel et al. 2007, variable soc10
	Incumbent running	Binary indicator for whether the incumbent stood for re-election	Hyde and Marinov 2012, variable nelda21
	Loser vote share	Percentage of votes for runner-up	Nohlen 2005; Nohlen, Krennerich, and Thibaut 1999; African Elections Database n.d.; Carr n.d.; Beck et al. 2001 (DPI version 2012)
	Poll type	Type of election, coded 0=legislative, 1=executive, 2=general	Hyde and Marinov 2012
	Past election violence	Number of people killed during election violence during the previous election	von Borzyskowski 2018 (see GEVD in appendix 1C)
	Fraud	Binary indicator for whether there were significant concerns that the election would be fraudulent	Hyde and Marinov 2012, variable nelda11
	Previous election suspended	Binary indicator for whether the previous election was suspended	Hyde and Marinov 2012, variable nelda1
	First multi-party election	Binary indicator for whether this was the first multi-party election	Hyde and Marinov 2012, variable nelda2
	Transitional government	Binary indicator for whether the country was ruled by a transitional government	Hyde and Marinov 2012, variable nelda10
	Uncertain election	Binary indicator for whether the previous election was suspended, it was the first multi-party election, or there was a transitional government	Hyde and Marinov 2012, variables nelda1, nelda2, nelda10
	Opposition competition	Binary indicator for whether opposition was allowed and more than one party was legal and there was a choice of candidates on the ballot	Hyde and Marinov 2012, variables nelda13, nelda4, nelda5

Variable	Description	Source
Previously observed	Binary indicator for whether any previous election was observed in this country	Hyde and Marinov 2012, variable nelda46
Economic wealth	GDP; measured in constant USD, lagged and logged	World Bank WDI 2012
Year	Indicator of calendar year	Hyde and Marinov 2012
UN peacekeeping	Binary indicator for whether United Nations peacekeeping troops were stationed in the country, lagged	Kathman 2013
Regime Type: Autocracy	Indicator for whether the Polity2 index is between −10 and −6, lagged	Marshall and Jaggers 2011 (PolityIV), variable polity2
Regime Type: Hybrid	Indicator for whether the Polity2 index is between −5 and 5, lagged	Marshall and Jaggers 2011 (PolityIV), variable polity2
Regime Type: Advanced Democracy	Indicator for whether the Polity2 index is between 6 and 10, lagged	Marshall and Jaggers 2011 (PolityIV), variable polity2
Judicial independence	5-point scale of extent to which the high court adopts government preferences despite its own view, lagged	Coppedge et al. 2015 (V-Dem), variable v2juhcind

APPENDIX TABLE 1C.2 Descriptive statistics

	VARIABLE	MEAN	STD. DEV.	MIN.	MAX.	N
Dependent variables	Pre-election casualties	14.43	74.48	0.00	980	476
	Post-election casualties	14.05	103.71	0.00	1,480	476
Independent variables	Technical election assistance	0.34	0.48	0.00	1.00	476
	Observation	0.65	0.48	0.00	1.00	439
	Observation and/or technical assistance	1.00	0.73	0.00	2.00	439
	Condemnation	0.10	0.30	0.00	1.00	438
Mechanism variables	Post-election loser challenge (GEVD)	0.22	0.42	0.00	1.00	462
	Post-election loser challenge (VDEM)	1.24	1.28	0.00	4.00	469
	Election commission capacity	2.30	1.25	0.00	4.00	476
	Election commission independence	2.11	1.31	0.00	4.00	476
	Clean voting	1.54	1.20	0.00	4.00	473
	Clean election index	2.03	1.33	0.00	4.00	463
Control variables	Executive constraints	4.31	1.98	1.00	7.00	439
	Post-conflict	0.37	0.48	0.00	1.00	476
	Economic development	6.97	1.16	4.28	10.23	471
	Natural resources	−2.91	7.18	−9.21	9.76	476
	Population size	15.93	1.36	12.90	19.08	475
	Ethnic fractionalization	0.54	0.25	0.06	0.94	476
	Incumbent running	0.38	0.48	0.00	1.00	476
	Loser vote share	25.03	12.80	0.00	49.80	440
	Poll type	0.85	0.85	0.00	2.00	476
	Past election violence	0.29	0.46	0.00	1.00	475
	Fraud	0.46	0.50	0.00	1.00	459
	Previous election suspended	0.16	0.36	0.00	1.00	468
	First multi-party election	0.08	0.27	0.00	1.00	470
	Transitional government	0.12	0.32	0.00	1.00	470
	Uncertain election	0.23	0.42	0.00	1.00	470
	Opposition competition	0.99	0.11	0.00	1.00	470
	Previously observed	0.76	0.43	0.00	1.00	470
	Economic wealth	22.74	1.85	18.67	27.47	470
	Year	2001.22	6.63	1990	2012	476
	UN peacekeeping	0.07	0.25	0.00	1.00	476
	Regime Type: Autocracy	0.14	0.34	0.00	1.00	475
	Regime Type: Hybrid	0.41	0.49	0.00	1.00	475
	Regime Type: Advanced democracy	0.45	0.50	0.00	1.00	475
	Judicial independence	2.13	1.06	0.00	4.00	476

APPENDIX TABLE 1C.3   Comparing election-related violence datasets

DATASET	ELECTORAL VIOLENCE?	TIME			SPACE REGION, # OF COUNTRIES	YEARS	MEASURE
		PRE	AT	POST			
AEVD (Straus and Taylor 2012)	✓	✓	×	✓	Africa, n=47	1990–2008	0–3
Lindberg (2009)	✓	combined		×	Africa, n=45	1990–2006	0–2
SCAD (Salehyan et al. 2012)	✓	✓	✓	✓	Africa and Latin America, n=59	1990–present	events
ACLED (Raleigh, Linke, Hegre 2012)	×	✓	✓	✓	Africa, n=50	1997–present	events
Arriola and Johnson (2012)	✓	combined		✓	global, n=154	1985–2005	0–3
Birch (2011)	✓	✓	✓	×	global, n=57	1995–2006	1–5
Beaulieu (2014)	✓	✓	✓	✓	global, n=121	1975–2006	0–1
NELDA (Hyde and Marinov 2012)	✓		combined		global, n=161	1946–2012	0–1
V-DEM (Coppedge et al. 2015)	?		Combined		global, n=174	1900–present	0–4
QED (Kelley 2010)	✓	✓	✓	×	global, n=171	1974–2004	0–3
GEVD (von Borzyskowski 2018)	✓	✓	✓	✓	global, n=161	1990–2015	number of people killed, injured, etc.

and after elections—because this information was not available elsewhere when I began this project. Since most data are created with a specific purpose in mind that differs from this project's goals, available data were not a perfect fit. To illustrate this, appendix table 1C.3 compares GEVD to other datasets; this shows that the information contained in other available datasets had either insufficient granularity (lacking counts of fatalities and injuries, for instance) or insufficient coverage (available for Africa only). Among those datasets, the African Electoral Violence Database (AEVD) seems best suited for the analyses in this book because it measures election violence *intensity* six months before and three months after elections and has clearly defined intensity thresholds from zero to three: no violence reported (0), violent harassment (1), violent repression with at least one fatality (2), and large-scale violence with at least twenty fatalities (3).[4] However, there are two drawbacks for the purpose of the analyses in this book. First, as a dataset on Africa, it obviously does not cover Latin America and thus makes it difficult to test the scope conditions of the argument. Second, the thresholds—while an improvement on violence dummies (0/1) in other datasets—still discard meaningful variation: twenty fatalities is quite different from hundreds of fatalities or more than a thousand fatalities, as in Kenya 2007 and Angola 1992.

The issue of thresholds also applies to a few other datasets. Among them is the dataset in Lindberg (2009) on elections and democracy in Africa, which provides information on whether elections were accompanied by significant, isolated, or no violence. In a similar vein, Arriola and Johnson (2012) rely on a promising data collection, although it has not yet been released publicly. Further, the Quality of Elections Dataset (QED) offers information on unrest/violence, defined as physical abuses, overall violent clashes, or manhandling of persons on election-day and the campaigning period. It includes a categorical variable (0–3) indicating no/minor/moderate/major problems. However, the category definitions and thresholds are somewhat unclear, except that ongoing war qualifies as a major problem.

Perhaps most useful for a cross-regional analysis—and frequently used in prior work on election violence—is the National Elections Across Democracy and Autocracy Dataset (NELDA, Hyde and Marinov 2012). The Nelda dataset provides information on government harassment (variable nelda15) and civilian deaths (variable nelda33). However, these are aggregated across all three electoral stages (before, on, after election-day) and, again, are binary in nature, such that "deaths=1" hides meaningful variation in the intensity of violence. A third indicator (nelda31) is focused on the aftermath of elections but only records government use of force; leaves unclear if the use of violence resulted in any injuries or fatalities; and is conditional on protests, in other words does not record violence in the absence of protests. Similarly, Beaulieu (2014) provides data on violence only if protests occurred. Birch (2011) captures intimidation before but not after elections, and there is no information on whether the intimidation turned violent.

While all of these datasets were useful for the purpose of their studies and have paved the way for more research, data on election violence intensity disaggregated by electoral stages—as needed for this book—were not available.

Event counts from ACLED[5] and SCAD[6] data have also been used in a few studies.[7] However, there are notable drawbacks to using these media-based event datasets as a measure of election violence.[8] Further, ACLED makes it difficult, if not impossible, to objectively filter out election-related events because it does not contain an election-related indicator. Instead of an issue indicator, ACLED features one-sentence descriptions of each incident, and a portion of the descriptions are ambiguous as to whether the event is election-related. Consequently, ACLED data make it difficult to objectively filter out electoral from all other forms of violence, such as militia fights over territorial control, rebels establishing new bases, communal conflicts, harassment, and protesting unrelated to elections. Further, the conceptual notion of "conflict" events is quite broad, as even peace campaigns are included.

Using SCAD to capture election-related violence seems conceptually more appropriate than ACLED because SCAD data allow filtering for election-related events and violence. SCAD's event counts can be either entirely peaceful or violent. SCAD provides an estimate of deaths (no estimate of injuries). Some studies using SCAD data include nonviolent events, such as vandalism and newspaper raids (Smidt 2016, 232), which do not necessarily involve any physical force or harm. Moreover, SCAD data rely on fewer media sources than ACLED, increasing concerns about systematic underreporting.[9]

Since available data were not suitable for the analyses in this book, I collected original data with an emphasis on disaggregating how many people were affected in which way and in which stage of the election.

To collect original data on election violence—including the number of people killed or injured—I used the printed version of *Keesing's Record of World Events*. *Keesing's* provides an objective and detailed monthly digest of political, economic, and diplomatic affairs for countries around the world, written mostly by academics and journalists. It relies on a large variety of sources, including reputable international periodicals,[10] regional news outlets,[11] country-specific news providers,[12] and radio broadcasts[13] as well as election-related sources and other non-news sources.[14] It originated in 1758 as the *Annual Register* and has been published continuously since 1931.

Keesing's was chosen over alternative information sources because it provides consistent coverage over time, is reasonably detailed, and has been used in other prominent data collection efforts on elections[15] and conflict.[16] *Keesing's* is preferable over WND (Facts on File) and World News Connection (WNC) because *Keesing's* draws on WND as one of its sources and has many others. To get at national elections worldwide, *Keesing's* also has better coverage: WNC uses only local media (as opposed to national) and WND uses almost exclusively English-language sources.[17]

Data were collected through human coding. Importantly, human coding allows the dataset to reflect more accurately whether violence in a given incident was in fact election-related. Determining whether conflict had an electoral dimension was important; otherwise the data would pick up other types of ongoing conflict as well that just happen to occur during election times. For example, persistent terrorist violence perpetrated by the Tuareg in Mali and the Taliban in Afghanistan was excluded from the coding unless it was clearly election-related. Bombing a polling center is coded as election violence, while bombing market places is not. I decided against machine coding to ensure the electoral "quality" of the conflict and because the main interest was not in event counts but in violence intensity. Each entry was coded by two research assistants. One research assistant coded the entire dataset. The second coding was done by three other research assistants. In this second round of coding, each research assistant coded a world region of personal expertise. Subsequently, inter-coder reliability and cleaning was done by two graduate assistants in close consultation with the author. All research assistants were given background information on elections, election violence, and manipulation and were trained extensively in coding procedures. They received a codebook and a memo for reference. Throughout the coding and cleaning process, regular consultations assured timely review of data quality to ensure that uncertainties and any divergence in standards would be detected early. To ensure replicability and transparency, all violence codes are accompanied with page numbers from the printed *Keesing's* in the respective variable notes.

Comparing GEVD to other datasets reveals a high rate of agreement on whether or not election violence occurred, while GEVD also provides additional information. As noted above, probably the best and most widely used measure of election violence to date is *nelda33* from Hyde and Marinov (2012), which is a binary indicator of whether there was "significant violence involving civilian deaths immediately before, during, or after the election." To compare this to GEVD, I generate two binary indicators from the counts: GEVD *deaths* (coded 1 if any election-related deaths occurred before, during, or after the election, 0 otherwise) and GEVD *casualties* (coded 1 if any election-related deaths or injuries occurred before, during, or after the election, 0 otherwise).

Comparing nelda33 to GEVD measures, both the rate of violence overall and the rate of agreement on individual elections are high. Globally from 1990 to 2012, the rate of violent elections reported is 21 percent in *nelda33*, 21 percent in GEVD *deaths*, and 24 percent in GEVD *casualties*. The rate of agreement is 86 percent between *nelda33* and GEVD *deaths*, and it is 85 percent between *nelda33* and GEVD *casualties*. Put differently, the two datasets disagree in only 14 percent of individual elections. Examining this set of elections shows that there is no clear trend in terms of one metric or the other usually over- or undercounting: both datasets have about eighty elections in which they indicate violence but the other dataset does not. A review of cases suggests that both datasets have some drawbacks. *Nelda33* captures violence that is not necessarily election-related. For example, the 2011 election in the Central African Republic was held during an ongoing civil war, with many attacks and extrajudicial killings carried out by the Lord's Resistance Army. Violence during the 1999 election in Guinea-Bissau was largely due to civil war. Similarly, after the legislative election May 2002, civil war resumes in Congo (Brazzaville), but the violence was part of the ongoing civil war rather than election-related. This is in line with the nelda33 definition of violence "around" (before/during/after) elections but not necessarily *related* to the election. In other words, the *nelda33* concept and measure are consistent (valid), but GEVD provides a cleaner measure of election-*related* violence. On the other hand, a review of cases also shows that GEVD under-counts in a few elections where unrest is reported without any casualty estimates or when the link of violence to elections is not clear. This underlines the conservative coding strategy, erring on the side of caution to minimize false positives, which at times risks false negatives (marking a violent election as peaceful). Again looking through the cases, this seems to be largely an issue of missing one, two, or a handful of affected people; undercounting larger numbers of people affected is rare.

Rates of agreement between GEVD and other datasets are also high. For example, the rate of agreement between AEVD (*repression, violence*) and GEVD *casualties* is 81 percent for pre-election violence and 89 percent for post-election violence. The rate of agreement with another new potential indicator of election violence from V-Dem (*v2elpeace, v2elintim*) is lower (72 percent), but V-Dem's agreement is even lower with *nelda33* (69 percent), which suggests substantial differences in the conceptual understanding of electoral violence in V-Dem data. A review of cases shows that V-Dem's discrepancies with nelda33 and GEVD arise because V-Dem includes more civil war and general societal unrest that happens to occur at election time but is not necessarily election-related. Overall, these comparisons suggest that GEVD data capture electoral violence fairly well and is in line with other prominent datasets of election experts (Hyde and Marinov 2012) and region experts (Straus and Taylor 2012). To the degree that there are differences, GEVD tends to be a more conservative measure, cleaner of other forms of violence that occur during the election without being election-related, but at times undercounting casualties when none are given in the source documents (*Keesing's*).

Post-Election Loser Challenge Data

For the empirical analyses in chapters 3 and 4, I employ data on loser challenges. This provides information on whether the losing party or candidate challenged the announced election result. These data were collected for Africa and Latin

America because until recently the only public data on this issue was restricted to sub-Saharan Africa before 2006.[18] Information on loser challenges comes from comprehensive searches of newspapers and newswires using the OneSearch meta search engine, which also searches within the popular LexisNexis database. Searches specified the name of the country, a date range up to three months after the election, and the following search terms: *election, elect, electoral, result, reject, refuse, annul, dispute, challenge, announce, court, demonstration*. The binary variable loser challenge is coded 1 when the electoral loser challenged the outcome of the election, and 0 otherwise. Loser challenges can take the form of statements, court proceedings, or demonstrations. As a robustness check, I use similar data from V-Dem on whether the loser accepted the outcome, invert the four-point scale to code challenges, and then collapse that to a binary measure.

Technical Election Assistance Data (TEAD)

Data on United Nations technical election assistance comes from two sources. Data on such assistance from 1990 to 2003 comes from von Borzyskowski (2016), which itself relies on the UN's internal compilation of election assistance projects published in Ludwig (2004b). These data are supplemented—mainly for 2004–2012—with original data on UN technical election assistance projects. These additional data were compiled from the UN Secretary General's biennial reports on election assistance and the UN's websites for election assistance.[19] Both sets of sources include information on the country name, the election for which assistance was provided, and the type of assistance. Only technical election assistance (by far the most frequent type of UN assistance) was included in the analysis. Data were coded by two research assistants and coding discrepancies were resolved in consultation with the author. UN technical election assistance is coded 1 when the UN provided such support and 0 otherwise.

Again, comparing these original data to similar data collection efforts shows high correlations and suggests a valid and reliable measure. Lührmann (2016) collected data on UN election support from 2007 to 2014. These data cover any forms of support, including technical election assistance and other forms, and are coded from the biennial reports of the UN Secretary General. Comparing Lührmann (2016) data to my original data for the years 2007–2012 globally shows a rate of agreement of 92 percent. More closely examining the 8 percent of elections with disagreements worldwide reveals that there are about a dozen cases where Lührmann's data report UN assistance but my data do not; this is unsurprising, as Lührmann's data go beyond technical election assistance to include other forms of election assistance. Further, a couple of these discrepancies are

APPENDIX TABLE 1C.4   Sample: Elections in 74 countries in Africa and Latin America, 1990–2012

Algeria	Jamaica
Angola	Kenya
Argentina	Lesotho
Benin	Liberia
Bolivia	Libya
Botswana	Madagascar
Brazil	Malawi
Burkina Faso	Mali
Burundi	Mauritania
Cameroon	Mauritius
Cape Verde	Mexico
Central African Republic	Morocco
Chad	Mozambique
Chile	Namibia
Colombia	Nicaragua
Comoros	Niger
Congo (Brazzaville)	Nigeria
Costa Rica	Panama
Cote d'Ivoire	Paraguay
Cuba	Peru
Dem. Republic of the Congo	Rwanda
Djibouti	Senegal
Dominican Republic	Sierra Leone
Ecuador	Somalia
Egypt	South Africa
El Salvador	Sudan
Equatorial Guinea	Surinam
Ethiopia	Swaziland
Gabon	Tanzania
Gambia	Togo
Ghana	Trinidad and Tobago
Guatemala	Tunisia
Guinea	Uganda
Guinea-Bissau	Uruguay
Guyana	Venezuela
Haiti	Zambia
Honduras	Zimbabwe

UN projects that started after an election (post-election reforms) but ended years before the next election and are thus not coded in my data (to ensure temporal priority of UN assistance before violence). In addition, about a dozen elections in my data record technical election assistance while Lührmann's data do not. In each of these cases, there are UN project documents or similar documentation showing technical support was indeed provided (but was apparently not listed in the SG biennial reports).

Appendix to Chapter 3

APPENDIX TABLE 3A.1 Effect of observer condemnation on post-election loser challenge

| | LATIN AMERICA AND AFRICA | | AFRICA | |
	(1)	**(2)**	**(3)**	**(4)**
Condemnation	1.408***	1.360***	1.382***	1.558**
	(0.397)	(0.436)	(0.475)	(0.551)
Fraud		0.176		−0.272
		(0.321)		(0.403)
Loser vote share	0.017	0.020	0.032*	0.034*
	(0.014)	(0.015)	(0.019)	(0.020)
Judicial independence	0.054	0.037	0.093	0.079
	(0.197)	(0.204)	(0.248)	(0.255)
Executive constraints	−0.125	−0.115	−0.001	−0.006
	(0.123)	(0.129)	(0.127)	(0.138)
Economic development	−0.080	−0.070	0.400*	0.438*
	(0.172)	(0.174)	(0.225)	(0.235)
Poll type	0.361	0.369	0.503*	0.536*
	(0.230)	(0.233)	(0.294)	(0.298)
Incumbent lost	−0.818**	−0.781**	−0.072	0.045
	(0.376)	(0.388)	(0.477)	(0.502)
Observations	239	235	149	146
Clusters	65	65	44	44
LL	−119.68	−117.41	−83.88	−81.05

Notes: The table reports estimates from logit models. The dependent variable is post-election loser challenge. The unit of observation is the national election. The sample is restricted to observed elections. Standard errors are clustered on country. ***, **, and * indicate significance at the 1%, 5%, and 10% levels.

APPENDIX TABLE 3A.2   Effect of loser challenge on post-election violence

	LATIN AMERICA AND AFRICA		AFRICA	
	(1)	(2)	(3)	(4)
Predicting violence intensity (count)				
Post-election loser challenge	2.726**	2.480**	3.135**	2.725
	(1.135)	(1.006)	(1.578)	(1.928)
Fraud		3.328**		1.806
		(1.359)		(1.694)
Executive constraints	−0.745***	−0.187	−1.140**	−0.902
	(0.260)	(0.576)	(0.535)	(0.757)
Post-conflict	−1.679	0.871	−1.135	0.061
	(1.669)	(1.436)	(2.322)	(2.527)
Economic development	0.916	1.403***	1.828	2.326
	(0.861)	(0.538)	(1.519)	(1.620)
Natural resources	−0.032	−0.091	−0.002	−0.031
	(0.142)	(0.075)	(0.117)	(0.124)
Ethnic fractionalization	−1.416	2.964	5.673*	7.835**
	(2.814)	(4.456)	(3.084)	(3.874)
Population size	0.965***	0.732*	0.445	0.567
	(0.316)	(0.432)	(0.305)	(0.370)
Poll type	0.051	−0.738	0.893	0.314
	(0.543)	(0.530)	(0.693)	(1.182)
Pre-election casualties	0.026	0.042**	0.002	0.007
	(0.018)	(0.017)	(0.006)	(0.023)
Loser vote share	−0.063	−0.003	0.045	0.071**
	(0.038)	(0.050)	(0.032)	(0.035)
Predicting zero violence				
Post-conflict	−0.871	1.070	−0.879	−0.427
	(0.803)	(2.604)	(1.356)	(1.629)
Economic development	0.640	2.718	0.519	0.710
	(0.428)	(2.956)	(0.413)	(0.503)
Log α	2.045**	2.973***	2.348***	2.417***
	(0.974)	(0.316)	(0.611)	(0.719)
Observations	240	236	150	147
Clusters	65	65	44	44
LL	−235.84	−233.23	−184.83	−183.44

Notes: The table reports estimates from count models (zero-inflated negative binomial models). The dependent variable is the count of election-related casualties in the three months after election-day. The unit of observation is the national election. The sample is restricted to observed elections. Standard errors are clustered on country. ***, **, and * indicate significance at the 1%, 5%, and 10% levels.

APPENDIX TABLE 3A.3 Effect of observer condemnation on post-election violence, accounting for potential endogeneity

	(1)	(2)	(3)	(4)
Main model predicting violence				
Condemnation	0.424	0.358	0.378	0.389
	(0.286)	(0.307)	(0.310)	(0.317)
Fraud		0.086	0.082	0.080
		(0.143)	(0.144)	(0.145)
Executive constraints	−0.035	−0.030	−0.030	−0.030
	(0.033)	(0.030)	(0.030)	(0.030)
Post-conflict	−0.037	−0.045	−0.045	−0.045
	(0.141)	(0.144)	(0.144)	(0.144)
Economic development	−0.070	−0.066	−0.067	−0.067
	(0.063)	(0.063)	(0.063)	(0.063)
Natural resources	0.004	0.004	0.004	0.004
	(0.010)	(0.010)	(0.010)	(0.010)
Ethnic fractionalization	0.433	0.432	0.433	0.433
	(0.266)	(0.265)	(0.265)	(0.265)
Population size	0.053	0.055	0.055	0.055
	(0.044)	(0.044)	(0.044)	(0.044)
Loser vote share	0.014***	0.015***	0.015***	0.015***
	(0.005)	(0.005)	(0.005)	(0.005)
Poll type	0.042	0.043	0.043	0.042
	(0.059)	(0.058)	(0.058)	(0.058)
Pre-election casualties (logged)	0.269***	0.266***	0.266***	0.266***
	(0.078)	(0.080)	(0.080)	(0.080)
First stage predicting condemnation				
Pre-election casualties (logged)	0.099	0.099	0.103	0.101
	(0.079)	(0.079)	(0.078)	(0.075)
Fraud	1.130***	1.136***	1.092***	1.063***
	(0.228)	(0.229)	(0.256)	(0.252)
ODA per capita	−0.065	−0.065	−0.063	−0.065
	(0.115)	(0.115)	(0.121)	(0.119)
First multi-party election	0.031	0.030	−0.001	−0.000
	(0.332)	(0.330)	(0.319)	(0.317)
Economic development			−0.099	−0.086
			(0.158)	(0.157)
Turnover				−0.370
				(0.268)
Rho	0.03	0.05	0.04	0.04
Wald test of independent equations ($\rho = 0$), $Pr(\chi^2)$	0.56	0.09	0.21	0.29
Observations	354	354	354	354
Clusters	70	70	70	70
LL	−614.75	−614.57	−613.97	−613.08

Notes: The table reports estimates from treatment effects models, which are linear regressions with an endogenous binary treatment variable in the first stage. The endogenous variable is observer condemnation. The dependent variable is post-election violence, i.e., the logged number of election-related casualties in the three months after election-day. The unit of observation is the national election. The sample is restricted to observed elections. Robust standard errors are clustered on country. ***, **, and * indicate significance at the 1%, 5%, and 10% levels.

Notes

INTRODUCTION

1. "What do election observers do?" *The Economist,* 21 June 2017.

2. Hyde 2007, 2008, 2010, 2011a, 2011b; Bjornlund, Bratton, and Gibson 1992, 408; McCoy, Garber, and Pastor 1991, 107–13; Garber and Cowan 1993; Donno 2013, 101–4; Kelley 2011, 2012, 129, 154. Some have raised caveats about the *extent* of positive effects (Kelley 2012, 168–69; Carothers 1997, 20–27; Bush and Prather 2017) and noted strategic adaptation by the incumbent (Simpser and Donno 2012; Ichino and Schündeln 2012; Hyde and O'Mahony 2010).

3. iPoll Databank 2005, 2009, 2011.

4. Carothers 2015b. See also Kumar 1998, 6; Kumar and Ottaway 1997, 38.

5. In this book, I use "(national) election commission" or "NEC" as a shorthand for election management body (EMB), i.e., the main institution responsible for administering electoral processes. EMBs can take several institutional forms, including election commissions (NECs), election councils, and election boards.

6. Election assistance can be technical, logistical, or financial and often involves several of these aspects. It often involves the election commission. I use "technical" election assistance to distinguish it more clearly from election observation/monitoring. I use "election assistance" and "technical election assistance" interchangeably. In this book, election "support" or "aid" means both technical election assistance and election observation.

7. Observer condemnation measures whether any reputable international observer group seriously questioned the winner of the election or the legitimacy of the process. Most observer reports are nuanced, include some criticism, and note some room for improvement; only those that are overtly negative are considered a condemnation. See Hyde and Marinov 2014, 343; data are from Hyde and Marinov 2012.

8. Hyde and Marinov 2012 and technical assistance dataset (see appendix 1C).

9. On the history of UN election assistance, see Ludwig 2004a; von Borzys-kowski 2016.

10. Organization for Economic Cooperation and Development/Development Assistance Committee (OECD/DAC), all donors, constant US dollars, sectors 150 and 15151. See stats.oecd.org/Index.aspx?DataSetCode=Table5# and www.oecd.org/dac/stats/documentupload/Budget%20identifier%20purpose%20codes_EN_Apr%202016.pdf, accessed 18 September 2018.

11. Norris 2017, 73.

12. UN 2010, 1.

13. UNDP 2012.

14. Abbarno 2017.

15. Norris 2017, 71.

16. Carothers 2015a, 72.

17. United Nations Human Rights Council 2010.

18. UNDP 2009, 2011; USAID 2010, 2013; ECDPM 2012; Atwood 2012.

19. Claes 2017; Claes and von Borzyskowski 2018.

20. EC-UNDP Joint Task Force on Electoral Assistance 2011 and www.usip.org/events/preventing-electoral-violence-in-africa-tools-policymakers, accessed 18 September 2018;

see also www.usip.org/education-training/courses/preventing-electoral-violence-asia-tools-practitioners-and-policymakers, accessed 18 September 2018.

21. Fischer 2002; IFES 2004, 2014; Kammerud 2011; Cyllah 2014.

22. IDEA 2013, 2015; Herrberg et al. 2012.

23. EISA 2009, 17, 14–19; AU Panel of the Wise 2010; UNDP 2014, 42.

24. Claes 2017; Claes and von Borzyskowski 2018; UNDP 2009, 51–93; Kumar and Ottaway 1997; Kumar 1998; Gillies 2011.

25. Three of the most prominent authors in this field—Thomas Carothers, Larry Diamond, and Peter Burnell—do not explore this phenomenon in their work. See Carothers 2004, 2006a, 2006b, 2010; Diamond 2008; Burnell 2000. But see Daxecker 2012, 2014.

26. Collier 2009, 20–21.

27. Author's calculation based on World Bank (2012) data and original Global Election Violence Data (GEVD) data.

28. Hyde and Marinov 2014; Hafner-Burton, Hyde, and Jablonski 2014.

29. Arriola and Johnson 2012.

30. Author's calculation based on data from Hyde and Marinov 2012, Nelda data, nelda11.

31. Author's calculation based on original data and Global Election Violence Data (GEVD).

32. Authors' calculation based on data from Beck et al. 2001.

33. I thank Thomas Risse for suggesting this term to me.

34. Hyde and O'Mahony 2010; Hyde 2011b; Kelley 2012.

35. Beaulieu 2014, 64; Beaulieu and Hyde 2009; Kelley 2011.

36. Beaulieu 2014, 73; Hyde and Marinov 2014; Kuhn 2012.

37. Daxecker 2012; Smidt 2016. Luo and Rozenas (2018) assume the condemnation-violence link to motivate a formal model.

38. For a discussion of ACLED and SCAD data quality to capture election-related violence, see appendix 1C; Eck 2012; von Borzyskowski and Wahman 2018.

39. Daxecker (2012, note 25) acknowledges explicitly that observer fraud reports are not measured.

40. Only 41 percent of observed elections with serious fraud are condemned by observers in Africa. Author's calculation based on the fraud measure used in these articles, i.e. State Department Human Rights reports issued up to a year after the election (see Daxecker 2012, 510; and Smidt 2016, 232–33; data from Kelley 2010 QED).

41. Atwood 2012, 22.

42. Kelley 2012, 72.

43. See Hyde and Marinov's (2012) Nelda data, nelda47.

44. Norris 2014, 203.

45. Ludwig 1995, 2004a, 2004b; Darnolf 2011; Soudriette and Pilon 2007.

46. Kumar 1998; Kammerud 2011; Santiso 2002; Steinorth 2011, 318–19.

47. Lührmann 2018.

48. Birch and Muchlinski 2018.

49. Birch and Muchlinski 2018, 397.

50. Norris 2017, 275.

51. Carothers and Samet-Marram 2015.

52. Norris 2014, ch. 5.

53. For accountability and credibility around elections, see the contributions by Robert Pastor and others in Schedler, Diamond, and Plattner 1999.

54. Norris 2014, 8–9, 21, 65; Norris, Frank, and Martínez 2015, 5.

55. Norris 2014, 2015, 2017. Note that researchers have used the term *election integrity* in earlier work; see, for example, Birch 2008; Beaulieu 2012.

56. Bjornlund 2004, 94–98; Elklit and Svensson 1997; Geisler 1993.

57. International organizations (IOs) include both international governmental (IGOs) and nongovernmental organizations (NGOs); see Pevehouse and von Borzyskowski 2016. Of course, IOs could potentially influence election violence through more ways than election support. One option is enforcing credible commitments, although that is rarely and unevenly done; see von Borzyskowski and Vabulas 2019. The book examines election support is one important mechanism.

58. As detailed in chapter 1, my focus is explicitly on reputable observer groups rather than facade monitors, that is, lenient groups with little monitoring effort and even less willingness to criticize elections. I use election "monitoring" and "observation" interchangeably.

59. Note that "manipulation" can encompass both violent and nonviolent means, whereas "violence" always entails physical force and "fraud" does not.

60. Author's calculation based on original GEVD data and V-Dem data, variable v2elembcap.

61. This is Colombia's 2002 election; the natural log of 45 is 3.8.

62. This is Angola's 1992 election; the natural log of 1,000 is 6.9.

63. Strictly speaking, *Latin America* refers to Spanish, Portuguese, and French-speaking countries and does not include English or Dutch-speaking countries like Guyana, Suriname, Trinidad and Tobago, and Jamaica. Thus the term *Latin America and the Caribbean* (LAC) is more accurate. For simplicity, I use "Latin America" as a synonym.

64. Bekoe 2009, 2012; Bekoe and Burchard 2017; Fjelde and Höglund 2016; Opitz, Fjelde, and Höglund 2013; Burchard 2015; Taylor, Pevehouse, and Straus 2017. One exception is Hafner-Burton, Hyde, and Jablonski 2014, 2018.

65. Note that selecting regions where support is more prevalent is *not* selecting on the independent variable because elections in these regions vary widely in the extent of international support. While selecting on the independent variable would be not be problematic per se, it would call for different inferential statements in terms of generalizability and certainty (King, Keohane, and Verba 1994, 137–38). However, both Africa and Latin America vary widely in the key explanatory variables.

66. Author's compilation based on original data as well as von Borzyskowski 2016, see appendix 1C; map made with Weidmann et al.'s (2010) cshapes package in R.

67. Author's compilation based on original data as well as von Borzyskowski 2016; Hyde and Marinov 2011, nelda46. Nelda46 has some missing values, thus reducing the number of observations here compared to figure I.3. Region coding with Arel-Bundock's R package countrycode, except that I group Canada and the U.S. with Europe instead of Latin America.

68. The focus on reputable observers as opposed to any international or domestic groups is based on prior research, as explained below.

69. Huntington 1991; Peeler 2009, 49.

70. Hagopian and Mainwaring 2005.

71. Lynch and Crawford 2011; Bratton and van de Walle 1997; Lindberg 2006.

72. Diamond 2011.

73. Von Borzyskowski and Vabulas 2019; OAS 2001a; on governance charters, see Börzel and van Hüllen 2015.

74. See Aniekwe and Atuobi 2016; and www.oas.org/eomdatabase/default.aspx?lang=en.

75. Author's compilation based on V-Dem data version 6.2, Coppedge et al. 2015.

76. For example, in Latin America, Haiti's election commission has had unusually low capacity impacting the organization of elections throughout the country in the 1990s and 2000s, along with serious deficits in Guyana and El Salvador in the early 1990s.

77. OSCE 2005, 1.

78. Dahl 1989, 221, emphasis added.

79. Kaplan 1997; Zakaria 2004; Pastor 1999b; Schmitter and Karl 1991.

80. Bratton 1998, 52.

81. Rod Nordland, Azam Ahmed, and Matthew Rosenberg, "Afghan Turnout Is High as Voters Defy the Taliban," *New York Times*, 6 April 2014, available at http://nyti.ms/1oA6bd1, accessed 6 April 2014.

82. Burchard 2015, 156–57.

83. Von Borzyskowski and Kuhn 2017.

84. Höglund and Piyarathne 2009, 299–300.

85. Wilkinson 2004.

86. Anders Kelto, "Violence Haunts Zimbabwe Ahead of Elections," NPR News, 19 May 2012, available at www.npr.org/2012/05/19/153076969/violence-haunts-zimbabwe-ahead-of-elections, accessed 6 April 2014.

87. Bratton 2008; Gutierrez-Romero and LeBas 2016; Mac-Ikemenjima 2017.

88. Such elections include Burundi 2010 and Kenya 2007, for instance; see Travaglianti 2014, ch. 6; Burchard 2015, 14; Bekoe and Burchard 2017; Hafner-Burton, Hyde, and Jablonski 2018.

89. Von Borzyskowski and Kuhn 2017.

90. Downs 1957.

91. Bratton 2008, 626; see also Höglund and Piyarathne 2009, 299; Birch 2010.

92. Bratton 2008, 626.

93. Höglund 2009, 417.

94. Pausewang, Trondvall, and Aalen 2002.

95. Chris McGreal and Julian Borger, "Mugabe Has Declared War and We Will Not Be Part of That War," *The Guardian*, 22 June 2008, available at www.theguardian.com/world/2008/jun/23/zimbabwe3, accessed 25 June 2010.

96. Bratton 2008, 626; Höglund 2009, 417; Klopp and Kamungi 2007/08, 15; Höglund and Piyarathne 2009, 299; Birch 2010.

97. Höglund 2009, 417; Klopp and Kamungi 2007/08, 15.

98. Pyne-Mercier et al. 2011.

99. Klopp and Kamungi 2007/08, 15.

100. Sisk 2008, 5; Hoeffler and Reynal-Querol 2003.

101. UNDP 2009, 5; Collier et al. 2003; Collier 2009; Patino and Velasco 2006.

1. CREDIBLE ELECTION THEORY

1. For introductions to the concept of election violence, see Höglund 2009; Straus and Taylor 2012.

2. Straus and Taylor 2012; Daxecker 2012, 2014; Birch and Muchlinski 2018.

3. Some countries shaded in white did not hold direct national elections since 1990: China, Saudi Arabia, Qatar, and Eritrea. Author's calculation based on original data, the Global Election Violence Data (GEVD). For details on data collection, see appendix 1C.

4. For example, in the U.S., Congresswoman Gabrielle Giffords was shot in the head at point-blank range in 2010 after her recent reelection. While Giffords survived, six other people died and twelve were injured. This may have been part of a rise of negative partisanship over the last few decades (Abramowitz and Webster 2016). In France, supporters of the far-right National Front party attacked and killed two immigrants, Ibrahim Ali and Brahim Bouraam, during their election activities in the 1995 presidential election. In the Netherlands, far-right LPF party leader and potential future prime minister Pim Fortuyn was assassinated during the 2002 campaign. In Spain, ETA has used violence to disrupt several elections.

5. Libya's 2012 election was violent as well, but it was the only direct election since 1965.

6. Straus and Taylor 2012, 29–30.

7. Burchard 2015.

8. Laakso 2007, 231–32, 243–44; Makumbe 2002, 91; Masunungure 2011, 55–57; Mehler 2009, 204–6.

9. Lehoucq 2003.

10. Höglund 2009; Birch 2011; Arriola and Johnson 2011; Hyde and Marinov 2014.

11. Schedler 2002; Birch 2011.

12. Cunningham, Dahl, and Fruge 2017.

13. Ritter and Conrad 2016.

14. Author's calculation based on original dataset, the Global Election Violence Data (GEVD).

15. Rod Nordland and Matthew Rosenberg, "Credibility of Afghan Vote in Doubt as Observers," *New York Times*, 29 March 2014; Adam Gallagher, "Afghan Voters Exhibit Enthusiasm Despite Election Flaws: Four Million Afghans Overcame Violence and Underperforming Election Administration to Cast Their Ballots," *USIP Olive Branch*, 6 November 2018, available at www.usip.org/blog/2018/11/afghan-voters-exhibit-enthusiasm-despite-election-flaws, accessed 7 November 2018.

16. "Boko Haram Threatens to Disrupt Nigeria Poll," Al Jazeera, 18 February 2015; "Boko Haram Kills 41 in Attack to Disrupt Nigeria Presidential Election," Associated Press, 28 March 2015.

17. Straus and Taylor 2012, 20; Wilkinson and Haid 2009.

18. Wilkinson 2004.

19. IFES 2004, 4–5.

20. Bratton 2008, 626; Höglund 2009, 417; Klopp and Kamungi 2007/08, 15; Höglund and Piyarathne 2009, 299; Birch 2010.

21. Pausewang, Tronvoll, and Aalen 2002; Chris McGreal and Julian Borger, "Mugabe Has Declared War and We Will Not Be Part of That War," *The Guardian,* 22 June 2008, available at www.theguardian.com/world/2008/jun/23/zimbabwe3, accessed 6 November 2018.

22. Travaglianti 2014, ch. 6; Burchard 2015, 14; Wilkinson and Haid 2009.

23. See Seeberg, Wahman, and Skaaning 2018.

24. Pastor 1999b; Lindberg 2006, 43–44.

25. See Riker 1983, 62; Przeworski 1991, 15; Nadeau and Blais 1993, 553.

26. Schedler 2001, 71; Anderson et al. 2005.

27. Anderson 2005 et al., 109.

28. Anderson 2005 et al., 101–104; Fuchs, Guidorossi, and Svensson 1998, 345.

29. Moehler 2009.

30. Focusing on the strongest runner-up is a simplifying assumption. While potentially all losing candidates or parties could challenge the result, in reality only the major contestants and often only the first runner-up have sufficient incentives to challenge result. Alternatively, we could conceptualize the "loser" as a group of losing contestants or further complicate the setup by modeling coordination dynamics within this group. The basic intuition in terms of interacting with the winner, however, remains the same.

31. In practice, this can precipitate the holding of new elections.

32. Assuming that both players are interested in winning the electoral competition, the costs of fighting would need to be prohibitively high to prevent either player from fighting. If fighting costs are low, both sides have a credible threat to fight. When conflict costs are high, then war need not happen. However, in the case of election violence, the use of force can be relatively small, such as a fight between the police and protesters, retaliatory violence against communities or assassination of individuals.

33. Chacon, Robinson, and Torvik 2011, 366.

34. Chacon, Robinson, and Torvik 2011; Londregan and Vindigni 2006; Wilkinson 2004; Steele 2011.

35. Londregan and Vindigni 2006, 25.

36. Chernykh (2014) and Beaulieu (2014) have examined these domestic post-election dynamics in some detail.

37. State Department 1992, 25, 29.

38. Arriola and Johnson 2011; Hafner-Burton, Hyde, and Jablonski 2014; Taylor, Pevehouse, and Straus 2017.

39. USAID 2010, 8–17; UNDP 2009, 7–18; Cyllah 2014.

40. See Hafner-Burton, Hyde, and Jablonski 2014; Krieger 2000; Kriger 2005; Klopp and Kamungi 2007/08; Wilkinson 2004; Bhasin and Gandhi 2013; Chaturvedi 2005; Fearon and Laitin 2003.

41. Kumar 1998; Kumar and de Zeeuw 2006; Kumar and Ottaway 1997, 1998; Lopez-Pintor 1997, 51; Gillies 2011.

42. Kumar 1998, 1, 5–7.

43. Kumar and Ottaway 1998, 229.

44. Collier 2009, 20–21; Collier and Rohner 2008.

45. Arriola 2013; Laakso 2007; Straus 2011; Wilkinson 2004; Wilkinson and Haid 2009; Varshney 2001.

46. On post-election protests—which can remain peaceful—see Kuntz and Thompson 2009; Thompson and Kuntz 2004; Bratton 2008; Kuhn 2012.

47. See Kuran 1995, 247; Tucker 2007; Kuntz and Thompson 2009, 56–257.

48. From a methodological perspective, including pre-election fraud to predict pre-election violence would induce simultaneity bias, as fraud would not temporally be prior to violence here, making inference problematic.

49. On foreign interference in election outcomes, Corstange and Marinov (2012, 655) calculate that there have been about two interventions by foreign powers per year. In recent years, about fifty national elections take place each year, which means that foreign meddling would affect about 4 percent of all elections.

50. See Bjornlund, Cowan, and Gallery 2007; Fischer 2007; Höglund 2009; Reilly 2002; Sisk and Reynolds 1998.

51. See Arriola and Johnson 2011, 41; Hafner-Burton, Hyde, and Jablonski 2014, 172.

52. Taylor, Pevehouse, and Straus 2017.

53. Hyde 2012.

54. Hyde 2011b, 2012, 45.

55. Hyde 2012, 58.

56. Hyde and Marinov 2012.

57. See Kerr 2013, 2014; Kerr and Lührmann 2017.

58. Höglund, Jarstad, and Kovacs 2009.

59. Kerr 2013; von Borzyskowski 2016.

60. Hyde 2012.

61. See www.ec-undp-electoralassistance.org/blog/2017/12/20/liberia-organizes-a-two-day-refresher-training-workshop-for-the-necs-hearing-clerks-and-hearing-officers/.

62. Von Borzyskowski 2016.

63. Hyde 2011b, 76.

64. Kelley 2012, 72.

65. Hyde 2011b.

66. For deterring fraud on election-day, see Alvarez, Hall, and Hyde 2008, 211; Hyde 2007. Note that some irregularities may just be displaced into neighboring, unobserved electoral districts (Ichino and Schündeln 2012).

67. Kammerud 2011, 163, emphasis in original.

68. Simpser 2013; Bjornlund 2004, 281–83; Beaulieu and Hyde 2009, 400–401; Kelley 2012, 78–80.

69. Kelley 2012, 100–101.

70. Hyde 2007, 2011b.

71. "Long Term and EU Observation Mission Statement Condemning Violent Protest," EU Press Statement for Guyana, 1 March 2001.

72. Tucker 2007.

73. See Donno 2010, 615–16; Donno 2013.

74. Von Borzyskowski and Vabulas 2019.

75. Hellquist 2014.

76. Hyde 2011b, 100–125.

77. Hyde 2011b, 120.

78. For detailed background to technical assistance, see Ludwig 1995, 2004; Kammerud 2011; Vickery 2011; Norris 2014, 201–2; Norris 2017, 65.

79. IO monitors usually issue press statements about the validity of the election process and outcome shortly after the election takes place. Longer statements, containing details and recommendations, are issued weeks after the election, and interim statements also may be issued depending on context. For simplicity, "report" here denotes any authoritative public statement by monitors after the election.

80. Hyde and Marinov 2014, 337.

81. See Carothers 1997, 23–25; Hyde 2012, 53.

82. Robertson 2015; Bush and Prather 2017.

83. Most manipulation is executed by incumbents and most incumbents win elections. See Gandhi and Lust-Okar 2009, 412; Simpser 2013, 76; Beaulieu and Hyde 2009, 400–402.

84. See Tucker 2007; Przeworski 1991.

85. See Kuntz and Thompson 2009, 256–57; Kuran 1995, 247; Trejo 2014.

86. Lohmann 1994, 50.

87. See Tucker 2007; Przeworski 1991, 2006; Weingast 1997.

88. Lührmann 2016, 2018.

89. Vickery 2011.

90. Birch 2011, 122.

91. Norris 2015, 151–52, 158.

92. Norris 2015, 159.

93. Opitz, Fjelde, and Höglund 2013.

94. Offe 1999, summarized in Warren 1999, 6.

95. Warren 1999, 7.

96. Laakso 2007; see also Fearon and Laitin 2003, 86.

97. Interview with Elizabeth Cote, IFES country director Guinea.

98. For example, IFES organized soccer matches in East Timor 2007 to "encourage friendships across clubs" and "promote peace." BELUN-EVER report No. 4, released 9 August 2007, 6. As for their impact on attitudes and behavior, local civil society organizations (who had implemented these matches) noted "youth showing respect for each other at parties where there were previous tendencies for violence to occur." BELUN EVER in Timor-Leste Final Report, 21 December 2007, 9.

99. Pastor 1999b.

100. Interview in Aljazeera, available at http://aje.me/ZZ3NOg.

101. On the color revolutions, see Tucker 2007; Thompson and Kuntz 2004; Kuntz and Thompson 2009; Hyde and Marinov 2014; Kuhn 2012.

102. Missingness on control variables reduces the sample in some of the regressions.

103. For multi-round elections, only the first round is coded; follow-up rounds are not coded because in practice it often remains unclear in such cases to which round violence is related, which risks double/multiple-counting and thus inflating the actual number of distinct cases.

104. Hyde and Marinov 2012, variable *nelda11*.

105. Hafner-Burton, Hyde, and Jablonski 2014, 167; Hyde and Marinov 2014, 340; Norris 2014, 156; Fjelde and Höglund 2016, 312; Hafner-Burton, Hyde, and Jablonski 2018, 471.

106. State Dept. Human Rights reports are usually issued in February or March of the subsequent year. Fraud measures based on that are in Kelley 2010 (QED); Daxecker 2012, 510; Smidt 2016, 232–33.

107. For example, sources contained in *Keesing's Record of World Events*; see appendix 1C.

108. Donno 2013, 203; Beaulieu 2014, 143.

109. Peace Research Institute Oslo (PRIO)'s Social Disturbance Database.

110. Long 1997.

111. For a similar application, see Hultman, Kathman, and Shannon 2014.

112. Kumar and Ottaway 1998; Kumar 1998; Gillies 2011.

113. Flores and Nooruddin 2016, ch. 7.

114. I say "treatment" in quotation marks because this language is usually used for random assignment (in experiments), but this book does not use random assignment.

115. Some have been successful in teaming up with individual observer groups for random assignment to examine within-country variation for individual elections. See Hyde 2007, 2010, 2011b.

116. Von Borzyskowski 2016.

117. These models build on prior research about selection (Hyde (2011, 77); von Borzyskowski 2016).

118. Imbens and Rubin 2015; using etregress in Stata 14.

119. For a similar application on UN election assistance, see Lührmann 2016. The outcome model (predicting violence intensity) uses a linear regression augmented with the endogenous treatment. To accommodate this model, the dependent variable is the logged casualty count.

120. Hyde and Marinov 2012.

121. For data sources and coding, see the appendix to this chapter.

122. Lührmann 2016.

123. Having attempted to collect UN project budget data consistently has proven unsuccessful as information varies even within individual projects and only a small share of projects documents offer such information in the first place. I leave these efforts to future research.

124. ICAI 2012, 8; Lührmann 2018, 2; Birch and Muchlinski 2018, 392; Bjornlund 2004, 54; Ludwig 1995, 342–43; UNDP 2012, 135; von Borzyskowski 2016.

125. Birch and Muchlinski 2018, 392.

2. SHAPING THE ELECTORAL ENVIRONMENT

1. Arriola and Johnson 2011, 2.

2. Collier 2009; Collier et al. 2003; Kumar and Ottaway 1998; Kumar 1998; Gillies 2011; Flores and Nooruddin 2016, ch. 7.

3. For count data, standard linear regression tends to produce inefficient and biased estimates (Long 1997), so standard OLS models are not run.

4. In the five hundred elections in 130 non-advanced democracies from 1990 to 2003 worldwide, 67 percent had observation and 18 percent had technical assistance. Technical support has become more frequent since the early 2000s. See von Borzyskowski 2016, 266.

5. The number of observations used in the analysis is lower than in the full sample (appendix table 1C.2) and varies across columns due to missing information in the observation variable (based on Nelda data) and some of the control variables.

6. Daxecker 2014, 238.

7. Another potential explanation for the difference in results is that Daxecker (2014) separates out election-day from the period before election-day. However, even replicating the models with separate measures of the dependent variables results in negative correlations for both pre-election minus election-day and election-day itself.

8. I use information criteria from model fit statistics to compare the standard and the zero-inflated models because recent work by Wilson (2015) has shown that the Vuong test is inappropriate for testing zero inflation because the negative binomial is not a nested model of the zero-inflated negative binomial. Xu et al. (2015) suggest that the Akaike Information Criterion (AIC) can be used to choose between these models and outperforms the Vuong test.

9. The alternative count models are standard negative binomial, standard Poisson, and zero-inflated Poisson.

10. In this specification, the coefficient of interest loses significance in models 5, 7, and 8. However, this is due to reduced sample size (and thus less statistical power) rather than the changed control variable.

11. Collier 2009.

12. Hyde 2011b.

13. Hyde 2011b.

14. Von Borzyskowski 2016.

15. Hyde 2011b, 77.

16. Von Borzyskowski 2016.

17. UNDP 2009.

18. Fortna 2003, 101.

19. I use Stata's etregress command with maximum likelihood estimation; to accommodate this model, the dependent variable (casualty count) is logged.

20. In model 5, observation is not an endogenous treatment variable because only one variable at a time can be modeled as endogenous.

21. In column 3 the Wald test is not significant, but note that all three predictors of selection added to columns 4 and 5 are important (those are *wealth, previously observed*, and the time trend.

22. Carothers 1997, 18.

23. For pre-election violence at these elections, see *Keesing's Record of World Events*, pp. 38084, 43892, 38898.

24. Ihonvbere 1996, 358.

25. Asunka et al. 2017.

26. Lansana Fofana, "Politics-Guinea: Violence Mars Elections Campaign," 11 December 1998, Inter Press Service.

27. *Keesing's Record of World Events*, pp. 39626, 39674, 42659.

28. State Department Human Rights Report, Guinea 1998.

29. The UN had provided assistance for the 2002 elections at the end of the civil war. While the 2007 elections were organized by domestic institutions, they were funded about 70 percent by the international community.

30. Almami Cyllah, IFES' Africa regional director, "Talking Points for International Peace Institute's Conference on Elections in Africa: Challenges and Prospects," New York, 19 July 2011.

31. GEVD; *Keesing's Record of World Events*, p. 40934.

32. IFES 2009.

33. European Union Election Observation Mission 2007a, 5, 20, 21.

34. UNDP 2005, 7–10; IFES 2009, 1, 3, 5.

35. European Union Election Observation Mission 2007a, 18.

36. European Union Election Observation Mission 2007a, 17.

37. IFES 2009.

38. Almami Cyllah, "Talking Points for International Peace Institute's Conference on Elections in Africa: Challenges and Prospects," New York, 19 July 2011.

39. UNDP 2009, 87.

40. UNDP 2009.

41. Burchard 2015, 108–9.

42. Claes and von Borzyskowski 2017, 2018.

43. Fromayan 2008, 41.

44. I thank both UNMIL and UNDP staff for sharing expertise and background information during interviews in Monrovia in March and November 2017.

45. See www.ec-undp-electoralassistance.org/blog/2017/12/20/liberia-organizes-a-two-day-refresher-training-workshop-for-the-necs-hearing-clerks-and-hearing-officers/.

3. THE DARK SIDE

1. Hyde 2011b; Hyde and Marinov 2014, 343; Hyde and Marinov 2012, nelda47; Hyde 2012, 45.

2. Hyde and Marinov 2014, 340; Hafner-Burton, Hyde, and Jablonski 2014, 167.

3. See Arriola and Johnson 2011, 41; and Hafner-Burton, Hyde, and Jablonski 2014, 172.

4. Taylor, Pevehouse, and Straus 2017, 406, 408–9; see also Straus and Taylor 2012, 20–21.

5. Follow-up analyses also test for—and cast doubt on—endogeneity more directly.

6. In column 2, condemnation and fraud are jointly significant; the inclusion of fraud increase multicollinearity.

7. When using a hurdle estimator for all models (logit and negative binomial), the coefficient of interest is still positive but reduces in significance. However, the model fit statistics indicate that the negative binomial model is not preferred.

8. Vogt et al. 2015.

9. V-Dem variable e_v2xel_frefair_3C. Note that this fraud measure, like many others, is possibly post-treatment, in contrast to the main measure of concerns about election fraud during the pre-election period from the main analyses.

10. Kelley 2010 (DIEM variable maxA1).

11. Tracy Wilkinson, "In Honduras, Vote Results Are Disputed." *Los Angeles Times*, 26 November 2013, A3.

12. Replicating these analyses with V-Dem data on loser challenges (binary or 5-point scale variable) yields similar results.

13. Chernykh 2014; Beaulieu 2014; Hyde and Marinov 2014.

14. This is estimated from model 4 with all other variables at their means.

15. This is based on model 3 of table 3A.2 with all variables set to their means.

16. Another potential concern is spuriousness (that fraud may drive both condemnation and violence); I address this in more detail elsewhere (von Borzyskowski 2019).

17. Kelley 2012, 198. IO-level measures are dropped because the present analysis is on the country-year level. The variable legal problems is dropped because many observations have missing data.

18. I use Stata's etregress command and the dependent variable is the logged casualty count.

19. Kelley 2012, 75.

20. I was able to collect these data for 71 of the 138 observed elections in Africa (1990–2008). Data are coded from observer reports and websites.

21. Carothers 1997, 18.

22. More extensive robustness checks are in von Borzyskowski 2019.

23. UNDP 2007a, 2007b.

24. Both elections had serious fraud on election-day, as measured by Beck et al. 2001.

25. European Union Election Observation Mission 2007a, 7; European Union Election Observation Mission 2007b, 31–32. One difference is the vote margin: Kenya's election was seven percentage points closer than Sierra Leone's, potentially making claims of a stolen election in Kenya more credible than in Sierra Leone. While it is not possible to rule this out (and it is impossible to find an election that was exactly identical on all dimensions), statistical results are substantively similar using vote margins instead of loser's vote share.

26. European Union Election Observation Mission 2007a, 1, 7.

27. Kandeh 2008, 628.

28. Jeffrey Gettleman, "Riots Batter Kenya as Rivals Declare Victory," *New York Times*, 30 December 2007.

29. Human Rights Watch 2008, 22.

30. See Jeffrey Gettleman, "Tribal Rivalry Boils Over after Kenyan Election," *New York Times*, 30 December 2007.

31. "Violence Erupts after Kibaki Sworn In," *The Nation*, 31 December 2007. EU 2008a, 1.

32. EU 2008a, 1, 3.

33. "Britain Urges Kenyan Leaders to Bring End to Violence," Agence France Press, 1 January 2008.

34. "EU Says Kenya Poll Flawed, Death Toll Nears 260," *The Daily Star*, 2 January 2008.

35. See "EU Calls for Inquiry into Allegedly Flawed Kenyan Poll Results," Deutsche Welle, 1 January 2008; Kenneth Ogosia, "Raila Calls for Million Man Protest," All Africa, 31 December 2007.

36. "Kenya under Pressure as Death Toll Rises," ABC News, 1 January 2008.

37. "Kenyans in U.S. Protest Disputed Election Results," Voice of America, 3 January 2008.

38. Atwood 2012, 22.

39. Kelley 2012, 72–73

40. Straus and Taylor 2012, 27.

41. Young-Jin Choi, "Statement on the Certification," UNOCI, 3 December 2010, available at www.un.org/ en/peacekeeping/missions/unoci/documents/unoci_srsg_certification_en_03122010.pdf.

42. Ouattara said, "All Ivorians know that Mr. Gabgbo has lost the elections, and this was certified by the United Nations." CSIS 2010, 7.

43. See Union Europeenne Mission d'Observation Electorale en Cote d'Ivoire, Election Présidentielle 2010, 1–2.; Union Europeenne Mission d'Observation Electorale en Cote d'Ivoire, Declaration Preliminaire Second Tour, 30 November 2010. See also Carter Center 2010, 7, 9.

44. See "Cote d'Ivoire: Statement by EU High Representative Catherine Ashton," 4 December 2010, available at http://allafrica.com/stories/201012040007.html; and Carter Center, "Statement on the Cote d'Ivoire Election," 4 December 2010, available at www.cartercenter.org/news/pr/cotedivoire-120410.html, accessed 5 November 2013.

44. "EU Foreign Affairs Chief Recognizes Ouattara Victory," Agence France Presse, 3 December 2010.

45. See "Kinshasa: ACP-EU declare support for Alassane Ouattara," Patriotic Vanguard, 5 December 2010; Korva Coleman, "EU to Ivory Coast's Gbagbo: Get Out," NPR, 17 December 2010, available at www.npr.org/blogs/thetwo-way/2010/12/17/132132112/eu-to-ivory-coasts-gbagbo-get-out.

46. "Cote d'Ivoire: Ouattara Claims Victory as Gbagbo Backlash Mounts," Radio France Internationale, 3 December 2010, available at www.english.rfi.fr/africa/20101203-ouattara-claims-victory-Gbagbo-backlash-mounts.

47. See Cote d'Ivoire events 47983, 47978–47980 in ACLED (Raleigh, Linke, and Hegre 2012); and events 4370244, 4370245 in SCAD (Salehyan and Hendrix 2016).

48. Tula World, 8 April 1997; New York Post, 28 November 2000.

49. "Incumbent Obiang Declares Victory in Equatorial Guinea Vote," Voice of America, 1 December 2009; New York Beacon, 3 December 2009.

50. Africa News Service, 29 March 2001, 27 February 2006.

51. Africa News Service, 6 and 21 May 2003.

52. Associated Press, 28 February 2006; New York Times, 9 December 2010.

53. The Australian, 12 December 2011.

54. Associated Press, 25 April 2007.

55. Washington Post, 2 March 1999.

56. Washington Post, 2 February 1999; Panafrican News Agency, 15 March 1999.

57. Philadelphia Inquirer, 4 March 1999; Keesing's Record of World Events, 1999, p. 42824.

58. Africa News, 9 November 1992.

59. Keesing's Record of World Events, 1992, pp. 39130, 39179.

60. Globe and Mail, 11 July 1996; Keesing's Record of World Events, 1996, p. 41178.

61. This violence was not preceded by a condemnation. Lindberg 2006, 60–61.

62. EISA post-election statement, 11 April 2008, 1.

63. State Department Human Rights Report 2009.

64. International Election Observation Mission, Preliminary Statement, 3 November 2003, 1, available at www.osce.org/odihr/elections/georgia/13138. This was a joint mission composed of the parliamentary assemblies of the OSCE, the Council of Europe, and the European Parliament.

65. Tucker 2007.

66. EU 2005, 37–40.

67. Carter Center 2009, 55.

68. "Ethiopian Protesters Massacred," BBC, 19 October 2006, available at http://news.bbc.co.uk/2/hi/6064638.stm, accessed 10 January 2015.

69. Mark Fineman, "70,000 Rally in Mexico to Protest Vote Fraud," Los Angeles Times, 28 August 1994.

70. NDI/IRI 1989, v, 79.

71. See "2005 Ethiopian Election: A Look Back," Voice of America, 16 May 2010; "Russia Concerned over Kyrgyz Protests," Agence France Presse, 21 March 2005.

72. Anderson et al. 2005, 6.

73. Thomas Grove, "Azeri Police Beat, Detain Demonstrators after Vote Protest Rally," Reuters, 12 October 2013.

74. Vanora Bennett, "Armenian Protests Turn Violent," *Los Angeles Times*, 26 September 1996.

75. Hyde and Marinov 2014; Kuntz and Thompson 2009.

76. UN 2005b, 4.

4. THE UPSIDE

1. This is because street protests can be violent themselves or might be peaceful but provoke clashes or repression by supporters of the winner or government forces.

2. Hafner-Burton, Hyde, and Jablonski 2014, 167; Hyde and Marinov 2014, 340.

3. Data from Coppedge et al. 2017.

4. Predicted from model 3 in table 4.1 with other variables set at their mean.

5. UN 2010, 1.

6. Lührmann 2016, 15.

7. Coppedge et al. 2017.

8. Coppedge et al. 2017.

9. P-values from the Wald test of independent equations ($\rho = 0$), $\Pr(\chi^2)$ are smaller than 0.01 in 5 of the twelve models, 0.03 other models, and insignificant in three independence models of commission.

10. P-values from the Wald test of independent equations are all above 0.17.

11. A third possibility is that election assistance does not influence challenges at all. A reading of cases, including those featured later in this chapter, cast doubt on that. However, distinguishing the different forms of loser challenges and its drivers is a promising research question ripe for future work. Currently, such fine-grained data are limited to elections in Eastern Europe and former Soviet Union states (Chernykh 2014).

12. For a more detailed description, see Claes and von Borzyskowski 2018.

13. Data from World Bank Development Indicators (2012). In 2011, Guyana's GDP per capita rose to $1,200. The population size is around 750,000 people.

14. The remaining population is of mixed heritage (17 percent) and of Amerindian descent (9 percent).

15. GEVD; see von Borzyskowski 2018.

16. See IFES 1993, 15–16; UNDP 2010a, 25; UNDP 2011b. During this period (1992–2011) the pre-election periods were largely peaceful except for two casualties before the 1992 election.

17. Commonwealth, "Hopes for Peaceful Elections in Guyana as Media Strike Deal," 13 April 2010, emphasis added, available at http://secretariat.thecommonwealth.org/new s/34580/34581/222429/1304codeofconductguyana.htm, accessed 6 April 2014.

18. GECOM head Surujbally, quoted in Chaubey 2011, 2.

19. Levitsky and Way 2010, 147.

20. International advisers from the Carter Center and the Commonwealth advised to postpone the election because they deemed preparations insufficient.

21. IFES 1993, 15–16.

22. Ibid.

23. Levitsky and Way 2010, 149. On the 1992 election, also see Carroll and Pastor 1993.

24. IFES 1998, 1, 26. UNDP coordinated between international observers. Two UNDP staff members were present but these were resident representatives, who also coordinate other economic, health, and education programs in the host country. Also see the government's account of elections, which does not mention the UNDP for 1997, at www.guyana.org/post_election97.htm, accessed 6 April 2014.

25. For a summary of all statements, see www.guyana.org/post_election97.htm, accessed 6 April 2014.

26. EAB, "Statement by the Government of Guyana on the Post-Election Situation," www.guyana.org/post_election97.htm.

27. Elections were held on 15 December 1997 with results announced 30 December 1997. Riots lasted into the new year.

28. See www.caricom.org/jsp/pressreleases/pres17_98.jsp.

29. Chaubey 2011, 3.

30. Chaubey 2011, 4.

31. EAB 2007, 13.

32. International monitors were the European Union, the Carter Center, and the Commonwealth. These IOs supported a domestic monitors under an umbrella organization, the EAB.

33. Violence data from GEVD; see von Borzyskowski 2018; see also Chaubey 2011, 2; Commonwealth 2006, 10, 37; and "A Small Riot in Guyana," *The Economist,* 12 April 2001, available at www.economist.com/node/569348, accessed 6 April 2014.

34. Much of the following discussion draws on Chaubey 2011.

35. Chaubey 2011, 6.

36. Chaubey 2011, 11.

37. Chaubey 2011, 8.

38. Chaubey 2011, 7.

39. Commonwealth quoted in Chaubey 2011, 12.

40. EAB 2007, 23.

41. For example, the fourth EAB-EVER report stated, "People's Progressive Party/Civic (PPP/C) party supporters stoned the house of and severely beat a People's National Congress/Reform One Guyana (PNC/R-1G) party candidate on August 8th at Hope West, Enmore, East Coast Demerara; PPP/C supporters were caught tearing down the posters of PNC/R-1G by the supporters of the PNC/R-1G at Industrial Site, Ruimveldt, Georgetown on August 11." EAB 2006a.

42. Chaubey 2011, 10.

43. GECOM release on 8 August 2006, available at www.gecom.org.gy/archived/pdf/release_polling_safeguards.pdf, accessed 6 April 2014.

44. Ibid.

45. Commonwealth 2006, 41.

46. UNDP 2009, 68.

47. EAB 2006b, 2.

48. Commonwealth 2006, 52.

49. UNDP 2009, 67.

50. Chaubey 2011, 2.

51. Limited UNDP assistance consisted of US$850,000 for the 2011 elections and US$400,000 for the 2015 elections instead of the nearly $4 million and comprehensive approach for the 2006 elections. See UNDP 2012, 38; UNDP 2011b; UNDP 2015.

52. The Carter Center attended in 1992, 2001, and 2006. The EU attended in 2001. The Commonwealth of Nations attended in 1997, 2001, and 2006.

53. UNDP 2014, 77.

54. Patterns of pre-election violence are quite similar, with high casualties before the February 1996 and 2001 elections and fewer casualties in the June 1996 and 2008 elections. The non-assisted 1991 election had several hundred pre-election casualties. The exceptions are the 2014 and 2018 elections, which had high pre-election casualties.

55. Anwar Hashim, "The Awami League's Post-Election Stance," *The Independent,* reprinted in *Holiday,* 30 November 2001.

56. UN 2010, 47; Transparency International Bangladesh, "Tracking the Election Process: An Analysis of the Violations of Electoral Code of Conduct by the Candidates of

the Postponed Ninth Parliamentary Election," available at www.ti-bangladesh.org/beta3/images/max_file/rp_ES_ElectionTracking3_07.pdf.

57. UNDP 2010b, 47.

58. UNDP 2014, 77; UNDP 2010b, 56, 74–107.

59. NDI, "NDI Election Watch: Bangladesh 2007 Elections, Issue no. 1," 21 December 2006, page 2, available at www.ndi.org/sites/default/files/2103_bd_watch1_122106.pdf, accessed 25 November 2018.

60. IFES, "Assessment of the Photo Voter List in Bangladesh: Final Report," 30 November 2008.

61. UNDP 2010b, 110.

62. UNDP 2010b, 85, 110.

63. UNDP 2010b, 111.

64. UNDP 2010b, 66.

65. UNDP 2010b, 120.

66. GEVD.

67. UNDP 2014, 84–85.

68. "Clashes and Boycott Mar Bangladesh Election," BBC News Asia, 5 January 2014.

69. Anjana Pasricha, "Opposition Boycott Casts Doubt about Credibility of Bangladesh Elections," Voice of America, 2 January 2014.

70. Gilligan and Sergenti 2008; Fortna 2008.

71. Hultman, Kathman, and Shannon 2013, 2014.

72. Doyle and Sambanis 2000, 2006; Jarstad and Sisk 2008.

73. Kumar 1998; Nooruddin and Flores 2016; Brancati and Snyder 2011, 2013; von Borzyskowski and Saunders 2019.

74. On the effect of UN multidimensional peacekeeping missions on violence, see Fortna 2008, 112. On their effect on democratization, see Fortna 2008, 65; Doyle and Sambanis 2000, 790–91; the latter measure "strict" mission success as an end to violence and a minimum level of democracy. In some analyses peacebuilding (meaning multidimensional missions) emerges as the only effective UN tool; see Doyle and Sambanis 2000, 790–91.

CONCLUSION

1. Martin and Simmons 1998.

2. Gourevitch 1978; Putnam 1988.

3. See Hyde and O'Mahoney 2010; Hyde 2011b; Kelley 2012; Ichino and Schündeln 2012.

4. See Gourevitch 1978; Pevehouse 2005.

5. See Fortna 2003, 2008; Kydd 2003, 2006; Beardsley 2008; Regan 2002.

6. See Hyde and Kelley 2011; Stremlau and Carroll 2011; Kelley 2012.

7. See Savun and Tirone 2011; Abouharb and Cingranelli 2006; Hartzell, Hoddie, and Bauer 2010; Simpser and Donno 2012; Busch and Reinhardt 2003; Shaffer, Sanchez, and Rosenberg 2008; Daxecker 2012, 2014.

8. The main exceptions are Goldstone et al. 2008; Newman and Rich 2004; Darnolf 2011.

9. See Ludwig 1995, 2004; Santiso 2002; Steinorth 2011, 318–19. Recent exceptions are Lührmann 2018; Birch and Muchlinski 2018.

10. Finkel, Pérez-Liñán, and Seligson 2007; Kalyvitis and Vlachaki 2012; Scott and Steele 2011; Carnegie and Marinov 2017.

11. Dietrich and Wright 2015; Perez-Linan, Finkel, and Seligson 2016.

12. Lührmann, McMann, and Ham 2017.

13. Dahl 1989, 233, 95.

14. For a discussion of domestic political will and the selection dynamics underlying international election support, see von Borzyskowski 2016.

15. Carothers 2015a, 72.

16. Hyde and Marinov 2014.

17. Von Borzyskowski and Kuhn 2017; see also Burchard 2015, 139, 157.

18. UN 2010, 1.

19. USAID 2010, 2013; ECDPM 2012.

20. Data from Hyde and Marinov 2012, nelda49.

21. OAS 2001b; Drennan 2015.

22. UN 2005a, 2005b.

23. UN 2005a, 4.

24. See also Hyde 2011b; Norris 2017, ch. 5.

25. Hyde 2012.

26. Hyde 2012. On a parallel finding on human rights NGOs, see Hill, Moore, and Mukherjee 2013.

27. Kelley 2012, 72b.

28. See UNDP 2009; USAID 2010, 2013.

29. For the USIP workshop, see www.usip.org/education-training/courses/preventing-electoral-violence-asia-tools-practitioners-and-policymakers.

30. Creative Associates International 2015; Fischer 2017.

31. Pastor 1999b, 18.

32. That is, if citizens do not trust their country's institutions *at all*, they may protest regardless of what international observers say. If citizens have *full* trust, they may not protest regardless of monitors' reports. Therefore the effect of observer verdicts on violence intensity after elections may vary by institutional trust.

APPENDIXES TO CHAPTER 1

1. The words "consent" and "concede" both mean that the respective player gives up, but different words were chosen to reduce ambiguity in the text as to which player and part of the game is referred to.

2. Let $c_i \in (0, 1)$ and $c_c < c_L < 1$. That is, I assume that the marginal cost of challenging is smaller than the fighting cost and smaller than the value of holding office.

3. The loser challenges as long as the payoff from challenge and concede $(1 - c_c)$ is greater than the payoff from consenting to the result (0).

4. Straus and Taylor 2012, 21–22.

5. Raleigh, Linke, and Hegre 2012.

6. Salehyan et al. 2012; Salehyan and Hendrix 2016.

7. For example, Daxecker 2012; Smidt 2016.

8. Von Borzyskowski and Wahman 2018.

9. Von Borzyskowski and Wahman 2018.

10. *The New York Times, The Economist,* The BBC, *The Financial Times, The Guardian, Le Monde Diplomatique.*

11. Africa News, *Al-Ahram Weekly, Middle East International,* ArabNews.com, *Caribbean and Central America Report.*

12. *The Hindu,* The Times of India Online, *China Daily, The Bangkok Post, Daily Mail and Guardian* (South Africa), *El Pais.*

13. The BBC Summary of World Broadcasts, Radio Free Europe.

14. Elections Around The World, United Nations Information Service.

15. Donno 2014, 203; Beaulieu 2014, 143.

16. Peace Research Institute Oslo (PRIO)'s Social Disturbance Database.

17. WNC is perhaps better known as a service provided by the Foreign Broadcast Information Service (FBIS); WNC shut down in late 2013.

18. Lindberg 2009.

19. See, e.g., UN Secretary General 2009, 17–18. UN's websites are UNDP Electoral Assistance website available at http://toolkit-elections.unteamworks.org/?q=node/175; UNDP Country websites available at www.undp.org/content/undp/en/home.html; and UNDP Project website available at http://open.undp.org/#2015/filter/focus_area-2.

References

Abbarno, Aaron. 2017. "The Culture of Success and Evidence-Based Foreign Assistance Programming." Blog post by Democracy International, 27 November 2017. Available at http://democracyinternational.tumblr.com/post/167947616692/the-culture-of-success-and-evidence-based-foreign.

Abouharb, Rodwan, and David Cingranelli. 2006. "The Human Rights Effects of World Bank Structural Adjustment, 1981–2000." *International Studies Quarterly* 50 (2): 233–262.

Abramowitz, Alan, and Steven Webster. 2016. "The Rise of Negative Partisanship and the Nationalization of U.S. Elections in the Twenty-First Century." *Electoral Studies* 41: 12–22.

African Elections Database. n.d. Available at http://africanelections.tripod.com, accessed 17 September 2018.

African Union Panel of the Wise. 2010. *Election-Related Disputes and Political Violence: Strengthening the Role of the African Union in Preventing, Managing and Resolving Conflict.* New York: IPI.

Alvarez, Michael, Thad Hall, and Susan Hyde. 2008. *Election Fraud: Detecting and Deterring Electoral Manipulation.* Washington, D.C.: Brookings Institution Press.

Anderson, Christopher, Andre Blais, Shaun Bowler, Todd Donovan, and Ola Listhaug. 2005. *Losers' Consent: Elections and Democratic Legitimacy.* Oxford, U.K.: Oxford University Press.

Aniekwe, Chika Charles, and Samuel Mondays Atuobi. 2016. "Two Decades of Election Observation by the African Union: A Review." *Journal of African Elections* 15 (1): 25–44.

Arel-Bundock, Vincent. 2017. "R Package Countrycode." See https://github.com/vincentarelbundock/countrycode.

Arriola, Leonardo. 2013. "Protesting and Policing in a Multiethnic Authoritarian State: Evidence from Ethiopia." *Comparative Politics* 45 (2): 147–68.

Arriola, Leonardo, and Chelsea Johnson. 2011. "Election Violence in Democratizing States." Working paper, 23 January 2012 version. Available at http://pscourses.ucsd.edu/poli120n/ArriolaJohnson2012.pdf, accessed 6 December 2018.

Asunka, Joseph, Sarah Brierley, Eric Kramon, and George Ofosu. 2017. "Electoral Fraud or Violence: The Effect of Observers on Party Manipulation Strategies." *British Journal of Political Science.*

Atwood, Richard. 2012. *How the EU Can Support Peaceful Post-Election Transitions of Power: Lessons from Africa.* Brussels: European Union, Directorate General for External Policies of the Union. EXPO/B/AFET/2012/06.

———. 1998. "Foreword." In *Postconflict Elections, Democratization, and International Assistance*, ed. Krishna Kumar. Boulder, Colo.: Lynne Rienner.

Beardsley, Kyle. 2008. "Agreement without Peace? International Mediation and Time Inconsistency Problems." *American Journal of Political Science* 52 (4): 723–40.

Beaulieu, Emily. 2014. *Electoral Protest and Democracy in the Developing World.* Cambridge, U.K.: Cambridge University Press.

———. 2012. "Intergovernmental Organizations and Election Integrity: Resolving Conflict and Promoting Democracy." Discussion Paper, International Institute for Democracy and Electoral Assistance.

Beaulieu, Emily, and Susan Hyde. 2009. "In the Shadow of Democracy Promotion: Strategic Manipulation, International Observers, and Election Boycotts." *Comparative Political Studies* 42 (3): 392–415.

Beck, George Clarke, Alberto Groff, Philip Keefer, and Patrick Walsh. 2001. "New Tools in Comparative Political Economy: The Database of Political Institutions." *World Bank Economic Review* 15 (1): 165–76.

Bekoe, Dorina, ed. 2012. *Voting in Fear: Electoral Violence in Sub-Saharan Africa.* Washington, D.C.: United States Institute of Peace.

Bekoe, Dorina, and Stephanie Burchard. 2017. "The Contradictions of Pre-election Violence: The Effects of Violence on Voter Turnout in Sub-Saharan Africa." *African Studies Review* 60 (2): 73–92.

Bhasin, Tavishi, and Jennifer Gandhi. 2013. "Timing and Targeting of State Repression in Authoritarian Elections." *Electoral Studies* 32: 620–31.

Birch, Sarah. 2011. *Electoral Malpractice.* Oxford, U.K.: Oxford University Press.

———. 2010. "Perceptions of Electoral Fairness and Voter Turnout." *Comparative Political Studies* 43: 1601–1622.

———. 2008. "Electoral Institutions and Popular Confidence in Electoral Processes: A Cross-National Analysis." *Electoral Studies* 27: 305–20.

Birch, Sarah, and David Muchlinski. 2018. "Electoral Violence Prevention: What Works?" *Democratization* 25 (3): 385–403.

Bjornlund, Eric. 2004. *Beyond Free and Fair: Monitoring Elections and Building Democracy.* Washington, D.C.: Woodrow Wilson Center Press.

Bjornlund, Eric, Michael Bratton, and Clark Gibson. 1992. "Observing Multiparty Elections in Africa: Lessons from Zambia." *African Affairs* 91 (364): 405–31.

Bjornlund, Eric, Glenn Cowan, and William Gallery. 2007. "Election Systems and Political Parties in Post-Conflict and Fragile States." In *Rebuilding Governance in Post-Conflict Societies and Fragile States: Emerging Perspectives, Actors, and Approaches,* ed. Derick W. Brinkerhoff, 108–47. New York: Routledge.

Börzel, Tanja A., and Vera van Hüllen, eds. 2015. *Governance Transfer by Regional Organizations: Patching Together a Global Script.* New York: Palgrave Macmillan.

Borzyskowski, Inken von. 2019. "The Risks of Election Observation: International Condemnation and Post-Election Violence." *International Studies Quarterly* 63.

———. 2018. "Introducing the Global Election Violence Dataset." Working paper.

———. 2016. "Resisting Democracy Assistance: Who Seeks and Receives Technical Election Assistance?" *Review of International Organizations* 11 (2): 247–82.

Borzyskowski, Inken von, and Patrick Kuhn. 2017. "Fear of Campaign Violence and Support for Democracy and Autocracy." Working paper.

Borzyskowski, Inken von, and Richard Saunders. 2019. "Peacemaking and Election Violence." In *Contemporary Peacemaking,* edited by Roger Mac Ginty and Anthony Wanis. London: Palgrave Macmillan.

Borzyskowski, Inken von, and Felicity Vabulas. 2019. "Credible Commitments? Explaining IGO Suspensions to Sanction Political Backsliding." *International Studies Quarterly.*

Borzyskowski, Inken von, and Michael Wahman. 2018. "Systematic Measurement Error in Election Violence Data: Causes and Consequences." *British Journal of Political Science.*

Brancati, Dawn, and Jack L. Snyder. 2013. "Time to Kill: The Impact of Election Timing on Postconflict Stability." *Journal of Conflict Resolution* 57 (5): 822–53.

———. 2011. "Rushing to the Polls: The Causes of Premature Postconflict Elections." *Journal of Conflict Resolution* 55 (3): 469–92.

Bratton, Michael. 2008. "Vote Buying and Violence in Nigerian Election." *Electoral Studies* 27 (4): 621–32.

———. 1998. "Second Elections in Africa." *Journal of Democracy* 9 (3): 51–66.

Bratton, Michael, and Nicolas van de Walle. 1997. *Democratic Experiments in Africa: Regime Transitions in Comparative Perspective.* Cambridge, U.K.: Cambridge University Press.

Burchard, Stephanie. 2015. *Electoral Violence in Sub-Saharan Africa: Causes and Consequences.* Boulder, Colo.: First Forum Press.

Burnell, Peter, ed. 2000. *Democracy Assistance: International Cooperation for Democratization.* London: Frank Cass.

Busch, Marc, and Eric Reinhardt. 2003. "Developing Countries and General Agreement on Tariffs and Trade/World Trade Organization Dispute Settlement." *Journal of World Trade* 37 (4): 719–35.

Bush, Sarah, and Lauren Prather. 2017. "The Promise and Limits of Election Observers in Building Election Credibility." *Journal of Politics* 79 (3): 921–35.

Carnegie, Allison, and Nikolay Marinov. 2017. "Foreign Aid, Human Rights, and Democracy Promotion: Evidence from a Natural Experiment." *American Journal of Political Science* 61 (3): 671–83.

Carothers, Thomas. 2015a. "Democracy Aid at 25: Time to Choose." *Journal of Democracy* 26 (1): 59–73.

———. 2015b. "Elections and Democracy Support." GSDRC Professional Development Reading Pack no. 7. Birmingham, U.K.: University of Birmingham.

———. 2010. "The Elusive Synthesis." *Journal of Democracy* 21 (4): 12–26.

———. 2006a. *Confronting the Weakest Link: Aiding Political Parties in New Democracies.* Washington, D.C.: Carnegie Endowment for International Peace.

———. 2006b. *Promoting the Rule of Law Abroad: In Search of Knowledge.* Washington, D.C.: Carnegie Endowment for International Peace.

———. 2004. *Critical Mission: Essays on Democracy Promotion.* Washington, D.C.: Carnegie Endowment for International Peace.

———. 1999. *Aiding Democracy Abroad: The Learning Curve.* Washington, D.C.: Carnegie Endowment for International Peace.

———. 1997. "The Observers Observed." *Journal of Democracy* 8 (3): 17–31.

Carothers, Thomas, and Oren Samet-Marram. 2015. "The New Global Marketplace of Political Change." Carnegie Endowment for International Peace.

Carr, Adam. n.d. Election Archive. Available at http://psephos.adam-carr.net/, accessed 10 April 2018.

Carroll, David, and Robert Pastor. 1993. "Moderating Ethnic Tensions by Electoral Mediation: The Case of Guyana." The Carter Center, Atlanta, Georgia. Available at www.cartercenter.org/documents/1205.pdf, accessed 6 April 2014.

Carter Center. 2010. Statement of Preliminary Findings and Conclusions, 30 November 2010. Available at www.cartercenter.org/resources/pdfs/news/peace_publications/election_reports/cote-divoire-prelim-113010.pdf, accessed 25 November 2018.

———. 2009. "Postelection Statement on Ethiopia Elections, 3 June 2005." In *Observing the 2005 Ethiopia National Elections,* 55–56. Atlanta: Carter Center.

Center for Strategic and International Studies (CSIS). 2010. "Discussion with Alassane Ouattara, President-elect of Côte d'Ivoire," 14 January 2010. Available at https://csis-prod.s3.amazonaws.com/s3fs-public/event/110114_Ouattara_Transcript.pdf, accessed 20 November 2018.

Chacon, Mario, James A. Robinson, and Ragnar Torvik. 2011. "When Is Democracy and Equilibrium? Theory and Evidence from Colombia's La Violencia." *Journal of Conflict Resolution* 55 (3): 366–96.

Chaturvedi, Ashish. 2005. "Rigging Elections with Violence." *Public Choice* 125 (1–2): 189–202.

Chaubey, Varanya. 2011. "Cooling Ethnic Conflict over a Heated Election: Guyana 2001–2006." Working paper. Princeton University ISS. Available at https://successfulsocieties.princeton.edu/publications/cooling-ethnic-conflict-over-heated-election-guyana-2001-2006, accessed 6 April 2014.

Chernykh, Svitlana. 2014. "When Do Political Parties Protest Election Results?" *Comparative Political Studies* 47 (10): 1359–1383.

Claes, Jonas. 2017. *Electing Peace: Violence Prevention and Impact at the Polls.* Washington, D.C.: United States Institute of Peace Press.

Claes, Jonas, and Inken von Borzyskowski. 2018. *What Works in Preventing Election Violence: Evidence from Liberia and Kenya.* Peace Works no. 143. Washington, D.C.: United States Institute of Peace Press.

———. 2017. *Preventing Election Violence in Liberia.* Peace Brief no. 229. Washington, D.C.: United States Institute of Peace Press.

Collier, Paul. 2009. *Wars, Guns, and Votes: Democracy in Dangerous Places.* New York: HarperCollins.

Collier, Paul, V. L. Elliot, Havard Hegre, Anke Hoeffler, Marta Reynal-Querol, and Nicholas Sambanis. 2003. *Breaking the Conflict Trap: Civil War and Development Policy.* Washington, D.C.: World Bank.

Collier, Paul, and Dominic Rohner. 2008. "Democracy, Development, and Conflict." *Journal of the European Economic Association* 6 (2–3): 531–40.

Commonwealth Secretariat. 2006. "Guyana General and Regional Elections 28 August 2006." Observer report.

Coppedge, Michael, John Gerring, Staffan Lindberg, Jan Teorell, David Altman, Michael Bernhard, Steven Fish, Adam Glynn, Allen Hicken, Carl Henrik Knutsen, Kelly McMann, Daniel Pemstein, Svend-Erik Skaaning, Jeffrey Staton, Eitan Tzelgov, Yi-ting Wang, and Brigitte Zimmerman. 2015. *Varieties of Democracy.* Dataset version 5. Varieties of Democracy Project.

Corstange, Daniel, and Nikolay Marinov. 2012. "Taking Sides in Other People's Elections: The Polarizing Effect of Foreign Intervention." *American Journal of Political Science* 56 (3): 655–70.

Creative Associates International. 2015. "Social Media and Forecasting Electoral Violence." Pilot project. Available at https://41pylqn86jp37e3n04us8vqq-wpengine.netdna-ssl.com/wp-content/uploads/2016/07/Guyana-_Pilot_Project.pdf, accessed 17 September 2018.

Cunningham, Kathleen, Marianne Dahl, and Anne Fruge. 2017. "Strategies of Dissent: Diffusion and Diversification." *American Journal of Political Science* 61 (3): 591–605.

Cyllah, Almami, ed. 2014. *Elections Worth Dying For? A Selection of Case Studies from Africa.* Washington, D.C.: International Foundation for Electoral Systems.

Dahl, Robert. 1989. *Democracy and Its Critics.* New Haven: Yale University Press.

Darnolf, Staffan. 2011. "International Election Support Helping or Hindering Democratic Elections?" *Representation* 47 (4): 361–82.

Daxecker, Ursula. 2014. "All Quiet on Election Day? International Election Observation and Incentives for Pre-Election Violence in African Elections." *Electoral Studies* 34: 232–43.

———. 2012. "The Cost of Exposing Cheating: International Election Monitoring, Fraud, and Post-Election Violence in Africa." *Journal of Peace Research* 49 (4): 503–16.

Diamond, Larry. 2011. "A Fourth Wave or False Start? Democracy after the Arab Spring." *Foreign Affairs,* 22 May.

———. 2008. *The Spirit of Democracy.* New York: Times Books.

Dietrich, Simone, and Joseph Wright. 2015. "Foreign Aid Allocation Tactics and Democratic Change in Africa." *Journal of Politics* 77 (1): 216–34.

Donno, Daniela. 2013. *Defending Democratic Norms: International Actors and the Politics of Electoral Misconduct.* Oxford, U.K.: Oxford University Press.

———. 2010. "Who Is Punished? Regional Intergovernmental Organizations and the Enforcement of Democratic Norms." *International Organization* 64 (3): 593–625.

Downs, Anthony. 1957. *An Economic Theory of Democracy.* 1st ed. New York: Harper and Row.

Doyle, Michael, and Nicholas Sambanis. 2000. "International Peacebuilding: A Theoretical and Quantitative Analysis." *American Political Science Review* 94 (4): 779–801.

———. 2006. *Making War and Building Peace: United Nations Peace Operations.* Princeton, N.J.: Princeton University Press.

Drennan, Justine. 2015. "Should International Groups be Monitoring Sudan's Elections?" *Foreign Policy,* 14 April.

Eck, Kristine. 2012. "In Data We Trust? A Comparison of UCDP GED and ACLED Conflicts Events Datasets." *Cooperation and Conflict* 47 (1): 124–41.

Electoral Assistance Bureau (EAB). 2007. "Final Report: General and Regional Elections, 28th August 2006, Co-operative Republic of Guyana." 7 March. Available at http://aceproject.org/regions-en/countries-and-territories/GY/reports/guyana-general-and-regional-elections-2006-final.

———. 2006a. "Guyana EVER Report #4." Review of 8–21 August 2006. EAB/IFES Election Violence Education and Resolution (EVER) Project.

———. 2006b. "Guyana EVER Report #6." Review of 29 August–6 October 2006. EAB/IFES Election Violence Education and Resolution (EVER) Project.

Electoral Institute of Southern Africa (EISA). 2009. "Preventing and Managing Violent Election-Related Conflicts in Africa: Exploring Good Practices." EISA Symposium. Available at https://docplayer.net/21944842-Preventing-and-managing-violent-election-related-conflicts-in-africa.html, accessed 17 September 2018.

Elklit, Jorgen, and Palle Svensson. 1997. "What Makes Elections Free and Fair?" *Journal of Democracy* 8 (3): 32–46.

European Centre for Development Policy Management (ECDPM). 2012. "Factsheet EEAS Mediation Support Project, Knowledge Product: Mediation and Dialogue in Electoral Processes to Prevent and Mitigate Electoral Related Violence." Brussels, Belgium. Available at http://ecdpm.org/wp-content/uploads/2013/11/EEAS-Mediation-Factsheet-Dialogue-Prevent-Mitigate-Electoral-Violence.pdf, accessed 17 September 2018.

European Commission–UNDP Joint Task Force on Electoral Assistance. 2011. "Thematic Workshop: Elections, Violence and Conflict Prevention." Summary Report, 20–24 June 2011. Available at www.ec-undp-electoralassistance.org/index.php?option=com_docman&task=doc_download&gid=396&Itemid=&lang=en, accessed 17 September 2018.

European Union Election Observation Mission. 2008. "Doubts about the Credibility of the Presidential Results Hamper Kenya's Democratic Progress." 1 January. Available at http://eeas.europa.eu/archives/eueom/pdf/missions/kenya_2007_final_preliminary_statement.pdf, accessed 20 September 2018.

——. 2007a. "Sierra Leone 2007 Final Report, Presidential and Parliamentary Elections." Available at http://eeas.europa.eu/archives/eueom/pdf/missions/eu_eom_sierra_leone_final_report.pdf.

——. 2007b. "Sierra Leone 2007 Second Round Presidential Election." 8 September.

——. 2005. *Ethiopia Legislative Elections 2005 Final Report.* Available at http://eeas.europa.eu/archives/eueom/pdf/missions/finalreport-ethiopia-2005.pdf, accessed 20 September 2018.

Fearon, James, and David Laitin. 2003. "Ethnicity, Insurgency, and Civil War." *American Political Science Review* 97 (1): 75–90.

Finkel, Steven, Andrew Green, Anibal Perez-Linan, Mitchell Seligson, and Neal Tate. 2007. "Cross-National Research on USAID's Democracy and Governance Programs—Code-book (Phase II)." Available at www.pitt.edu/~politics/democracy/downloads/Codebook_Phase_2.pdf, accessed 17 September 2018.

Finkel, Steven, Anibal Pérez-Liñán, and Mitchell Seligson. 2007. "The Effects of U.S. Foreign Assistance on Democracy Building, 1990–2003." *World Politics* 59: 404–39.

Fischer, Jeff. 2017. "Social Media Monitoring of Electoral Conflict: Use of the Aggie Platform in Ghana." Presentation at the 12th Implementation Meeting of the Declaration of Principles for International Election Observation, hosted by the OAS, 14 December 2017.

——. 2007. "Managing Elections in Fragile States: A Comparative Analysis of Post-Conflict Electoral System Design in Nepal and Kosovo." Available at www.ec-undp-electoralassistance.org/index.php?option=com_docman&task=doc_download&gid=396&Itemid=&lang=enjefffischerelectionsinfragilestates, accessed 17 September 2018.

——. 2002. "Electoral Conflict and Violence: A Strategy for Study and Prevention." IFES White Paper. Available at www.ifes.org/sites/default/files/econflictpaper.pdf, accessed 17 September 2018.

Fjelde, Hanne, and Kristine Höglund. 2016. "Electoral Institutions and Electoral Violence in Sub-Saharan Africa." *British Journal of Political Science* 46 (2): 297–320.

Flores, Thomas, and Irfan Nooruddin. 2016. *Elections in Hard Times: Building Stronger Democracies in the Twenty-First Century.* Cambridge, U.K.: Cambridge University Press.

Fortna, Page. 2008. *Does Peacekeeping Work? Shaping Belligerents' Choices after Civil War.* Princeton, N.J.: Princeton University Press.

——. 2003. "Inside and Out: Peacekeeping and the Duration of Peace after Civil and Interstate Wars." *International Studies Review* 5 (4): 97–114.

Fromayan, James. 2008. "National Election Commission, Sierra Leone." In *Elections in Post-Conflict Countries: Lessons Learned from Liberia, Sierra Leone, DR Congo, and Kosovo,* edited by Tobias von Gienanth, Tobias Pietz, Hendrik Wantia, and Samuel Atuobi, 37–41. Berlin: Zentrum für Internationale Friedenseinsätze (ZIF).

Fuchs, Dieter, Giovanna Guidorossi, and Palle Svensson. 1998. "Support for the Democratic System." In *Citizens and the State,* ed. Hans-Dieter Klingemann and Dieter Fuchs, 323–53. Oxford, U.K.: Oxford University Press.

Gandhi, Jennifer, and Ellen Lust-Okar. 2009. "Elections under Authoritarianism." *Annual Review of Political Science* 12: 403–22.

Garber, Larry, and Glenn Cowan. 1993. "The Virtues of Parallel Vote Tabulations." *Journal of Democracy* 4 (2): 95–107.

Geisler, Gisela. 1993. "Fair? What Has Fairness Got to Do with It? Vagaries of Election Observations and Democratic Standards." *Journal of Modern African Studies* 31 (4): 613–37.

Gillies, David. 2011. *Elections in Dangerous Places: Democracy and the Paradoxes of Peacebuilding*. Montreal: McGill–Queen's University Press.

Gleditsch, Nils Petter, Peter Wallensteen, Mikael Eriksson, Margareta Sollenberg, and Håvard Strand (2002). "Armed Conflict 1946–2001: A New Dataset." *Journal of Peace Research* 39 (5).

Goldstone, Jack, Larry Garber, John Gerring, Clark Gibson, Mitchell Seligson, and Jeremy Weinstein. 2008. *Improving Democracy Assistance: Building Knowledge Through Evaluations and Research*. Committee on Evaluation of USAID Democracy Assistance Programs, National Research Council. Available at www. nap.edu/catalog/12164.html, accessed 17 September 2018.

Gourevitch, Peter. 1978. "The Second Image Reversed: The International Sources of Domestic Politics." *International Organization* 32 (4): 881–912.

Gutierrez-Romero, Roxana, and Adrienne LeBas. 2016. "Does Electoral Violence Affect Voting Choice and Willingness to Vote? Evidence from a Vignette Experiment." CSAE Working Paper WPS/2016-35.

Hafner-Burton, Emilie, Susan Hyde, and Ryan Jablonski. 2014. "When Do Governments Resort to Election Violence?" *British Journal of Political Science* 44 (1): 149–79.

——. 2018. "Surviving Elections: Election Violence, Incumbent Victory, and Post-Election Repercussions." *British Journal of Political Science* 48 (2): 459–88.

Hagopian, Frances, and Scott Mainwaring. 2005. *The Third Wave of Democratization in Latin America*. Cambridge, U.K.: Cambridge University Press.

Hartzell, Caroline A., Matthew Hoddie, and Molly Bauer. 2010. "Economic Liberalization via IMF Structural Adjustment: Sowing the Seeds of Civil War?" *International Organization* 64 (2): 339–56.

Hellquist, Elin. 2014. "Punishment at Home and Abroad: The Duality in the European Union's Approach to Sanctions." Working paper.

Herrberg, Antje, Raphaël Pouyé, and Fabio Bargiacchi. 2012. "Missing a Trick? Building Bridges between EU Mediation and EU Electoral Support in conflict-Affected Countries." mediatEUr Discussion Paper.

Hill, Daniel, Will Moore, and Bumba Mukherjee. 2013. "Information Politics Versus Organizational Incentives: When Are Amnesty International's 'Naming and Shaming' Reports Biased?" *International Studies Quarterly* 57: 219–32.

Hoeffler, Anke, and Marta Reynal-Querol. 2003. "Measuring the Costs of Conflict." Working paper. Available at www.conflictrecovery.org/bin/2003_Hoeffler_Reynal-Measuring_the_Costs_of_Conflict.pdf, accessed 20 September 2018.

Höglund, Kristine. 2009. "Electoral Violence in Conflict-Ridden Societies: Concepts, Causes, Consequences." *Terrorism and Political Violence* 21 (3): 412–27.

Höglund, Kristine, Anna Jarstad, and Mimmi Söderberg Kovacs. 2009. "The Predicament of Elections in War-Torn Societies." *Democratization* 16 (3): 530–57.

Höglund, Kristine, and Anton Piyarathne. 2009. "Paying the Price for Patronage: Electoral Violence in Sri Lanka." *Commonwealth and Comparative Politics* 47 (3): 287–307.

Hultman, Lisa, Jacob Kathman, and Meghan Shannon. 2014. "Beyond Keeping Peace: United Nations Effectiveness in the Midst of Fighting." *American Political Science Review* 108 (4): 737–53.

Human Rights Watch. 2008. "Ballots to Bullets: Organized Political Violence and Kenya's Crisis of Governance." *Human Rights Watch* 20 (1A). Available at www.hrw.org/reports/2008/kenya0308/kenya0308web.pdf, accessed 6 April 2017.

Huntington, Samuel. 1991. *The Third Wave: Democratization in the Late Twentieth Century*. Tulsa: University of Oklahoma Press.

Hyde, Susan. 2012. "Why Believe International Election Monitors?" In *Credibility and Non-Governmental Organizations in a Globalizing World: When Virtue is Not Enough*, ed. Peter Gourevitch, David A. Lake, and Janice Gross Stein, 37–61. New York: Cambridge University Press.

——. 2011a. "International Dimensions of Elections." In *Dynamics of Democratization*, ed. Nathan Brown, 266–81. Baltimore: Johns Hopkins University Press.

——. 2011b. *The Pseudo-Democrat's Dilemma: Why Election Monitoring Became an International Norm*. Ithaca, N.Y.: Cornell University Press.

——. 2010. "Experimenting in Democracy Promotion: International Observers and the 2004 Presidential Elections in Indonesia." *Perspectives on Politics* 8 (2): 511–27.

——. 2008. "How International Election Observers Detect and Deter Fraud." In *Election Fraud: Detecting and Deterring Electoral Manipulation*, ed. Michael Alvarez and Thad Hall, 201–15. Washington, D.C.: Brookings Institution Press.

——. 2007. "The Observer Effect in International Politics. Evidence from a Natural Experiment." *World Politics* 60: 37–63.

Hyde, Susan, and Judith Kelley. 2011. "The Limits of Election Monitoring: What Independent Observation Can (and Can't) Do." *Foreign Affairs*, 28 June. Available at http://fam.ag/AF7Q8I, accessed 6 December 2018.

Hyde, Susan, and Nikolay Marinov. 2014. "Information and Self-Enforcing Democracy: The Role of International Election Observation." *International Organization* 68: 1–31.

——. 2012. "Which Elections Can Be Lost?" *Political Analysis* 20 (2): 191–210.

Hyde, Susan, and Angela O'Mahony. 2010. "International Scrutiny and Pre-Electoral Fiscal Manipulation in Developing Countries." *Journal of Politics* 72 (3): 1–14.

Ichino, Nahomi, and Matthias Schündeln. 2012. "Deterring or Displacing Electoral Irregularities? Spillover Effects of Observers in a Randomized Field Experiment in Ghana." *Journal of Politics* 74 (1): 292–307.

Imbens, Guido, and Donald Rubin. 2015. *Causal Inference for Statistics, Social, and Biomedical Sciences*. New York: Cambridge University Press.

International Commission for Aid Impact (ICAI). 2012. "Evaluation of DFID's Electoral Support through UNDP." Report No. 8.

International Foundation for Electoral Systems (IFES). 2014. "Election Violence Education and Resolution (EVER)." Available at www.ifes.org/sites/default/files/ever_one_pager_august_2014.pdf, accessed 20 November 2018.

——. 2009. "Supporting Democratic Elections in Sierra Leone." Washington, D.C.: IFES.

——. 2004. "Electoral Violence Education and Resolution (EVER) Assessment Mission to Ghana." Related document available at www.ifes.org/sites/default/files/ghanaever.pdf, accessed 20 September 2018.

——. 1998. "Technical Assistance Project Guyana: Final Report." 30 April. Washington, D.C.: IFES. Available at www.ifes.org/sites/default/files/r01638.pdf, accessed 6 December 2018.

——. 1993. "Final Report, Guyana Election Assistance Project, October 1990 to November 1992." Washington, D.C.: IFES. 31 January. Available at www.ifes.org/sites/default/files/r01633_0.pdf, accessed 20 September 2018.

International Institute for Democracy and Electoral Assistance (IDEA). 2015. Secure and Fair Elections Workshop.

——. 2013. "Electoral Risk Management Tool." Available at www.idea.int/data-tools/tools/electoral-risk-management-tool, accessed 20 November 2018.

iPoll Databank. 2011. German Marshall Fund, Transatlantic Trends 2011 Survey, May 2011, survey question USTNS.2011GMF.Q38A. TNS Opinion and Social Institutes. Roper Center for Public Opinion Research, Ithaca, New York.

——. 2009. Program On International Policy Attitudes, University of Maryland. PIPA/ Knowledge Networks Poll, May 2009, survey question USUMARY.090809.R01. Roper Center for Public Opinion Research, Ithaca, New York.

——. 2005. Chicago Council on Foreign Relations/PIPA/Knowledge Networks Poll, September 2005, survey question USUMARY.092905.R27B. Roper Center for Public Opinion Research, Ithaca, New York.

Ihonvbere, Julius. 1996. "Where Is the Third Wave? A Critical Evaluation of Africa's Non-Transition to Democracy." *Africa Today* 43 (4): 343–67.

Jarstad, Anna, and Timothy Sisk. 2008. *From War to Democracy: Dilemmas of Peacebuilding.* Cambridge, U.K.: Cambridge University Press.

Kalyvitis, Sarantis, and Irene Vlachaki. 2012. "When Does More Aid Imply Less Democracy? An Empirical Examination." *European Journal of Political Economy* 28 (1): 132–46.

Kammerud, Lisa. 2011. "Merging Conflict Management with Electoral Practice: The IFES Experience." In *Elections in Dangerous Places: Democracy and the Paradoxes of Peacebuilding,* ed. David Gilles, 147–70. Ithaca, N.Y.: McGill-Queens University Press.

Kandeh, Jimmy. 2008. "Rogue Incumbents, Donor Assistance, and Sierra Leone's Second Post-Conflict Elections of 2007." *Journal of Modern African Studies* 46 (4): 603–35.

Kaplan, Robert. 1997. "Was Democracy Just a Moment?" *The Atlantic* (December).

Kathman, Jacob. 2013. "United Nations Peacekeeping Personnel Commitments, 1990–2011." *Conflict Management and Peace Science* 30 (5): 532–49.

Kelley, Judith. 2012. *Monitoring Democracy: When International Election Observation Works, and Why It Often Fails.* Princeton, N.J.: Princeton University Press.

——. 2011. "Do International Election Monitors Increase or Decrease Opposition Boycotts?" *Comparative Political Studies* 44 (11): 1527–1556.

——. 2010. "Data on International Election Monitoring: Three Global Datasets on Election Quality (QED), Election Events and International Election Observation (DIEM)." Available at https://sites.duke.edu/kelley/data/, accessed 12 October 2013.

Kerr, Nicholas. 2014. "EMB Performance and Perceptions of Electoral Integrity in Africa." In *Advancing Electoral Integrity,* ed. Pippa Norris, Richard W. Frank, and Ferran Martínez i Coma, 189–210. New York: Oxford University Press.

——. 2013. "The Causes and Consequences of Electoral Administration Reform in Africa." Dissertation, Michigan State University.

Kerr, Nicholas, and Anna Lührmann. 2017. "Public Trust in Manipulated Elections: The Role of Election Administration and Media Freedom." *Electoral Studies* 50: 50–67.

King, Gary, Robert Keohane, and Sidney Verba. 1994. *Designing Social Inquiry: Scientific Inference in Qualitative Research.* Princeton, N.J.: Princeton University Press.

Klopp, Jacqueline, and Prisca Kamungi. 2007/08. "Violence and Elections: Will Kenya Collapse?" *World Policy Journal* 24 (4): 11–18.

Krieger, Norma. 2000. "Zimbabwe Today: Hope against Grim Realities." *Review of African Political Economy* 85: 443–68.

Kriger, Norma. 2005. "ZANU-PF Strategies in General Elections, 1980–2000: Discourse and Coercion." *African Affairs* 104 (414): 1–34.

Kuhn, Patrick. 2012. "Elections, Information, Fraud, and Post-Electoral Protest." Working paper.

Kumar, Krishna, ed. 1998. *Postconflict Elections, Democratization, and International Assistance.* Boulder, Colo.: Lynne Rienner.

Kumar, Krishna, and Marina Ottaway. 1998. "General Conclusions and Priorities for Policy Research." In *Postconflict Elections, Democratization, and International Assistance*, ed. Krishna Kumar, 229–37. Boulder, Colo.: Lynne Rienner.

——. 1997. "From Bullets to Ballots: Electoral Assistance to Post-Conflict Societies." USAID.

Kumar, Krishna, and Jeroen de Zeeuw. 2006. *Promoting Democracy in Postconflict Societies*. Boulder, Colo.: Lynne Rienner.

Kuntz, Philipp, and Mark R. Thompson. 2009. "More Than Just the Final Straw: Stolen Elections as Revolutionary Triggers." *Comparative Politics* 41 (3): 253–72.

Kuran, Timur. 1995. "Why Revolutions Are Better Understood than Predicted: The Essential Role of Preference Falsification: Comment on Keddie." In *Debating Social Revolutions*, ed. Nikki Keddie, 27–35. New York: New York University Press.

Kydd, Andrew. 2006. "When Can Mediators Build Trust?" *American Political Science Review* 100 (3): 449–62.

——. 2003. "Which Side Are You On? Bias, Credibility, and Mediation." *American Journal of Political Science* 47 (4): 597–611.

Laakso, Liisa. 2007. "Insights to Electoral Violence in Africa." In *Votes, Money, and Violence: Political Parties and Elections in Sub-Saharan Africa*, ed. Matthias Basedau, Gero Erdmann, and Andreas Mehler, 224–252. Scottsville, South Africa: University of KwaZulu-Natal Press.

Lehoucq, Fabrice. 2003. "Electoral Fraud: Causes, Types, and Consequences." *Annual Review of Political Science* 6: 233–56.

Levitsky, Steven, and Lucan Way. 2010. *Competitive Authoritarianism: Hybrid Regimes after the Cold War*. Cambridge, U.K.: Cambridge University Press.

Lindberg, Staffan. 2009. "Elections and Democracy in Africa, 1989–2007." Available at www.clas.ufl.edu/users/sil/downloads.html, accessed 20 January 2013.

——. 2006. *Democracy and Elections in Africa*. Baltimore: Johns Hopkins University Press.

Lohmann, Susanne. 1994. "Dynamics of Informational Cascades: The Monday Demonstrations in Leipzig, East Germany, 1989–1991." *World Politics* 47 (1): 42–101.

Londregan, John, and Andrea Vindigni. 2006. "Voting as a Credible Threat." Working paper.

Long, Scott. 1997. *Regression Models for Categorical and Limited Dependent Variables*. Thousand Oaks, Calif.: Sage.

Lopez-Pintor, Rafael. 1997. "Reconciliation Elections: A Post-Cold War Experience." In *Rebuilding Societies after Civil War: Critical Roles for International Assistance*, ed. Krishna Kumar, 43–61. London: Lynne Rienner.

Ludwig, Robin. 2004a. "The UN's Electoral Assistance. Challenges, Accomplishments, and Prospects." In *The UN Role in Promoting Democracy: Between Ideals and Reality*, ed. Edward Newman and Roland Rich, 169–87. New York: United Nations University Press.

——. 2004b. "Free and Fair Elections: Letting the People Decide." In *The United Nations: Confronting the Challenges of a Global Society*, ed. Jean Krasno, 115–62. Boulder, Colo.: Lynne Rienner.

——. 1995. "Processes of Democratization: The New Role of the United Nations in Electoral Assistance." *Ecumenical Review* 47 (3): 339–43.

Lührmann, Anna. 2018. "United Nations Electoral Assistance: More than a Fig Leaf?" *International Political Science Review*.

——. 2016. "UN Electoral Assistance: Does It Matter for Election Management?" Varieties of Democracy Working Paper Series.

Lührmann, Anna, Kelly McMann, and Carolien van Ham. 2017. "The Effectiveness of Democracy Aid to Different Regime Types and Democracy Sectors." V-Dem working paper.

Luo, Zhaotian, and Arturas Rozenas. 2018. "The Election Monitor's Curse." *American Journal of Political Science* 62 (1): 148–60.

Lynch, Gabrielle, and Gordon Crawford. 2011. "Democratization in Africa, 1990–2010: An Assessment." *Democratization* 18 (2): 275–310.

Mac-Ikemenjima, Dabesaki. 2017. "Violence and Youth Voter Turnout in Sub-Saharan Africa." *Journal of the Academy of Social Sciences* 12 (3–4): 215–26.

Makumbe, John. 2002. "Zimbabwe's Hijacked Election." *Journal of Democracy* 13 (4): 87–101.

Marshall, Monty G., and Keith Jaggers. 2011. "Polity IV Project: Political Regime Characteristics and Transitions, 1800–2010. Dataset User's Manual." University of Maryland, College Park. Available at www.systemicpeace.org/inscr/p4manualv2010. pdf, accessed 18 September 2012.

Martin, Lisa, and Beth Simmons. 1998. "Theories and Empirical Studies of International Institutions." *International Organization* 52 (4): 729–57.

Masunungure, Eldred. 2011. "Zimbabwe's Militarized, Electoral Authoritarianism." *Journal of International Affairs* 65 (1): 47–64.

McCoy, Jennifer, Larry Garber, Robert Pastor. 1991. "Pollwatching and Peacemaking." *Journal of Democracy* 2 (4): 102–14.

Mehler, Andreas. 2009. "Introduction: Power-Sharing in Africa." *Africa Spectrum* 44 (3): 2–10.

Moehler, Devra. 2009. "Critical Citizens and Submissive Subjects: Election Losers and Winners in Africa." *British Journal of Political Science* 39: 345–66.

Nadeau, Richard, and Andre Blais. 1993. "Accepting the Election Outcome: The Effect of Participation on Losers' Consent." *British Journal of Political Science* 23 (4): 553–63.

National Democratic Institute for International Affairs (NDI) and National Republican Institute for International Affairs (IRI). 1989. "Transcript of the 8 May Press Conference." In *The May 7, 1989 Panamanian Elections: International Delegation Report*, 79.

Newman, Edward, and Roland Rich. 2004. *The UN Role in Promoting Democracy: Between Ideals and Reality*. New York: United Nations University Press.

Nohlen, Dieter, ed. 2005. *Elections in the Americas. A Data Handbook*. Vols. 1 and 2. Oxford, U.K.: Oxford University Press.

Nohlen, Dieter, Michael Krennerich, and Bernhard Thibaut. 1999. *Elections in Africa: A Data Handbook*. New York: Oxford University Press.

Norris, Pippa. 2017. *Strengthening Electoral Integrity: The Pragmatic Case for Assistance*. New York: Cambridge University Press.

——. 2015. *Why Elections Fail*. New York: Cambridge University Press.

——. 2014. *Why Electoral Integrity Matters*. New York: Cambridge University Press.

Norris, Pippa, Richard Frank, and Ferran Martínez i Coma, eds. 2015. *Contentious Elections: From Ballots to the Barricades*. New York: Routledge.

Offe, Claus. 1999. "How Can We Trust Our Fellow Citizens?" in *Democracy and Trust*, ed. Mark E. Warren, 42–87. Cambridge, U.K.: Cambridge University Press.

Opitz, Christian, Hanne Fjelde, and Kristine Höglund. 2013. "Including Peace: The Influence of Electoral Management Bodies on Electoral Violence." *Journal of Eastern African Studies* 7 (4): 713–31.

Organization of American States (OAS). 2001a. "Inter-American Democratic Charter, Lima (Peru)." Available at www.oas.org/charter/docs/resolution1_en_p4.htm, accessed 20 September 2018.

———. 2001b. "Report of the Electoral Observation Mission to Peru 2001." Washington, D.C. Available at http://aceproject.org/regions-en/countries-and-territories/PE/reports/peru-general-elections-2001-report-of-the/at_download/file, accessed 20 September 2018.

Organization for Security and Cooperation in Europe (OSCE). 2005. "International Election Observation Mission, Parliamentary Elections, the Kyrgyz Republic, 27 February 2005." Statement of preliminary findings and conclusions. Available at www.osce.org/odihr/elections/kyrgyzstan/41882?download=true, accessed 17 September 2018.

Pastor, Robert A. 1999a. A Brief History of Electoral Commissions. In *The Self-Restraining State: Power and Accountability in New Democracies*, edited by Andreas Schedler, Larry Diamond, and Marc F. Plattner, 75–81. Boulder, Colo.: Lynne Rienner.

———. 1999b. "The Role of Electoral Administration in Democratic Transitions: Implications for Policy and Research." *Democratization* 6 (4): 1–27.

Patino, Patrick, and Djorina Velasco. 2006. "Election Violence in the Philippines." Friedrich Ebert Stiftung. Available at http://library.fes.de/pdf-files/bueros/philippinen/50071.pdf, accessed 20 September 2018.

Pausewang, Siegfried, Kjetil Tronvoll, and Lovise Aalen, eds. 2002. *Ethiopia since the Derg: A Decade of Democratic Pretension and Performance.* London: Zed Books.

Peeler, John. 2009. *Building Democracy in Latin America.* Boulder, Colo.: Lynne Rienner.

Pérez-Liñán, Anibal, Steven E. Finkel, and Mitchell Seligson. 2016. "Under What Conditions Does Democracy Assistance Work?" Paper presented at the Annual Meeting of the Midwest Political Science Association, Chicago, Illinois, April.

Pevehouse, Jon C. 2005. *Democracy from Above: Regional Organizations and Democratization.* Cambridge, U.K.: Cambridge University Press.

Pevehouse, Jon, and Inken von Borzyskowski. 2016. "International Organizations in World Politics." In *The Oxford Handbook of International Organizations*, ed. Jacob Katz Cogan, Ian Hurd, and Ian Johnstone, 3–32. Oxford, U.K.: Oxford University Press.

Przeworski, Adam. 2006. "Self-Enforcing Democracy." In *The Oxford Handbook of Political Economy*, ed. Donald Wittman and Barry Weingast. New York: Oxford University Press.

———. 1991. *Democracy and the Market: Political and Economic Reforms in Eastern Europe and Latin America.* Cambridge, U.K.: Cambridge University Press.

Putnam, Robert. 1988. "Diplomacy and Domestic Politics: The Logic of Two-Level Games." *International Organization* 42 (3): 427–60.

Pyne-Mercier, Lee, et al. 2011. "The Consequences of Post-Election Violence on Antiretroviral HIV Therapy in Kenya." *AIDS Care* 23 (5): 562–68.

Raleigh, Clionadh, Andrew Linke, and Havard Hegre. 2012. "Armed Conflict Location and Event Dataset (ACLED) Codebook." Version 2.

Regan, Patrick M. 2002. "Third Party Interventions and the Duration of Intrastate Conflict." *Journal of Conflict Resolution* 46 (1): 55–73.

Reilly, Ben. 2002. "Electoral Systems for Divided Societies." *Journal of Democracy* 13 (2): 156–70.

Riker, William. 1983. "Political Theory and the Art of Heresthetics." In *Political Science: The State of the Discipline*, edited by Ada Finifter, 47–67. Washington, D.C.: APSA.

Ritter, Emily, and Courtenay Conrad. 2016. "Preventing and Responding to Dissent: The Observational Challenges of Explaining Strategic Repression." *American Political Science Review* 110 (1): 85–99.

Robertson, Graeme. 2015. "Political Orientation, Information, and Perceptions of Election Fraud: Evidence from Russia." *British Journal of Political Science* 47 (3): 589–608.

Ross, Michael. 2012. *The Oil Curse: How Petroleum Wealth Shapes the Development of Nations*. Princeton, N.J.: Princeton University Press.

Salehyan, Idean, and Cullen Hendrix. 2016. Social Conflict Analysis Database (SCAD) codebook.

Salehyan, Idean, Cullen Hendrix, Jesse Hamner, Christina Case, Christopher Linebarger, Emily Stull, and Jennifer Williams. 2012. "Social Conflict in Africa: A New Database." *International Interactions* 38 (4): 503–11.

Santiso, Carlos. 2002. "Promoting Democratic Governance and Preventing the Recurrence of Conflict: The Role of the United Nations Development Programme in Post-Conflict Peace-Building." *Journal of Latin American Studies* 34 (3): 555–86.

Savun, Burcu, and Daniel Tirone. 2011. "Foreign Aid, Democratization, and Civil Conflict: How Does Democracy Aid Affect Civil Conflict?" *American Journal of Political Science* 55 (2): 233–46.

Schedler, Andreas. 2002. "Elections without Democracy: The Menu of Manipulation." *Journal of Democracy* 13 (2): 36–50.

——. 2001. "Measuring Democratic Consolidation." *Studies in Comparative International Development* 36 (1): 66–92.

Schedler, Andreas, Larry Diamond, and Marc Plattner. 1999. *The Self-Restraining State: Power and Accountability in New Democracies*. London: Lynne Rienner.

Schmitter, Philippe, and Terry Lynn Karl. 1991. "What Democracy Is . . . and Is Not." *Journal of Democracy*: 2–16.

Scott, James, and Carie Steele. 2011. "Sponsoring Democracy: The United States and Democracy Aid to the Developing World, 1988–2001." *International Studies Quarterly* 55 (1): 47–69.

Seeberg, Merete Bech, Michael Wahman, and Svend-Erik Skaaning. 2018. "Candidate Nomination, Intra-Party Democracy, and Election Violence in Africa." *Democratization* 25 (6): 959–77.

Shaffer, Gregory, Michelle Ratton Sanchez, and Barbara Rosenberg. 2008. "Winning at the WTO: The Development of a Trade Policy Community within Brazil." Working Paper No. 14, Area de Relaciones Internacionales FLACSO/Argentina.

Simpser, Alberto. 2013. *Why Governments and Parties Manipulate Elections: Theory, Practice, and Implications*. New York: Cambridge University Press.

Simpser, Alberto, and Daniela Donno. 2012. "Can International Election Monitoring Harm Governance?" *Journal of Politics* 74 (2): 501–13.

Sisk, Timothy D. 2008. Elections in Fragile States: Between Voice and Violence. Paper presented at the International Studies Association Annual Meeting, 24–28 March 2008, San Francisco, California.

Sisk, Timothy, and Andrew Reynolds, eds. 1998. *Elections and Conflict Management in Africa*. Washington, D.C.: United States Institute of Peace.

Smidt, Hannah. 2016. "From a Perpetrator's Perspective: International Election Observers and Post-Electoral Violence." *Journal of Peace Research* 53 (2): 226–41.

Soudriette, Richard, and Juliana Geran Pilon, eds. 2007. *Every Vote Counts: The Role of Elections in Building Democracy*. Washington, D.C.: IFES Democracy Collection.

State Department. 1992. Country Reports on Human Rights Practices for 1991. Washington, D.C.: State Department. Available at https://archive.org/details/countryreportson1991unit, accessed 6 November 2018.

Steele, Abbey. 2011. "Electing Displacement: Political Cleansing in Apartado, Colombia." *Journal of Conflict Resolution* 55 (3): 423–45.

Steinorth, Charlotte. 2011. "The United Nations, Post-Conflict Institution-Building and Thin Concepts of Democracy." In "The Future of Statebuilding: Ethics, Power and Responsibility in International Relations," special issue of *The Journal of Intervention and Statebuilding*, University of Westminster.

Straus, Scott. 2011. "'It's Sheer Horror Here': Patterns of Violence during the First Four Months of Cote d'Ivoire's Post-Electoral Crisis." *African Affairs* 110 (440): 481–89.

Straus, Scott, and Charlie Taylor. 2012. "Democratization and Electoral Violence in Sub-Saharan Africa, 1990–2008." In *Voting in Fear: Electoral Violence in Sub-Saharan Africa*, ed. Dorina A. Bekoe, 15–38. Washington, D.C.: United States Institute of Peace Press.

Stremlau, John, and David Carroll. 2011. "Monitoring the Monitors: What Everyone Gets Wrong about Election Observers." *Foreign Affairs*, 14 September 2011. Available at http://fam.ag/wy1Zsk, accessed 12 June 2013.

Taylor, Charlie, Jon Pevehouse, and Scott Straus. 2017. "Perils of Pluralism: Electoral Violence and Incumbent in Sub-Saharan Africa." *Journal of Peace Research* 54 (3): 397–411.

Thompson, Mark R., and Philipp Kuntz. 2004. "Stolen Elections: The Case of the Serbian October." *Journal of Democracy* 15 (4): 159–72.

Travaglianti, Manuela. 2014. "Threatening Your Own: Electoral Violence within Ethnic Groups in Burundi and Beyond." Dissertation, New York University.

Trejo, Guillermo. 2014. "The Ballot and the Street: An Electoral Theory of Social Protest in Autocracies." *Perspectives on Politics* 12 (2): 332–52.

Tucker, Joshua A. 2007. "Enough! Electoral Fraud, Collective Action Problems, and Post-Communist Colored Revolutions." *Perspectives on Politics* 5 (3): 535–51.

United Nations. 2010. "Department of Political Affairs of the United Nations Secretariat and United Nations Development Programme: Revised Note of Guidance on Electoral Assistance." New York. Available at http://content-ext.undp.org/aplaws_publications/2545621/Note%20of%20Guidance%20Final%20September%202010.pdf, accessed 17 September 2018.

——. 2005a. "Code of Conduct for International Election Observers." New York.

——. 2005b. "Declaration of Principles for International Election Observation." New York.

United Nations Development Programme (UNDP). 2015. Guyana Social Cohesion Project II: Supporting Stakeholder engagement and Capacities for Social Cohesion in Guyana in Preparation for Next Elections and Beyond. Available at https://info.undp.org/docs/pdc/Documents/GUY/GSCPII%20Project%20Doc.pdf, accessed 25 November 2018.

——. 2014. *The Longer Term Impact of UNDP Electoral Assistance: Lessons Learned*. New York: UNDP.

——. 2012. *Evaluation of UNDP Contribution to Strengthening Electoral Systems and Processes*. New York: UNDP.

——. 2011a. *Understanding Electoral Violence in Asia*. New York: UNDP.

——. 2011b. "Violence Free Elections in 2011." Available at www.gy.undp.org/content/guyana/en/home/ourwork/democraticgovernance/successstories/Sample_Success_Story_2/, accessed 25 November 2018.

——. 2010a. *Assessment of Development Results, Evaluation of UNDP Contribution: Guyana*. New York: UNDP.

——. 2010b. *Elections in Bangladesh 2006–2009: Transforming Failure into Success*. New York: UNDP.

——. 2009. *Elections and Conflict Prevention: A Guide to Analysis, Planning and Programming*. New York: UNDP.

——. 2007a. *The 2007 Kenya Election Assistance Programme*. New York: UNDP. Available at http://toolkit-elections.unteamworks.org/?q=webfm_send/644, accessed 25 November 2018.

——. 2007b. *UNDP and Government of Sierra Leone 2007: Project Document Support to Electoral Reform and the National Electoral Commission*. New York:

UNDP. Available at www.undp.org/content/dam/undp/documents/projects/SLE/ 00049276_Project_document-v2.pdf, accessed 25 November 2018.

———. 2005. *Government of Sierra Leone and United Nations Development Programme. Project Document: Support for Electoral Reform and the National Election Commission.* New York: UNDP.

United Nations Human Rights Council. 2010. *Report of the Special Rapporteur on Extrajudicial, Summary or Arbitrary Executions, Philip Alston.* A/HRC/14/24/ Add.7. Available at https://documents-dds-ny.un.org/doc/UNDOC/GEN/ G10/135/53/PDF/G1013553.pdf?OpenElement, accessed 25 November 2018.

U.S. Agency for International Development (USAID). 2013. *Best Practices in Electoral Security: A Guide for Democracy and Governance Programming.* Washington, D.C.: USAID.

———. 2010. *Electoral Security Framework: Technical Guidance Handbook for Democracy and Governance Officers.* Washington, D.C.: USAID.

Varshney, Ashutosh. 2001. "Ethnic Conflict and Civil Society: India and Beyond." *World Politics* 53 (3): 362–98.

Vickery, Chad. 2011. *Guidelines for Understanding, Adjudicating, and Resolving Disputes in Elections.* Washington, D.C.: IFES.

Vogt, Manuel, Nils-Christian Bormann, Seraina Ruegger, Lars-Erik Cederman, Philipp Hunziker, and Luc Girardin. 2015. "Integrating Data on Ethnicity, Geography, and Conflict: The Ethnic Power Relations Data Set Family." *Journal of Conflict Resolution* 59 (7): 1327–1342.

Warren, Mark E. 1999. *Democracy and Trust.* Cambridge, U.K.: Cambridge University Press.

Weidmann, Nils, Doreen Kuse, and Kristian Skrede Gleditsch. 2010. "The Geography of the International System: The CShapes Dataset." *International Interactions* 36 (1): 86–106.

Weingast, Barry. 1997. "The Political Foundations of Democracy and the Rule of Law." *APSR* 91 (2): 245–63.

Wilkinson, Steven. 2004. *Votes and Violence: Electoral Competition and Ethnic Riots in India.* Cambridge, U.K.: Cambridge University Press.

Wilkinson, Steven, and Christopher Haid. 2009. "Ethnic Violence as Campaign Expenditure: Riots, Competition, and Vote Swings in India." Working paper.

Wilson, Paul. 2015. "The Misuse of the Vuong Test for Non-Nested Models to Test for Zero-Inflation." *Economics Letters* 127: 51–53.

World Bank Development Indicators. 2012. Available at http://data.worldbank.org/ indicator, accessed 10 April 2012.

Xu, Lizhen, Andrew Paterson, Williams Turpin, and Wei Xu. 2015. "Assessment and Selection of Competing Models for Zero-Inflated Microbiome Data." *PLoS ONE* 10 (7): e0129606.

Zakaria, Fareed. 2004. *The Future of Freedom: Illiberal Democracy at Home and Abroad.* New York: W.W. Norton.

Index

CPSIA information can be obtained
at www.ICGtesting.com
Printed in the USA
BVHW030919030519
547017BV00003B/35/P